Raising Your Children With Hypnosis

Donald J. Mottin

Director

MOTTIN & JOHNSON INSTITUTE OF HYPNOSIS
3466 Bridgeland #212
Bridgeton, MO 63044
1-800-288-3065

www.donmottin.com

Published by ASC
HypnoClassics

ISBN: 1-885846-10-X

Dedication

When selecting whom to dedicate this book, it became an impossibility to only select one person. There have been so many people who have shaped my life in a positive way, which in turn, has made this book a possible.

While growing up, my father, *Jim Mottin*, constantly taught me that we have a choice whether to look at an event in a positive or a negative way. My Dad could encounter a situation that would have made another individual stressed out, but he would find the positive side in all events.

As I grew older, I was fortunate to keep these positive influences around me. My wonderful wife of 25 years, *Brenda Mottin*, always believed in me and reinforced that I could accomplish anything that I set my mind to.

The National Guild of Hypnotists is the largest certifying body in the world. The President of the NGH is *Dr. Dwight Damon*. He has been involved with hypnosis for over 50 years. I cannot imagine this book ever going to press without the encouragement of Dr. Damon. I met him about ten years ago at a seminar. Within six months, I considered him one of my best friends. He has this unique ability to be both professional and personable at the same time.

The Executive Director of the National Guild of Hypnotists is a fantastic lady named *Melody Bachand*. Although I do not see Melody in person nearly enough, there is rarely a week go by when we are not speaking by phone. From the onset of this book, she has helped tremendously with her insight and expertise in publishing matters.

For several years, I procrastinated in finishing this book. It wasn't until my good friend, colleague and right-hand assistant, sat down and read what had been written that my procrastination rapidly changed to motivation. This very special person is *Bree Ferrario*. Without Bree's encouragement and dedication, it would have been impossible to move this project from a thought into reality. She spent countless hours compiling an abundance of my material from different sources, along with her own experience and sage advice. Bree made this project come alive.

And last, but not least, *Carolyn Bozwell*, my friend and colleague who initially typed this manuscript.

It is impossible to ever select just one person who has impacted your life in a positive manner. We may tend to consciously forget the various encounters in our lives, but you can be certain that even the brief exchanges with another person can, and will, have an effect upon you.

Table of Contents

Introduction

This book was written with two objectives in mind. The first allows adults to deliver positive suggestions to children *without* the use of a formal hypnotic induction. These techniques are perfect for parents, teachers, clergy, nurses, school counselors and babysitters that may simply wish to improve their communication skills with children.

The second objective of this book is to teach simple and safe techniques to hypnotize children. The techniques described in this book have been written in a nonintimidating manner; free of excess clinical terms and definitions.

There have been classes taught and books written for almost every area of our lives, with the exception of communicating with our children on a subconscious level.

The reader can anticipate mastering the secrets of delivering positive messages to children that will change behaviors and allow their children to become the best that they can be. The techniques found in this book are not based on theory, but rather have been successfully employed for decades.

Once the reader masters these techniques, it would seem impossible to ever go back to the old method of consciously working with children. Children today are faced with more complex problems than ever before in history. The time has come for a more successful means of communicating and leading them in the right direction.

Parents and therapists have used a variety of methods to influence children. There was the strict disciplinarian approach, there was the permissive approach of allowing the child to decide for him/herself, and then there was the old standby of reward and punishment. The one thing that all of these techniques have in common, is that they attempt to influence behavior externally.

It has been proven that when we are dealing with an individual's external motivation, it will always be temporary. For a more permanent change, the motivation must be internal. This is where proper communication skills, namely hypnosis, have been proven so effective. The child wants to improve for his/her own benefit, rather than for the benefit of the parent or therapist.

CHAPTER 1

What Is Hypnosis?

There have been dozens of different definitions for hypnosis *"an altered state of awareness"*, *"a state of hyper-suggestibility"* and *"a trance"* are just a few. In this book the author feels that it is more important for the parents and therapists to know what transpires in the hypnotic state rather than delving into complex definitions.

Although hypnosis has been around for hundreds of years, it is still one of the most misunderstood of all the sciences. Much of the misinformation can be traced back to television, movies and novels. The average adult encountering hypnosis in a private session realizes that the media is not an accurate portrayal of hypnotism. However, if the myth is the only exposure that a person has with hypnosis, they may believe that it is similar to the television version.

Misconceptions

There are three basic misconceptions surrounding hypnosis. The first is that a person under hypnosis is out of control. This is not true. In fact, **a person never loses control with hypnosis** but, instead, takes control of a part of their life that, perhaps, they did not have control over prior to the hypnotic session.

A person can never be made to do something against his or her own will under hypnosis. The question that comes to mind is, *"What if the child does not want to change?"* I have heard hundreds of times, *"I don't want to do better in school"*. In reality the child is saying, *"I don't think I can do better"*. It is an easy task to ascertain whether the child honestly does not want to change or simply doubts his or her own abilities.

If the parent or therapist would ask the child one simple question, they would have the true answer. ***"If I had a magic button that you could push and then you would instantly do better at _____, would you want to push the button?"*** We have seen this same technique work with adults that say, *"I don't want to stop smoking"*. When they are faced with the scenario of the magic button, they almost always say that they would push the button. We realize that in most cases it is not a situation that the child does not want to change but, rather, a strong belief that they *cannot* change.

After understanding that ***hypnosis cannot be used to trick a person into a behavior that they are opposed to***, most parents and therapists feel more comfortable in using hypnosis. If your goal is to create a household of totally obedient, glassy-eyed children, then hypnosis is not the answer for you.

The second common misconception about hypnosis is that the person under hypnosis must always tell the truth. **Hypnosis does not operate as a lie detector;** in fact, a person would be a better liar under hypnosis.

Imagine asking a six-year-old, *"Did you eat the last cookie?"* As they responded with, *"No, not me"*, in a conscious state, they would be looking up at the ceiling, arms swinging around them and doing a lot of fancy footwork. In a hypnotic state, when the child is totally relaxed, the only response would be their calm words of *"No, not me"*

Many people associate hypnosis with truth, serum after reading articles about the police departments using hypnosis in their criminal cases. The police are not hypnotizing the suspects; they are using hypnosis with the victims or witnesses of a crime. More often than not, when a witness is asked to describe a suspect, their only conscious memory is about how large the gun appeared! Under a hypnotic regression most witnesses and victims can recall the entire event with great accuracy.

The third common fear of being hypnotized is the fear of not coming out of the hypnotic state. **There has never been a case of an individual failing to exit the hypnotic state.** In reality, it would be impossible for a person to stay hypnotized, even if they chose to do so. Once again, we need to give the movies credit for spreading this false information. In the movies, if a person is hypnotized and something would happen to the hypnotist, the hypnotized subject would be doomed to a state of hypnosis for all eternity. (It works great in the movies!)

In actuality, if a person was hypnotized and the parent or hypnotist left the room, the child would simply fall into a natural state of sleep. He/she would then awaken once rested, or in the same manner that you would awaken the child each morning. So, if hypnosis is such a natural state, why is it portrayed in such an eerie manner on television? If they showed hypnosis accurately in the movies, it would be boring.

Imagine a movie showing hypnosis the way it truly is. The hypnotized subject is commanded to divulge all of his deepest secrets and then told to go out and rob the nearest bank. The subject opens his eyes and says, *"I'm not telling you anything. I am not robbing a bank. In fact, I'm leaving"*. Not a very exciting plot.

The next question that normally comes to mind is, *"If it is so natural, how does it work?"*

How Hypnosis Works

Hypnosis works because it bypasses the critical part of the mind. If someone walked into the room and said, *"This room is becoming very cold"*, you would not experience any change in the temperature of the room. However, without even being aware of it, your critical mind begins to analyze that statement. A window has not been opened, the air-conditioner has not been adjusted, and so the room is not cold. All of this information was processed by the critical part of your mind in a fraction of a second.

If the critical part of the mind was bypassed and the same statement was made about the room becoming cold, your mind would have accepted that idea as reality, and send a message that the body was feeling cold.

Bypassing the Critical Mind

There are **five** means of bypassing the critical part of the mind:

1. Repetition is the most common of all of the bypass methods being used today. With repetition, the same message is delivered over and over again until the desired results are achieved. Let's examine our earlier example of the room becoming cold. If someone verbally said many times that the room seemed cold or if others remarked in kind, eventually we might begin to experience a slight chill.

Children learn their multiplication tables through this technique of repetition. As the child hears or says, *"two times two equals four"*, dozens of times, the mind locks onto the thought that, *"two times two **does** equal four"*. Repetition is used in all parts of our lives in order to get the subconscious part of the mind to accept new ideas. **Once the subconscious accepts a thought as reality, it then responds automatically without any need for conscious assistance.**

When you first began to drive a car, you thought about each movement that you made. By repeatedly driving a car for a number of years, you can now operate that vehicle subconsciously. You do not think, *"I need to turn the wheel thirty degrees to the right, while applying a small degree of pressure to the brake, as I check the mirrors."* All of the required responses to operate the car have now become automatic for you.

There may have been a time when you drove several miles and passed your exit because your subconscious had taken over the responsibility of operating the vehicle. This is truly an example of bypassing that critical part of your mind through repetition.

2. Emotions can also allow the critical part of the mind to be bypassed. **Situations involving fear, confusion, depression or excitement are common sensations that allow the critical part of the mind to be totally or partially bypassed.** The following case history illustrates how an emotional upset can enable the critical part of the mind to be bypassed:

Story of Paul

Paul was a twelve-year-old who was failing every subject in school. Paul's parents stated that they had tried everything to help motivate their son.

Paul's mother had tried the reward system. She had promised her son that if he did better in school she would give him his own color television for his bedroom, and Paul improved slightly for approximately a week. Then Paul's father stepped in and used the threat of punishment if the grades did not improve. Once again Paul's performance improved modestly for the first week, but then he reverted back into the routine of not turning in assignments and failing simple tests.

Further discussion with the parents revealed that Paul used to be a very good student and the dramatic change seemed to occur about 18 months earlier. After having the parents wait in the reception area, I had Paul come into the office. He was a very intelligent twelve-year-old that had an intense desire to do better. Paul stated that it seemed the harder he tried to improve, the worse he did. He truly wanted to improve, not only for his parents, but also for himself. He knew he had the ability, but did not understand why he was failing.

After inducing hypnosis, Paul remembered a time when he was ten-years-old. Paul had ridden his new bike down to the corner store to get a candy bar. He came out of the store and was devastated when he realized that in those few moments, someone had stolen his new bike. Paul walked home feeling as though his whole world had come crashing down around him. By the time he reached his front yard, Paul was crying hysterically. His father was in the front yard and immediately inquired what was wrong.

Paul replied, "I know that you told me to lock my bike, but I forgot and someone stole it." Paul's father screamed, "You stupid idiot! You will never, ever learn." That did it; Paul's subconscious mind had just picked up on a suggestion. The suggestion was that he was stupid and that he would never, ever learn.

This subconscious thought is known as an **imprint**. **An imprint is a thought that has been registered at the subconscious level of the mind at a time of great emotion or stress, causing a change in behavior**. It is especially effective when the statement is made from an authority figure (parents, teachers, police officer, etc.) or someone who we admire or look up to (sibling, friend, celebrity, etc.). We all have hundreds of different imprints that affect the way we respond.

The imprint is not always a destructive thought. A child that is always well mannered may have an imprint that he is polite. A child that is proficient at sports may have an imprint that she is a great athlete. We will be covering imprints, how they are acquired and what techniques can be utilized to remove them, in another chapter. **A parent that understands the power of their words can actually create positive imprints on their children on a regular basis.**

I travel the country facilitating classes and giving lectures. The evaluations I have received reveal that I have a natural knack for public speaking, but people are not born with most natural abilities. They need to be cultivated, nurtured. There has never been an eight-pound baby public speaker born in a hospital delivery room.

To this day, I can recall a time at Christmas visiting my Grandmother's house, when I was about ten-years-old. I was the middle child of three children. My older brother had always demonstrated a certain amount of musical ability. He was playing the guitar and receiving much attention from all of the aunts and uncles. I was feeling a little depressed from the lack of attention, when one aunt asked my father if I was also musically inclined. He said no, my brother had all of the musical talent in the family, but when it comes to talking to people, I was the best that he had ever seen. Although my father knew nothing about hypnosis or imprints, he had just created a positive subconscious thought that has been with me my entire life.

3. Relaxation is the third way of bypassing the critical part of the mind. When we are relaxed, the critical part of the mind becomes more passive than in a normal alert state. Children have known this for years.

When it is imperative for a child to receive a *"Yes"* response from a parent, they usually wake up the parent, just halfway, to ask the question. While Dad is half asleep, the child will ask, *"Could I have a pet alligator?"* Dad mumbles, *"Sure, that would be nice"*. **In the state between consciousness and sleep, the subconscious mind is receptive to suggestions.**

In the 60s, many people became excited about the potential of *"sleep learning"*. The theory was that you could play a record while you were sleeping and, thus, learn new information throughout the night. The theory sounded wonderful. It was later discovered that the only time the mind responded to the recorded message was just prior to entering sleep and the few moments of exiting sleep.

Although the sleep learning technique was not proven to be beneficial, it did provide useful information regarding the times when the mind is receptive to new messages. If it had been true, imagine the positive effectiveness that parents could have on their children. There are literally thousands of opportunities for the parents to deliver positive messages to the subconscious level of the mind.

Every parent realizes that a young child can fall asleep in almost every position imaginable. Where does your child fall asleep? In your arms? While watching television? While riding in the car? Just as they are ready to drift off is a great time to give them a positive suggestion to instill confidence, quick learning and healthy self-esteem.

4. Concentration is the fourth way of bypassing the critical part of the mind and allowing a message to be received at the subconscious level. **When a person is concentrating intensely, the subconscious is open to suggestions without any conscious interference.**

The following demonstration has been conducted many times:
An individual at a movie theater is sitting on the edge of his seat, totally involved in the movie. A second person, sitting behind the first person, leans forward and in a firm voice says, "Stand up!" In the middle of the movie, the first person would jump to his feet. In this example, the individual concentrating on the movie did not analyze the demand to stand up. The suggestion had bypassed the critical part of the mind because he was so focused on the movie, and he simply responded to the words "stand up!"

Our first inclination might be to think that children do not possess this degree of concentration. Children actually have a higher degree of concentration than most adults. For many children, the house could blow away while they were busy playing with their favorite toy!

All children have the wonderful ability to become totally absorbed in what they are doing. What the average child might be lacking in what adults consider a good concentration level, the child makes up for with his/her imagination. The child's way of concentrating might be daydreaming. It could be playing with an imaginary friend or have an intense conversation with a stuffed animal. Children are in an altered state over half the time. This allows the learning process to be accelerated.

Never underestimate a child's ability to focus his/her attention. A child's attention span may be shorter than that of an adult, but it is normally more intense.

5. Belief is the one element that can create almost magical, immediate results in the child. **If we can create a true belief pattern in the child, the elements of concentration, emotions, repetition, and relaxation would not be needed.** Children and the use of placebos truly go hand in hand.

I recall a time when one of my neighbors was having an argument with her daughter. I asked her what the problem was and she stated that her daughter wanted a band-aid in order to stop the hurt. When I inquired why she did not want to put a band-aid on the injured area, she replied that her daughter had a headache.

*After a brief discussion, she agreed and placed a band-aid in the center of her daughter's forehead and gave her a kiss. Within five minutes her daughter reported that she felt "all better". Was it the band-aid, the kiss or a combination of the two? It was the little girl's **belief** that this procedure would make a difference.*

My colleague and assistant, Bree Ferrario, had her own hypnosis office for three years before she came to work with me. She told me about a situation that, also, involved the belief system.

*A man called inquiring about hypnosis sessions regarding weight. He said that his 14-year-old son wanted to come in for a session. Bree asked him several questions and then the man said that his son wanted to **gain** weight. She continued discussing the process and how it would help his son. There was complete silence on the other end of the phone. She asked if he was still there, and with a surprised tone in his voice he said, "You are the first person who hasn't laughed when I said that he wanted to **gain** weight."*

*Bree explained that whether a person needed to lose or gain weight, it is just as serious to that person as it is to the other. The man felt more comfortable and explained that his son was initially doing all of the calls to get information and prices. When he would explain that he wanted to gain weight, the other person would laugh and say, "That's funny, most of my clients want to **lose** weight!"*

*Since he was a sensitive young man, the humor escaped him. He told his father that he **believed** that hypnosis could help him. He insisted that his father continue his search.*

When they came in for the session, the father told Bree that his son would only eat a particular food from a specific restaurant. Every night when he came home from work, he had to stop at this restaurant to pick up this special dinner for his son. He didn't mind doing it, as he loved his son very much. He was concerned, however, because he was so limited in what he would eat. The boy was extremely thin. The father knew that this wasn't healthy.

In the first session, Bree asked the boy about the foods that he liked and dis-

liked. She asked if it was the smell, texture or look of the food that repelled him. He gave her the details that she needed. When asked what was the one food that he hated the most in the whole wide world, his answer was "mashed potatoes".

Bree asked this boy if he would make a deal with her. She asked him to try two foods that he hasn't been eating over the next few weeks. That would be one new food each week. She said that all he had to do was to eat one spoonful. If he really didn't like it, he did not have to eat any more. If it was okay, he would finish the serving.

Two weeks later he came in for his second and last session. Bree asked him if he tried any new foods over the past few weeks and he said that he did. She asked if he liked either or both of them. He said that he did. When asked which food he liked, he shyly smiled and said, "mashed potatoes". Amazing! The food he hated the most in the whole wide world two weeks prior was now one that he enjoyed.

Before this second session the father gave Bree more information. He told her that not only does his son eat just that specific food at that one restaurant, he didn't eat food that the family prepared, he didn't eat the food at school, he didn't even eat fast foods when he was out with his friends. He told her that his son was very shy and didn't feel that he fit in with the other kids at school.

With this information, Bree knew that he needed to receive suggestions that made him feel confident and that he fit in. She gave him suggestions that when he was with his friends, he would feel the comradery and enjoy their company. When he was with his family, he would feel their love and support. She told him that when he ate with these people he would feel comfortable eating the same foods that they did and that he would feel the wonderful feelings even more. She put in suggestions that he would only eat the amount of food his body needed and would stop eating when he was full. (She didn't want him coming back in a few years to lose weight!)

Several months later after the new school year began, Bree received a "Thank You" note from this boy. He told her that he was now eating the same foods as the rest of the people in his life. He thanked her for helping him to do what he never thought he could do before. His life was now more fun and exciting. For a hypnotist, this is the best reward that we can receive.

You have now learned the five different elements that allow the analytical part of the mind to be bypassed, and all of them can be done without inducing the hypnotic state. You also have an example of what dramatic change can take place when hypnosis is used.

By this point, the reader should have made some initial observations. First, the **techniques used in hypnosis happen automatically** throughout our daily lives. The second observation is that since these changes occur naturally, there is **not a danger** when they are used during a hypnotic session. Our goal with hypnosis is to deliver positive suggestions that will create a cycle of progress and improvements. **You cannot remove negative behaviors with negative suggestions.** Scare tactics don't work!

Let's now examine other areas of our life where these same hypnotic principles can be used effectively. Advertisers have been using each of these five techniques successfully for a number of decades.

Repetition of a television commercial will cause the consumer to automatically think of a specific product. Through repetition, various companies have the American public programmed to think of their product. When we think of hamburgers, we tend to think in terms of advertisements. The *"Golden arches"* belong to _____. The person who lives at the golden arches is *"Ronald _____"*. Even the person who says they have trouble remembering names can think of *"Ronald Mc Donald"*. The name comes to mind instantly because of the repetition of commercials. This is simply one example of hundreds of associations with companies that we have all learned through repetition.

Emotions have always been used in selling products and services. Advertisers have used almost every emotion to help drive home their selling point. A house is totally destroyed by fire but, luckily, *"They were in good hands with All State Insurance"*.

A family is totally happy and content after driving cross-country in their Ford van. Many advertisers realize their prospective customers are **relaxing** while watching television and, as they relax, the selling message is delivered.

This type of approach does not cause the consumer to rush right out and purchase the product, but rather the information is stored in the mind. A consumer may be in need of motor oil and, while at the auto parts store, remembers hearing good things about a certain brand of motor oil. Since the consumer heard the message initially while in a relaxed state, he may or may not recall that the wonderful things he heard were actually from a commercial.

In using **concentration** in advertisement, the advertiser is not concerned with whether or not you are concentrating on the commercial. This technique is known as *"distracting the conscious mind"*. These commercials are usually so indirect that, even if you are concentrating on the commercial, you may not even be aware of what is being sold. The message is still being recorded by your subconscious mind for later use.

The last tool used is to create the correct *belief* system. There are two ways in which advertisers use this technique. The first is to have a celebrity that the public holds in high regard to endorse the product by lending his/her credibility to the product. The message is, *"If it is good enough for this celebrity, it is good enough for me"*. The second technique is to show documentation or live demonstrations of the product performing. Infomercial are prime examples of this.

Once the belief system has been created, the consumer may actually begin recommending the product to others, even if they have not personally used it. One of the most obvious examples of advertisers bypassing the critical part of the mind was in a shampoo commercial. This specific commercial ran successfully for a number of years under the premise of being concerned for your safety.

In each version of the commercial, one member of the family would be in the shower and request someone else to hand them the shampoo. The family member would toss them the shampoo and it would bounce off the shower wall and come to rest on the floor. The individual in the shower made several gallant attempts to catch the shampoo before it fell. The family member that did the tossing would then say, *"Don't worry, it now comes in a new, unbreakable tube"*.

The public believed that the unbreakable tube would provide them with the added safety they needed. The selling feature was an unbreakable tube. Have you ever seen a tube that does break? The average consumer never thought about the silliness of the commercial. They only heard the words, *"Don't worry, it's an unbreakable tube"*. We can accomplish so much by accidentally bypassing the critical part of the mind. Imagine the wonderful things that could be achieved by working at it!

In a following chapter, you will learn how to word suggestions in a manner that will increase the likelihood of being accepted by the subconscious. You will also learn techniques that will enhance your communication skills.

History: How It All Began

Now that you know what hypnosis is and how it works, you may be interested in how hypnosis began. It has been said that hypnosis began before any recorded history. It was used in religious and healing ceremonies. The procedure was different then than it is at this time. Inductions were primitive, consisting of chanting and monotonous drum beating as the eyes became strained from staring at a particular spot.

It is surprising to discover that in the early 1770s, the modern history of hypnosis began with Father Gassner, a Catholic priest. At that time, it was believed that people who were ill were possessed by demons and could only regain good health when the demons were cast out of their bodies.

Physicians would observe **Father Gassner** as he *"cured"* his patients. It was quite a spectacle. Father Gassner would make a grand entrance in a long, black cape, holding a gold crucifix high up in the air. Patients had been told in advance that when the priest touched them with the crucifix, they would fall to the floor and remain there until they were instructed to do otherwise. The patients were told to actually *"die"* while lying on the floor. A physician would examine the individual to assure that there was no pulse, no heartbeats and would pronounce the person as being dead. During this time, the Father would cast out the demons, and then the patient would revive and awaken, restored to a healthy life again. Mesmer was said to have witnessed a number of these sessions and is responsible for introducing the phenomena to the medical profession.

Franz Anton Mesmer did not believe, as Father Gassner did, that patients were possessed by demons. He determined that the metal crucifix held by the Father was responsible for magnetizing the patient. Mesmer developed his idea into the theory of animal magnetism. He would later name this *"Mesmerism"*, after himself.

Even though Mesmer was called a fraud by the French government, in 1784, Benjamin Franklin, who was a member of the investigating committee, stated that this phenomenon was worthy of further consideration. Although Mesmer tried to convince the commission that he had a secret worth knowing, he continued to hide the extreme simplicity of his procedure by camouflaging it with complicated machinery and superfluous instructions.

It was believed that the more the individuals were in a state of nature, the better. It was necessary that the person be open to suggestions and would obey them without question. Passive obedience in the individual and sustained patience in the operator were the key ingredients to success. By being naked during the procedure, the individual would be more *"submissive"* and psychologically *"defenseless"*. This put them in the frame of mind that would be advantageous for Mesmer's procedure.

Having his patients in a tub filled with water and iron fillings protruding from which were larger iron rods, Mesmer would suggest to them that as he touched them with his magnetic rod, they would become magnetized. He said that they would have a reaction, somewhat startling – like a seizure, and then would be cured. It was Mesmer's belief that this *"seizure"* was absolutely necessary for the cure to be effective. Mesmer, much like Father Gassner, was very dramatic in his long-flowing robe. The image of him holding his magnetic rod as he circled his clinic commanded authority.

His student, **Marquis de Puysegur** would do the same procedure, but forgot to tell them in advance that they would have a startling reaction. Because of this omission, they entered into a state of quiet relaxation, which he called ***"Artificial Somnambulism"***, because the patients did not have the startling reaction.

Marquis de Puysegur was responsible for describing the three main features of hypnosis, which are **concentration of the senses** on the hypnotist, **accepting suggestions without question** and **amnesia for events** that have transpired while in a trance. It was later determined in 1814, that it wasn't the animal magnetism that created the positive results in the individuals, instead, it was due to the suggestions that had been given to the patients that had been accepted.

In 1842, **Dr. James Braid** coined the term *"Hypnosis"*. He renamed *"Mesmerism"* after the Greek word *"Hypnos"*, which means *"Sleep"*. He later tried to rename it again, once he realized that hypnosis was not a true sleep, but hypnosis had become so well known by this name that he abandoned his efforts. What would he have called it? **Monoideism**, which means *"the state or condition of devotion to one idea or thought"*

Dr. Braid had a good understanding of how powerful and helpful hypnosis is in working in conjunction with medical treatment. Hypnosis was capable of curing many diseases for which there had not been a cure. He realized that it needed to be used along with medication and medical remedies in order to achieve the best results. He was truly ahead of his time.

On April 4, 1845, **Dr. James Esdaile** performed his first operation under hypnosis. He was the groundbreaker who used hypnosis as an anesthesia. He did much research in Calcutta, India trying to promote further use of hypnosis in the medical field. As he was performing hundreds of surgeries using hypnosis, chloroform was introduced as an anesthesia. Physicians who felt that his patients were hysterical dismissed his findings regarding the value of hypnosis as an anesthesia. When a prize of $10,000 was offered in 1853 to the discoverer of the anesthetic properties of ether, which was described as the earliest anesthetic, Esdaile sent a letter in protest stating that he had performed hundreds of painless surgeries under hypnosis for years before anyone had ever heard of ether. Chloroform had proceeded ether and, as with hypnosis, was not recognized as being the first anesthetic.

Sigmund Freud is probably the best-known person associated with hypnosis. Unfortunately, he was a poor hypnotist, so his rejection of it sent hypnosis into obscurity. Because of Freud's great brilliance and popularity in psychoanalysis, his denunciation of hypnosis rendered it useless and unworthy.

World War I created a new era of hypnosis. There were few psychiatrists available at that time and with numerous paralytic and amnesia cases with psychogenic origin, the value of hypnosis was once again on the forefront. Many new experts came forth, including many stage hypnotists.

In 1955, the *British Medical Association* officially endorsed the teaching of hypnosis in all medical schools. A university course in hypnosis was established for medical and dental professions. The *American Medical Association* conducted a three-year exhaustive study, which culminated in an official endorsement of hypnosis in 1958.

Milton Erickson, a maverick psychiatrist, was highly effective with his countless innovative and creative techniques. Brief therapy, solution focused therapy, systemic family therapy, child psychology and even sports performance training have all been influenced by Milton Erickson's work and ideas. He was the master of indirect hypnosis; he used metaphors, surprise and humor in his work.

In the 1970s *John Grinder* and *Richard Bandler*, initiators of Neuro-Linguistic Programming, incorporated Ericksonian hypnosis into their work. With the culmination of these techniques, progress has been accelerated in personal improvement.

As we look back over the years, we realize just how far hypnosis has come. It has been used in medical and dental procedures. 44,000 operations were done in 1960 under hypnosis without a single anesthetic death. 52,000 were done in 1961, and 68,000 in 1962. That was over 40 years ago. One can only imagine how many procedures are performed today using hypnosis.

A countless number of sessions have been conducted for pre and post-surgery clients. We had the privilege of performing a hypnosis session in a hospital for a lady who had rejected her kidney transplant. After only one session, her improvement allowed her to return home after just a few days. The power of one's mind should never be underestimated.

When you consider the modern history of hypnosis and realize that a Catholic priest was the one who brought this procedure to our modern world, it is no surprise that the Catholic Church approved hypnosis for therapy in 1957. We've come a long way, but there is still a long way to go.

CHAPTER 2

How Can Hypnosis Help To Raise Children?

It is important to understand what your child is thinking and experiencing. When we are able to get onto their level, we are able to communicate with them in a way that they understand.

Children are basically in a state of hypnosis most of the time! When we give suggestions that they accept, the goals are reached. But, what if they don't accept the suggestions? That's easy. It doesn't work! This is why you need to know what motivates your children. When you know what is important to them, you will be able to utilize this to your advantage.

Now, you may think that this is manipulative, and it is! But, you are the parent(s). It is your responsibility to teach and guide your children into being healthy, happy, successful adults. You want them to be socialized so that they fit into society. When parents cater to their children, they are doing them a disservice. How? In the real world, you don't always get what you want. There may be times when you want something, but may have to work harder for it, or have to wait longer to achieve it. If a child is conditioned to always get what they want when they want it, they will become quite frustrated in their adult life when the rest of the world doesn't see things their way.

With hypnosis, we are working with positive suggestions. **You cannot remove negative behavior with negative suggestions.** Since we focus on the positive, this is the outcome that will be achieved.

Whatever we think about, whether it is positive or negative, we are putting energy into it. Whatever we put energy into, is what we are creating in our lives. Since it takes the same amount of energy to create either a positive or a negative outcome, doesn't it make more sense to focus on what you *do* want?

Conscious Mind vs. Subconscious Mind
The conscious mind is very practical and analytical. This is the part of the mind that we refer to when we say that we are **"thinking"** about something. The **subconscious mind** takes things literally. It does not *read between the lines*. The subconscious is the **"reacting"** part of our mind. It works quickly, automatically.

Let's take a scenario and look at it in two different ways:

Imagine that on the floor there is a 2"x 4" piece of board that is about 10 feet long. You practice walking on the board and can do it with ease. You may even clown around doing fancy footwork to show off how adept you are walking on this board. You are so skilled; you never fall off of it. You may even find that you can run across the board and still keep your footing.

Now, imagine that we take this same board and place it between two buildings that are 20 stories high. Would you be able to run and play on the board as you did when it was placed on the floor? The board didn't get any smaller; the consequences became greater.

This is how different the conscious and the subconscious minds are. The subconscious mind does things quickly and automatically. Once you've learned something, you can do it with ease without much thought; like typing, riding a bike or driving a car. When the conscious mind kicks in, it is practical and analytical. It hinders our progress at times because it *thinks too much!*

Of course, we don't want to make poor choices that put us in harm's way. The illustration above shows that you can be doing the same thing, but when the consequence is too high, we may end up getting in our own way.

Imagine that you are asked to recite your ABCs. Someone will time you to see just how fast you can say them. Without thinking, you automatically rattle off the letters without second thought.

Now, the person timing you tells you that they are going to cut your work in half; you only have to say "half" of the alphabet. You get excited thinking that you're going to break the world's record for this! That's right, you only need to say "half" of the alphabet – every "other" letter!

If you even attempted to do this, it would take you at least ten times more in order to finish. Why? Because you have to "consciously" think about each letter in order to know which ones to skip.

As you can see, the conscious and subconscious parts of our minds have their own purposes and benefits. If used in the way they are intended, we reap the rewards. If, however, they are not used in the manner in which they were created, there may be drawbacks or disappointments.

As an example, imagine that your child does his/her homework every night and feels very comfortable with what they have learned. The next day the teacher says that there is going to be a pop quiz. If they pass this one test, they will pass the class. If they fail, they will be held back for another year. All of a sudden, the consequences have become greater. Your child felt secure studying at home, but if this one test can make that big of a difference, it puts added pressure on them. This is when they will usually engage their *conscious* mind to *think* of the right answers. Instead, if they would just *relax* and let the *subconscious* mind take over, the answers would come to them quickly and easily.

The subconscious mind stores everything that we have ever seen, heard, thought, read or experienced. It is all there. It is filed away so that when we need it, we have it. When the conscious mind tries to take over, it tries too hard to get the information. It's like trying to catch a feather; the more you grasp at it, you are actually *pushing* it away. When you relax with your hand open, the feather will gently float down onto the palm of your hand.

Hypnosis allows your children to focus on what would bring them the most success in life. It opens up a world of possibilities. Individuals who use hypnosis are basically very positive, happy, up-beat people. They focus on what they want, and they get it. Isn't this what you want for your children?

Hypnosis is effective because there are techniques that you can use in the waking state without inducing hypnosis. Throughout this book, you will be given tried and true techniques that stand the test of time. These are not just theories, but actual applications that have been utilized over decades.

Basic Reasons For Behavior

The downfall of many books and classes is the failure to explain that there is not only one single way of communicating. If we were all exactly the same, there would be just one single way for us to do this. If we were all exactly the same, then delivering a message would be much easier.

When delivering suggestions, either in a conscious or a subconscious state, it is important to ascertain the type of individual that we are dealing with. Children, like adults, fall into some predictable categories. These categories have been determined through trial and error. The child has experimented with different types of behaviors trying to determine which behavior is most likely to lead them to the ultimate goal.

When we are working with toddlers, it is different than with older children. You cannot reason with a two-year-old. Sometimes bad behavior is the only way that they know how to communicate because they get a reaction. It works, so they continue to do it.

For example, some toddlers have learned to bite in order to get their message across. Giving your child *"time out"* for this type of behavior is not effective. You need to get down to their level, look your child in the eye and in an authoritative voice say, *"Stop, no biting!"* By looking them in the eye, you have their attention. By telling them in short, specific terms what you want, they will learn.

Since this is the only way that your toddler knows how to get what they want, they continue to do it. But, if you take a look at the situation, you will be able to determine what it is that they are trying to communicate to you.

Let's say that your toddler is playing with another child who has a toy that they both like. Your child bites the other in order to get the toy. In the past it worked because when your child bit the other one, they dropped the toy and, *viola*, your child got what they wanted – the toy!

Since you don't want your child being known as *"jaws"*, it's important to find another way to resolve this issue. First of all, if you know that your child has a special toy that other children may want to play with as well, put the toy away when other children are around. No toy. No problem. Second option would be for you to keep an eye on your toddler. When the first sign comes that they are getting ready to chomp down on someone's flesh, that's when you look them in the eye and say, *"Stop – no biting!"* If the toy is what you think your child wants, look at your toddler and acknowledge that you understand the situation. Tell him/her, *"You want that toy, don't you?"* Repeat it as often as you need to for the child to understand that you know what they want. When the child feels that they are getting their message across, the biting won't be necessary.

Children need to know that if they choose a certain action that the consequence will *always* be the same. They need consistency. If you tell your child that they cannot watch TV if their homework is not finished, you must stick with that. *No exceptions.* If they don't finish their homework, they *choose* not to watch TV. Make them responsible for their decisions. Let them know that they are in control of the outcome. If they want to watch TV, they will make sure that their homework is completed.

If *"time out"* is used, you need to put your child in a place where there are no distractions. They should remain in *"time out"* for one minute for each year in their age. (Example: for a *three*-year-old child, the *"time out"* would be for *three* minutes.)

When I was growing up, life was much simpler. If one of us kids started to get out of line, all it took was *"the look"* from one of our parents and we knew they meant business. We knew for sure what would happen if we didn't shape up. They set the boundaries and we knew just how far we could push them.

What happens with some parents is that they will give in when the child begs, screams, cries or throws a tantrum. At first, you may encounter this, but if you stick with your rules, soon the child will realize that you are not budging. They will learn that they are accountable for their own actions. This will make life a lot easier at home, as well as help your child to adjust to the outside world. When they go to school or work, your child will realize that the world does not revolve around them. Other personalities come into play. It's quite different than it was in their safe haven at home.

When my daughter, Angie, would get upset, I had a sure-fire cure for her ranting and raving. In the heat of the moment, when she was yelling and getting mad, I would interrupt her and tell her that if she wanted to be mad, she had to take off her *left shoe* and put it on top of the TV set.

When she did this, she lost her momentum. After putting her shoe on top of the TV, she couldn't get back into the anger in the same way as she had done before. By interrupting the behavior and having her change her focus from being mad to taking off her *left shoe*, we cancel out the bad behavior. She had to think about her *left shoe* and then she had to place it on top of the TV. Once that is done, so is the tantrum.

As much as they may deny it, children *want* discipline. This shows that you love and care about them. If you didn't, you would let them do whatever they wanted whenever they wanted. By setting down some practical rules, your children will feel the love and care that you have for them. Even if all of the other children are doing something and your child is not able to participate, at first they may be disappointed, but in the end will realize that you only said *"No"* because you care about their wellbeing.

Children need you to be their parent(s), not their friend(s). There will be plenty of time for that when they become adults. Until then, your role is to love them, guide them, teach them and protect them. Children do not have the experience or information that you do. They cannot anticipate possible outcomes, where you have that knowledge.

You may be amused in the future when your children tell you, *"Remember the time you wouldn't let me _____?"* They may surprise you by saying that they really didn't want to do that and were happy that you told them that they couldn't. You were their excuse, their *"fall guy"*. Be the best parent as they are growing up, and you may be their best friend when they are adults.

There are **four reasons** for a child to respond in a manner that is not acceptable:

1. To Get Attention

We are all striving for attention. As a three-year-old, the child might roll on the floor. This is his/her way of saying, *"Look at me!"* As a twelve-year-old, he/she can no longer get attention by rolling on the floor. They must find another way of getting attention. They could then choose to join a gang or become involved with drugs. These choices would surely get the attention that they are seeking. More positive choices might have been to excel in sports, music or be at the top in their class for grades.

As a teenager and adult, he/she will be seeking attention. Without verbally saying so, we are all saying, *"Look at me!"* As adults we might be saying it with the fancy car we drive. Elaborate clothing or jewelry might be our way of saying, *"Look at me!"* Some people accomplish this undertaking through their careers. From an early age as a toddler to an elderly senior citizen, we are always trying to get attention and approval from others.

2. To Beat Adults At A Power Game

Many children learn, either directly or indirectly from their parents, that the most important thing in our life is to win. Parents that are always boasting about outdoing someone else are indirectly sending a message to the child that everything is fair as long as you win. A child that is raised in an environment where he/she hears Dad or Mom constantly talking about taking advantage of someone will naturally emulate this behavior. The parents' behavior may also be a direct suggestion. The parent that is preoccupied with always winning may consciously teach the importance of winning to their child.

I had a friend that was sharing a story with me about his son. He stated that his little boy had thrown a deck of cards on the floor and had refused to pick them up. He told the child he was not going to leave until he had picked up all of the cards. The child began to test in order to see if Dad really meant what he said. Would he have to pick up all fifty-two cards? He picked up about a dozen and asked Dad, "How is that"? The father replied, "I told you to pick them all up." The child, testing once again, picked up another ten or twelve cards and then asked, "How is that"? This time the parent said that was enough. I think my friend could see the surprise on my face as he related this story. His response was, "I also need to teach him to win".

There is nothing wrong with teaching a child to win. The parent must also teach the child to follow rules set down by those in an authoritative position. With this type of learning, the child will view rules set down by the parents, teachers, coaches, etc. as a power game.

Children can be very manipulative. They may *"push the envelope"* at times to see how much they can get away with.

I remember a time when I was a little boy and I got some markers and drew on my Mother's dresser. When she saw the damage that was done, she scolded me and sent me to my room. Now, my Mom was a smart lady. She knew that my older brother was too old to be doing something like that, and my younger sister was too young. So, that left me. She was right, but then that power trip kicked in!

As I was in my room, I could hear my Mom coming down the hallway. I acted like I was crying, and began to say out loud, "Dear God, please forgive my Mom for getting mad at me. She doesn't know that I'm not the one who drew on her dresser, but at least you know!" Moments later, my Mom rushed into my room, scooped me up in a hug filled with apologies. I was really glad that I wasn't my older brother that day!

3. <u>To Get Revenge On Their Parents Who Refused To Give Them Attention Through More Acceptable Means</u>

There are hundreds of different ways in which children strive to get revenge upon their parents. Early in their lives, it might be by throwing a fit at a family function, but as time goes on, the child has a tendency to select the exact opposite of what the parent wants. A parent that is against dancing lessons may find a child that is preoccupied with dancing. Many years ago experts called this *"reverse psychology"*. They suggested that parents tell the child the exact opposite of what they wanted them to do.

In today's times, children are far too knowledgeable to be taken in by that technique. For most children the revenge phase is short-lived. However, it is not unheard of for the child to mature into adulthood continuing to get revenge or rebel in some fashion against one or both of their parents.

There have been many cases where a daughter will marry someone that her parents are totally against. If the desire for revenge or rebellion is strong enough, a child could actually ruin her own life just to get back at her parents. Some child and teen suicides have been traced back to the desire to teach the parents a lesson.

4. <u>To Be Sickly Or Non-Productive</u>

Children in this category are usually failing in school or plagued by unfounded illnesses. The attention received may not be from the parents directly, but rather from doctors, nurses or tutors. The child has made the decision that since he is not going to receive the attention from inside the home, he is now going to get it from outside sources.

Sometimes bad behavior is not really intentional. A child may do something without the thought or intention of hurting anyone. You may find that your child has a great imagination that can get them into trouble from time to time.

When my little sister and I were kids, she had a little kitchen set like most girls did at her age. My sister had blonde, curly hair. It was full and beautiful. One day I got a thought. My imagination ran wild. "I wonder..." I thought. "How do they make cotton candy?" I thought I had it all figured out. I got my sister's mixer from her kitchen set and as I turned it on, I placed it in the center of her golden locks. "This is how they do it!" I was sure I had the answer. I couldn't wait to make some. I would certainly share it with my sister. As she ran screaming to my Mother with the mixer caught in her hair, I realized that I didn't have it figured out after all.

Bad habits, bad grades, irrational fears, problems with self-esteem and many other behavioral problems may be based on an imprint. We know there can be positive imprints, as well. **Any change in behavior that began as the result of something we've seen, heard, felt or experienced is an *imprint*.** This behavior resides in the subconscious part of the mind. The individual may experience an intense emotion when this experience occurs and may not even remember in a conscious state when the behavioral change took place.

A child in pain with an ear infection is told that they are *"just like Uncle Joe"*, who was always sickly. This child may develop an obsession about becoming sick.

Sometimes, however, the imprint is neither positive nor negative:

I have an imprint that involves drinking water. I'm one of the few people I know that prefers to drink warm water. Using self-hypnosis, I regressed myself back in time and discovered an imprint that occurred when I was about eight or nine years old.

It was summertime and I was locked out of the house in the July heat. I was so thirsty; I thought I was dying from lack of water. I tried every door and window, but couldn't get into the house. About this time, convinced that I was going to die, I thought, "Here I come, God!" (Even then I was a positive thinker, assuming I was headed to Heaven!) Suddenly, I remembered the garden hose. When I turned it on and began to drink, it was very warm, but it was the best water I had ever tasted. As an eight or nine-year-old, I was convinced that it saved my life. Even today, I prefer my water warm or at least room temperature. Cold water just doesn't quench my thirst as well.

I was very impressionable as a child. Now, as an adult, I realize why I have some of the imprints that I do. I like to carry a fair amount of money in my pocket wherever I go. Looking back, I realize where this imprint started.

As kids, my brother, sister and I would go to the movies. Since he was the oldest, my brother carried all of the money. My parents gave him money for the show and refreshments that we wanted to have while we were there. My brother paid for the show, but when we asked him for some popcorn, he said, *"No"*. I realize now that he wanted to pocket that extra money for himself. It has been a habit of mine ever since to make sure that I always have money in my pocket.

Another imprint that I have comes from watching horror movies as a kid. Remember those movies where the killer hid in the basement and as the person walked down the stairs he would grab their ankles so that they would fall down so he could kill them? Boy, it certainly made an impression on me! To this day, whenever I am going up or down the basement stairs, I take two steps at a time! Eventually, I decided to close in the back of the basements stairs and carpet it. Even though, consciously, I know that there is no killer hiding underneath my basement stairs, I feel a lot better with the stairs closed off!

Brain Development

It's amazing to discover that a baby's brain is only about 25% of its approximate adult weight; it is not fully developed at birth. By three-years-old, the brain is about 80% of its adult size; it grows to 90% by age five. Babies' brains grow very rapidly taking years to complete. The development in the early years is quite dramatic. A baby's and young child's brain is extremely more active and complex than you may think.

The *cerebral cortex* is the part of the brain that is responsible for all of our conscious thoughts, feelings, memories and voluntary actions. When a baby is born, this part of the brain is very immature and is not functioning as it will in the future. Babies' brains develop first in their *vision cortex or primary touch area of the cortex.* Later the *temporal and frontal lobes* develop. These are the areas of the brain that are involved in higher cognitive and emotional functions.

The brain is quite complex. It weighs only three pounds, but is the body's most vital organ. All of the brain cells that a brain has are present at birth. No more are developed. Although we have enough brain cells to learn anything, if they are not used they die off. As the old saying goes, *"Use it or lose it!"*

Between the ages of three and ten is our learning peak. This is the time to expose your child to as much as you can in order to strengthen their learning ability. Classical music, like Mozart, was believed to help them develop their math and spatial reasoning because it is in the same areas of the brain. However, this has not yet been proven. During this age span, it would be easier for a child to learn different languages.

Get in the habit of talking with your child. Whatever activity you may be doing, tell your child step-by-step about the process. Name items that you are using, tell them the name of each item of clothing as you are dressing them, tell them what color it is, count how many buttons are on their shirt. The more information you give them, the quicker they learn. It helps to strengthen their brain cells.

A baby's emotions are developed between 10 and 18 months. Long-term memory is connected with emotions. The *limbic system* regulates emotional impulses and assists us to determine what the appropriate response would be; should we fight, run, hide, cry, whine, or react in some other way. Children learn by example. Whatever response is taught to the child, it will become permanent. If something happens and is followed by a certain action, it makes an imprint on the brain. The response that the child is taught is what they will do; the more vivid the memory, the stronger the imprint.

Did you know that a three-year-old can hold two different emotions in their mind at the same time? They can be sad that they broke a toy, yet happy that it is Christmas.

The more loving and patient you are with your children, the more secure they feel. When children are ignored or not nurtured during this impressionable time, they do not fully develop all areas of their brains.

Nutrition plays a big role in a baby's development, for brain as well as body, and is most sensitive between mid-gestation and two years of age. The mother's nutrition during pregnancy, and if she breast-feeds her baby, is critical to the child. After the baby is born, the quality of the baby's nutrition is a determining factor. When fetuses and infants are malnourished, it can result in deficient brain growth, which contributes to behavioral, as well as learning problems.

It is also necessary to realize the importance that nurturing plays in the development of your child. Simple activities such as holding, feeding and comforting your baby does impact the way the baby's brain develops.

You may be surprised to learn that babies prefer listening to a person talk or sing than any kind of sound. This, and the nurturing provided by holding and rocking them, is the best kind of stimulation for their brain development. Just loving your baby is the best thing that you can do for their health and wellbeing.

A friend of mine babysat her nephew one day each week for a good portion of his first year of life. She loved to hold him, read and sing to him as they spent their time together. She would talk with him when she fed him as if he knew and understood what she was talking about. He loved motion, so she would rock him and *"dance"* with him as she sang. After his first birthday, the weekly assistance was no longer necessary, as her sister grew stronger and felt more comfortable in her motherly role.

After not seeing her nephew for a length of time, she was pleased to find that when she did see him when he was walking, he would see her and run right to her. She felt so good, thinking that all of her singing, talking, reading and cooing made a positive impression on him. When she would hold him and sing a song that she used to sing before putting him to bed, he would put his head on her shoulder and relax his whole body. The memory had never left.

Research shows that one of the best ways to assist a child in their critical brain-building years is to talk, read and sing to them. This will help the child to improve their language skills and stimulate their brain development. When you talk to them, use a higher voice or a more animated inflection. They respond better to this style than a normal speaking voice that would be flatter or monotonous. When teaching them words, over-enunciate the words. This will help them to remember the words and learn pronunciation.

Over the years it has been determined that when adults talk to their babies, they should talk to them in the actual terms that they would use with each other, rather than using *"baby talk"*. As an example: when getting ready to feed your infant, refer to the bottle as a *"bottle"*, not a *"ba-ba"* or other cutesy term that you may come up with. By talking to babies in your usual vocabulary, they will learn more quickly. If you think about this, it makes sense. If they *think* that a bottle is a ba-ba, they will one day have to re-learn that a ba-ba is *really* a bottle. They have to learn one thing *twice*.

The human brain begins forming just about three weeks after conception.

However, don't let this confuse you. It actually is a life-long process for the brain to fully develop. In some ways, it never does because we are always taking in new information. The brain stores everything that we have ever seen, heard, felt or experienced. This affects our perception. Although a child's brain is more open to learning and taking in new information than an adult, it is also more vulnerable to their environment, whether it is positive or negative.

Genes and environment play crucial roles in a child's development. The genes provide each of us with our potential or foundation. Environment influences our perception, which creates mannerisms and habits.

A good example of this would be obesity. Our genes may dictate that we have the *potential* to be overweight, but the environment in which we live influences the eating habits that we adopt. If a child is raised in a family where everyone is overweight; they eat the wrong kind, wrong amounts of food with little or no physical activity, they, too, will be overweight if they choose the same eating patterns and lack of activity as the rest of the family. However, if a child has the *potential* to be overweight in their genes, but is raised in a family that eats healthy foods in the appropriate amount with an active lifestyle, they will not be overweight.

The difference between these two children would be their environments and choices that they make in their lives. If a child is raised in the first scenario, but chooses to eat right and be active, although the rest of the family is obese, they will not be. Just as if the child in the second scenario decided to binge or eat unhealthy and be inactive, they will gain weight, even though the rest of their family is healthy and in shape.

When comparing male vs. female for brain development, the male brains are slightly larger in size, but the females are more advanced. Another comparison is that the male and female brains are *"wired"* differently.

Baby girls will develop more quickly as far as being able to see, hear and touch. Baby girls are more advanced with memory, fine motor skills and ability to talk, language skills.

By the age of three, the boys will have a tendency to catch-up with the girls and actually be more advanced in the area of visual-spatial integration. Boys will be able to move about more easily and be more adept in their hand-eye coordination.

Many times we are amazed when we see that little boys are drawn to playing with trucks and cars or building blocks and little girls are drawn to dolls or playing with other children. This is actually the way that their brains are *"wired"*. Since boys are better with their hand-eye coordination, it would make sense that they would like to build or move something. Since girls are more social and are better at language, playing with dolls is natural because they are *"talking"* for the dolls while playing with a sibling or friend.

To assist your children in balancing their abilities, one may choose to converse more with a little boy or play word games to help him develop his social and language skills. When playing with a little girl, working a jigsaw puzzle or building blocks may assist her in improving her visual-spatial abilities.

Overall, males are better at mental rotation, being able to imagine how an object would look if it were turned 90 degrees; while females are better with verbal skills and being able to identify different emotional expressions in others. Perhaps, this is why women are more compassionate, as a rule, than males. The female brain is aligned with varying emotions, so are able to relate or respond more effectively with others.

This, of course, is generally speaking. Every person is unique and individual. There are many men who may be more compassionate than women, while many women excel in their visual-spatial abilities. It is unfair to say that *all* males are *this way* and *all* females are *this way*. Many things factor into our individual development.

Teenagers: Have They Lost Their Minds?

A child's brain is still developing until their early 20s. Behind the forehead is a part of the brain called the *frontal lobe* that associates with **reasoning, critical thinking and problem solving**. Since this is **not fully developed**, there may be times when your child may spew obscene remarks that may even surprise them. When they get emotionally charged, their reasoning factors may have vanished totally. They make poor choices and harmful decisions. We ask them, *"Have you lost your mind?"* In a way, they never had one; they haven't fully developed theirs yet .

Research shows that the brain of a teenager responds differently to the outside world than an adult brain. The teenage brain doesn't think things through in a reasonable manner; instead, they have more of an impulsive behavioral response. They don't think about the consequences or the probable repercussions. They want it, they do it, and then reality sinks in after the fact. Teens are more spontaneous and less inhibited than adults.

Since their reasoning capabilities are still under construction, we cannot expect them to be able to determine appropriate decisions for all situations. That's what parents are for. You need to look around the corners for them, since they aren't able to do this for themselves.

An interesting study was conducted where teens and adults were shown facial expressions and asked how they perceived them. A facial expression that expressed *fear* was not acknowledged by teens in that way, although adults did identify that facial expression accurately. Teens perceived it as *shock, sadness, or anger.* Knowing that teens actually *see* things differently, is there any wonder that we have problems with communication?

Never assume that just because you gave them specific information that they understood it the way you meant it. They may understand what you said, but in a totally different way than you had desired. Keep in mind that they are not always trying to be difficult, their brains are just processing the information in a different manner.

Sleep, or lack of it, affects teens' ability to think, perform and their mood. Research says that teens should get nine-and-a-quarter hours of sleep each night in order to be at their best. Surveys show that most teens are not getting the right amount of sleep.

ADD / ADHD In Children

Neurologists have tests that can be given to your child to determine if they have *ADD (Attention Deficit Disorder) or ADHD (Attention Deficit and Hyperactivity Disorder).* An EEG determines the brain waves to see if there is a pattern that shows the presence of this disorder. There is also a Spectrogram that looks at the dynamics of the brain and how it takes in glucose. One out of 20 is diagnosed with ADD or ADHD.

Children with this condition often have trouble with change. They need routines in their life so they know what to expect. If there are any changes that come up, it is important to notify the child as far ahead of the change as possible so that they can focus better.

Now we are going to examine the symptoms of ADD or ADHD. Those who have a child or children already diagnosed with this condition will recognize many of these:

SYMPTOMS OF ADD/ADHD

Poor academic achievers
Tend to take things literally
Demonstrate anti-social behavior
The majority of cases are males
Self-conscious XE "conscious" about appearance
Will spend hours doing 30 minutes of homework
If given a list of tasks, normally only remember the last one
Tend to have the ability to manipulate people
Rarely appear to be listening
Have difficulty remaining seated
Interrupt conversations of others
Normally passive and sensitive
Demonstrate difficulty in following directions
Seem to be always fidgeting
Increased likelihood of becoming involved with substance abuse in the future

There are many positive qualities found in those individuals with ADD/ADHD. People with this condition tend to be very likable. They are normally warm, friendly, intuitive people with high energy levels. They tend to be very trusting, have a good sense of humor and are very caring, empathetic to others.

Children with ADD/ADHD tend to take things very literally. During sessions, I've given the suggestion that their eyes are locked shut and asked them to try to open their eyes. I tell them that they'll discover their eyelids are locked shut, only to have the child reach up and try to lift their eyelids with their hands. If told to open their eyes and pick one spot on their hand on which to concentrate, they would literally point to the spot with the other hand.

While parents may report that it takes the child hours to finish a small amount of homework, they also find that the child may appear to have intense concentration when it comes to a topic that is of interest to them. Make their homework assignments fun so that they are more interesting to the child. ADD/ADHD students may do poorly on assignments that they find boring. Sometimes the child shows great ability to focus on a particular task, but if given a list of tasks, may only remember the last one.

You may want to help your child by keeping the list short, just two or three items, and having the most important item the last one on the list. In time, gradually make the list longer, always ending with the most important task or information.

The intelligence level can be very high; they can be very manipulative with others. Their need for attention can present itself as anti-social behavior. Some will do whatever it takes to get attention. It's important to be aware of the increased risk of substance abuse. This is an extreme way to get attention, as well as go off into their own little world.

Obviously, all children are unique with individual personalities. There are children with personalities that do not conform to the standard ADD/ADHD behaviors. We've found that hypnosis can help a child overcome some of the negative behaviors, retain the positive qualities and achieve a high degree of success in life.

An important factor about raising children with this condition is that the parents need to be unified in raising their child and how they react to the behavior issues. Children with ADD/ADHD need structure, discipline and consistency. This is vital in keeping their behavior in check.

Food can affect their behavior. Certain foods interact poorly with the child's brain at a neurological level. Fried foods usually make children sleepy. The more natural the food, the easier it is for the brain to metabolize and use it properly.

Children can learn to control their own brain patterns and activity to the point that it can affect their ADD/ADHD. Biofeedback monitors biological functioning. A child can learn to raise one brain wave and reduce another. Psychologists and psychiatrists who perform biofeedback training can teach children to do this. This can help children to awaken their brains in the right areas.

Many parents complain because medication seems to create side affects like no appetite, insomnia, headaches and lethargy. Working with well-informed doctors can help create a balance that helps the child in their development.

Hypnosis plays an integral part because the subconscious part of the mind is in control of automatic functions and habits. Giving positive suggestions to your child under hypnosis helps them to accept these suggestions without interruption from the conscious mind.

Children with ADD/ADHD sometimes need to have a place where they can unwind and reduce stress. Hypnosis is a perfect way for them to do just that.

Using Audiotapes For ADD/ADHD
There are important elements in working with ADD/ADHD. We will cover these, as well as some of the benefits you can expect. All benefits may not be present in all children.

There are pros and cons for using audiotapes. I tend to disagree with the use of tapes. With repetition, comes familiarity and boredom. With boredom, the child loses interest in listening to the tape.

There are *eight* basic rules for making audiotapes, if you choose to record them:

1. *Keep the length around 15 minutes.*
2. *Use the same background music as you played during the session. The child will instantly associate the music with the hypnotic session.*
3. *Use only direct suggestions. Children with ADD/ADHD tend to have less success with metaphors or indirect suggestions.*
4. *Have the child listen to the tape an average of **three times each week**. Increasing the amount of times the tape is used will not increase its benefits.*
5. *The best time for the child to use the tape would be just prior to falling asleep at night.*
6. *It is very valuable to personalize the tape for the child.*
7. *After 21 days of use, change or alter the tape. Typically, a tape will begin diminishing in effectiveness after that amount of time. This will counteract the familiarity and boredom that tends to develop.*
8. *Keep the suggestions simple and precise. The use of repetition in suggestions has been proven especially beneficial when working with children with ADD/ADHD.*

Years ago ADD/ADHD was considered simply a conduct problem and the solution was more discipline. Once the condition was recognized and diagnosed, the normal treatment became medications. Often these prescriptions created an over-medicated, zombie-like child that still had difficulty concentrating in school.

Hypnosis has proven to be very successful in treating ADD/ADHD. While not all children will have the same results, there are many positive outcomes a parent can anticipate for the child:

POSITIVE EFFECTS FROM HYPNOSIS
Decrease in amount of medications needed
Elimination of medications
Improved concentration span
Improved self-confidence
Noticeable improvement, even after a single session
Improved organizational skills
Improved control over physical movements; fidgeting
Improved grades
The child is happier and has improved perception of what the future holds for them

It's important to include the type of stimulants that can affect a child with ADD/ADHD. Both external and internal exert an influence and is essential to keep in mind that the child can perceive these either as a positive or a negative experience.

INTERNAL

The use of self-talk by the child
Anger that the child may experience when frustrated
Self-satisfaction from perceiving improvements
Daydreaming, in or out of school

EXTERNAL

Comments from teachers
Report Cards
Comments from friends or other students
Medications
Comments from parents
Visual stimulants in or out of the home

There are immeasurable benefits to teaching self-hypnosis XE "hypnosis: definitions for" to the child with ADD. With self-hypnosis XE "hypnosis:definitions for", the child will have the needed reinforcement that is needed in between sessions.

There are *seven* basic steps to teaching self-hypnosis to the child:
1. *Sell the benefits of self-hypnosis to the child*
2. *Teach progressive relaxation*
3. *Teach the use of visualization*
4. *Teach the correct use of positive suggestions*
5. *Teach how to deepen the state*
6. *Teach the procedure for exiting from hypnosis*
7. *Reinforce the importance of practice*

Self-hypnosis is a tool; the more you use it, the better you will get. Conversely, if you don't use it, you tend to lose it. You will find a greater degree of success if your child gets in the habit of using self-hypnosis on a regular basis.

Most Commonly Asked Questions

Can anyone be hypnotized?

This is probably the most asked question about hypnosis. If someone *wants* to be hypnotized and has, at least, normal intelligence, they can be hypnotized. The person going into hypnosis is always in control. You *cannot* be made to do anything against your will or your moral beliefs. The more an individual is able to relax, the more effective the session will be.

Are there any side effects from hypnosis?

Since hypnosis is a natural state, our bodies are conditioned to going in and out of the hypnotic state on a regular basis. Most people comment that they slept better after being hypnotized. This may be related to the fact that they were able to relax during the session, and this peaceful feeling carried over into their nightly sleep. The only side effects that would be associated with hypnosis would be positive.

Is there anything dangerous about hypnosis?
No. Hypnosis is very safe and natural. We do require a doctor's written prescription whenever we do sessions for pain control or pain management. The reason we are adamant about this is if hypnosis were used to reduce or eliminate pain or discomfort, but the doctor was not aware of this, the doctor would not have a barometer in order to gauge the individual's discomfort. We do not want to mask any symptoms that the doctor may need in order to make a proper diagnosis.

Should I stop taking medication before or after I'm hypnotized?
Hypnosis works in conjunction with medical treatment, *not in place of it.* Always follow your doctor's instructions. It is advisable to check with your physician first before making any changes with your medication or medical treatments.

Will I be able to drive after the session?
If you were able to drive to the office for the session, you will be able to drive afterwards. Hypnosis is very relaxing. Some individuals report that they feel as if they had several hours of sleep when they come out of the hypnotic state. Some people feel more energized. It is a truly rewarding experience that contributes to your feelings of health and wellbeing.

What does hypnosis feel like?
The best way to describe it would be that if you were lying down in front of the television and someone came into the room and asked you to turn off the TV, but you didn't move because you were so comfortable, that's what it feels like. You are awake; you are aware. You can hear everything that is being said, but you are just so relaxed, you do not want to disturb the wonderful feeling that you are experiencing.

Would the session be ruined if I were to cough or sneeze during the session?
Not at all! It's amazing how many people will cough, sneeze, scratch their nose, or move about during the session. It has no bearing on the outcome. The most important factor is your ability to relax and keep an open mind.

What is the youngest age for a child to be hypnotized?
As a rule, five-years-old is the youngest age for a hypnosis session, although this may vary depending on the hypnotist. For children under five year old, use the positive suggestions that we give you throughout this book to help them in a positive way in the waking state.

Will my child get stuck in hypnosis?
Since hypnosis is a natural state, a person would not get stuck. If an individual were hypnotized and then left alone, the person would fall asleep after a certain

amount of silence, and then wake up after they felt rested. They would just go into a natural sleep.

Will my child's personality change after the session?
An individual will only change what they want to change. Hypnosis is NOT brainwashing. We cannot make your child do anything. Depending on what they want to use hypnosis for will determine the amount of change that takes place. For example, if they are using hypnosis to become more confident or outgoing, changes may occur in these areas. There are no negative side effects from hypnosis. By giving suggestions for more confidence or to be more outgoing, they are not going to become a bully or mean-spirited from hypnosis. The results would all be positive.

Is there any difference between an adult or a child being hypnotized?
The difference would be in the way that the session is conducted. Children have short attention spans, so we would not be able to induce hypnosis and have them sit still for 30 minutes. It just won't happen! Therefore, we combine several small sessions into one. We induce hypnosis, give positive suggestions, bring them out of hypnosis and talk or play games with them for a short period of time. We would then re-induce the hypnotic state and give more positive suggestions. Depending on the child and the topic, we may do this procedure several times within the session.

Does my child have to do anything to prepare for the session before coming into your office?
No, not a thing. There is nothing that needs to be done in order to prepare for hypnosis, other than allowing yourself to relax and keep an open mind. Children are relieved to hear that they will NOT be getting any shots at the hypnotist's office!

How long will the session take?
The average session takes about one hour. When working with children, we like to allow a little more time because we talk privately with one or both parents before bringing the child into the office. Sometimes we are able to have an informative conversation over the telephone with a parent when they are booking the appointment, so there would be little or no need to converse with them again. We do need to acquire certain information from the parent or guardian in order to make the most of the session with the child.

Can I sit in on the session?
We find that we are more successful in our sessions when we work one-on-one with our clients, but if the child feels more comfortable having a parent sit in, then it would be advantageous for the parent to be there. Some children feel more comfortable with the parent in the room initially, but don't feel the need to have the parent stay during the entire session. After asking questions to get informa-

tion about the child's goal, the parent may leave before we induce hypnosis. We determine each session on an individual basis, depending on the needs and comfort level of our clients.

Will the improvements from the session last forever; if not, how long will they last?

Hypnosis is effective until it is bombarded either internally or externally by negativity. When a client accepts suggestions, they may last forever. However, if they doubt that the change will last or if someone who has influence over them states that it will not work or last, then the results will be short-lived. Reinforcement sessions would be advisable to strengthen the positive results from the suggestions that were given in the hypnotic session.

How many sessions will it take?

This depends on the topic and the individual being hypnotized. Everyone is different. Our goal is to be successful in as few sessions as possible. We want our clients to be in control and feel confident that the power of their own mind is what determines the outcome.

Will my child understand what you are doing in the session?

We talk with children at their level of comprehension. They will understand what we are saying to them. Like adults, they may not know why we do or say something in particular, but they understand that we are on their side, wanting them to reach their goal as easily as possible.

What happens if my child doesn't want to achieve the goal that we came to work on?

We cannot make anyone do something against their will. With children, however, we may work on a dual goal in order to get their cooperation. For example, if the child is having a session to improve their schoolwork or grades, they may not be motivated to work on this goal. If, however, we incorporate something that they are interested in, like sports or music, to improve on, the child is more willing to put forth the effort. We call this *"compounding"*. We give suggestions that as their schoolwork or grades improve, they may discover that their skills or abilities in (whatever they choose) are getting better, too.

CHAPTER 3

How To Get Started

Knowing what goal you want to reach is the first step in being successful. Imagine, just think about what would happen if someone handed you a dart and told you to hit the target. If you didn't have a target, you wouldn't be able to hit it. If you had several goals, your focus would be split and you wouldn't know at which target to aim. You need to be clear what it is that you want to achieve.

When working with children, we need to be realistic. Just because Mom or Dad would like junior to be the best shortstop on the baseball team doesn't mean that this would be his desire. Music may be the main focus for this child. It is important to cultivate the talents and abilities in our children, but they need to want to do this as well. It may just be a matter of timing.

The wonderful thing about using hypnosis to raise your children is that it is easy to do. You can utilize hypnotic techniques when your children are wide-awake! You can achieve great results by using these techniques as they are falling asleep or just waking up in the morning. You will learn basic hypnosis so that you will be able to induce the hypnotic state and achieve goals in this manner. The possibilities are endless!

Visualization

An easy technique to use when wanting to reach a goal or make a change is *visualization*. The conscious mind is practical and analytical, while the subconscious mind takes things literally. When using visualization to reach goals or make changes, we focus on the positive outcome that we desire.

Successful athletes on a regular basis use this technique. If you interviewed any sport, you would discover that the athletes who *thought* about their performance ahead of time were able to repeat what they had imagined.

A study was conducted with three groups of students. The test was to see which group could throw the most balls through the basketball hoop while standing at the free throw line. The first group was told to do nothing in preparation for the test. The second group was instructed to practice throwing the balls into the hoop every day for a designated time. The third group was told to just "imagine" throwing the ball through the hoop every day for a designated time.

When the three groups of students were physically tested to determine which group would get the most balls through the hoop, which group would you pick?

If you were like most people, you would pick the second group. However, the winners were the third group.

This may seem strange to most people because one would think that the more you do it, the better you would get. Practice makes perfect, right? Yes and no. When you think about each group, it is easy to dismiss group one because they put no effort into reaching their goal. The second group practiced. However, they did not always get the ball through the hoop each attempt that they made. The third group used visualization. If you are thinking about throwing a basketball through the hoop, aren't you going to *always imagine* getting the ball into the hoop? Of course you are! Hence, the difference.

The more you practice (visualize) reaching your goal, the subconscious mind *believes* that it has actually happened. The subconscious mind takes everything literally, so when you imagine throwing a basketball through the hoop, it goes in. The mind and body assume, then, that every time you physically throw a basketball, it goes in. When you are standing at the free throw line, whenever you throw the ball, your mind has already done it successfully hundreds of times before. Why should this time be any different?

Practice thinking about achieving whatever your goal is. The more you think about achieving your goal in a positive way, the easier it will be to manifest it because your mind will have already achieved it successfully every time that you thought about it.

There is something to be said for a positive attitude. You get what you expect to get. This, then, can also be negative.

A man took his young son to the circus. As they were watching the huge elephants in the center ring, the little boy looked up at his father and asked, "Daddy, why does the elephant just stand there? It is so big and strong, couldn't it just pull the rope and get away?"

The father smiled as he explained to his son, "When the elephant was a baby, it was much smaller than it is now. At that time, the trainer would attach a strong, steel chain around its ankle and drive a huge, stake deep into the ground. No matter how hard or how much the baby elephant would pull, it just couldn't get loose. The baby elephant tried many, many times, yet, could never break the chain that was attached to its ankle."

"As the baby elephant grew bigger, it still could not break the chain. When the elephant became an adult, it stopped trying to break away because of all of the previous times that it failed. Now, the trainer just needs to tie a rope gently around its ankle because it no longer tries to break free."

Isn't it sad to think that if the elephant would try *just one more time*, it would be successful? Unfortunately, this is what happens to us at times. We may try over and over again to achieve a goal, but give up after constantly failing. If we would only change the way that we look at a goal and try one more time, there is always the possibility for us to be successful. Sometimes people give up too soon, just like the elephant.

Affirmations

An *affirmation* **is a positive statement that is worded in the present tense that has power and meaning for you.** When setting goals or creating a thought to focus on, make sure that it is a positive statement. You *cannot* remove negative behavior with a negative suggestion. Keep your wording short and to the point. It is easier to remember and easier to repeat. Put positive emotion into your statement; avoid saying it by rote. You need to feel it in order to believe it.

When creating affirmations to assist your children in reaching their goals, determine what it is that you and your children want to accomplish. Do they want to improve their grades? Be more social? Feel more confident? Improve their sports performance? Once you have decided what their specific goal is, you can create a statement that puts your children in the right frame of mind. Remember to word the affirmations in language that your children would use. Keep it age appropriate.

Examples of affirmations for your children could be:

I complete my homework every day.
I remember and understand what I read and learn.
I am happy being me.
I like people and people like me.
Every day I feel better than the day before.
Each game I play, I improve my performance.

It is helpful to create an affirmation and say it, write it and think it to yourself whenever possible. The more you do it, the quicker it takes effect. I like to do my affirmations as I am driving to and from work or when running errands. This helps me to do something productive, as I am en route. I feel better taking advantage of this time that might have otherwise been wasted. Have your children find a time that is comfortable for them. The subconscious mind is very suggestible just as we are waking up or falling asleep. These are excellent times to state affirmations. Great way to start and end a day!

The Power Of Words

Have you ever had a time in your life when someone said something to you that made such an impact that you never forgot it? If it was something negative, it may have held you back from achieving goals or being the best that you can be. If the statement was positive, it might be something that you say over and over again to yourself during times when you need to be motivated. Either way, what we say to others may impress them more than we realize. If you went back to the person who made the statement to you, they may not even remember the event. But, for you, it is unforgettable. Be aware of what you say and how you say it. A slip of the tongue for you may create a lasting impression on someone else.

My grandson, Elijah, is two-years-old. When he goes shopping with my daughter, Angie, he can be quite a handful. One day Angie told me about Elijah's latest thing that he does. When they're shopping, he will walk up to a lady, tug at her clothes or reach for her hand and say, *"Pretty."* Now, what woman wouldn't melt when they hear that? Children are so innocent that they say things like they are. They don't hold any punches. It doesn't matter how old the woman is or what she looks like, Elijah will call her, *"Pretty"*. I'm sure that this one little word has made the day of many female shoppers. It is something that will stay with them for a long time.

Imagine if one of the women who Elijah would call *"Pretty"* was told all of her life that she was ugly. Even if she were only told once that she wasn't very appealing, she would repeat that to herself over again. It would soon become her belief. Now, here comes a sweet, little boy who calls her, *"Pretty"*. She would feel the impact of this compliment more than the other women who knew that they looked good.

When we hear a statement over and over again, it makes an impression on our brain. It doesn't matter if it is something that is being said to you, or if you are thinking it in your own mind. Either way, if the suggestion is accepted, the subconscious mind will deem it as being true, even if the statement is false.

Children are most likely to accept statements as being true when they are said to them from an authority figure or from someone they admire or fear.

Two children from the same family, experiencing the same event, may remember it in two totally different ways. If you have siblings, ask them about an event that occurred when you were together when you were very young. Before telling how you recall it, ask them what they remember. You might be surprised!

Timing Is Everything

Everyone is different. Something that is said to one person may be accepted as an insult, where another person may dismiss the statement all together. Emotions play a big part in our understanding. If a person had just experienced a situation that upset them and shortly afterwards they were introduced to someone they had never met, chances are the upset individual would not like the new person. Even if the new person is the nicest person in the world, the upset person subconsciously associates the new person with the event that was upsetting. Timing is everything.

Delivering Suggestions In Waking State

When giving suggestions, it is important to tell people what you want, not what you don't want. So many times we fall into the habit of stating the obvious, something that we don't like. The subconscious mind does not process negative statements as one would think. For example, if I told you **not** to think of a pink elephant, you would first have to think of it before you would not think of it. This defeats the purpose.

Let's say that your children are playing outside with some friends. You are concerned about their safety, as the street has a fair amount of traffic. The parent looks out the front door, and tells the children, *"Don't play in the street!"* You would think this would be effective, right? Wrong! If the parent looked outside in about ten minutes, they would probably find the children *playing in the street*; the very thing that they were told *not* to do. Why? Because when the mind processes the information, it doesn't pick up *"Don't"*. The mind interprets the statement as, *"Play in the street!"* With this in mind, it would be more effective to say, *"Have fun playing in the yard!"* This sounds more positive and does not contain any negative words that can be misconstrued.

This same principle relates to sports. Imagine a coach studying the opposing team to discover their weaknesses. After watching their rivals bat a few times, the coach tells the pitcher, "Don't throw low and inside." He repeats it several times to make sure that the pitcher got the message. As his arm is winding up for the pitch, the athlete hears the message, "Don't throw low and inside. Don't throw low and inside. Throw low and inside!" Sure enough, a home run for the opposing team.

Since the mind does not pick up the negative word "Don't", the message gets changed to doing exactly the opposite of the desired goal.

Now let's take a look at a very common situation; your child's messy bedroom. When parents pass by and see everything on the floor, except for the floor, they may make a remark like, *"This room is a pig pen. Clean it up!"* Even if the child follows orders and cleans up the mess, chances are that a few days later, it will be right back to the way it was before. Why? Because the parent has claimed and affirmed that the room is a pig pen. This thought stays with the subconscious mind and, thinking that it is indeed a pig pen, will revert back to its origin – being a pig pen! Instead, the parent may state, *"This room has the potential of being neat and orderly. Clean it up!"* The thought of being neat and orderly stays with the subconscious mind and, viola, a neat and orderly room.

We have a tendency to do this with ourselves more times than we are aware. Imagine that you have gained a few pounds, but would like to wear a particular pair of pants to a special event. You go to put the pants on, but they won't come up passed your knees. You may think to yourself, *"Oh, I'm getting too fat!"* or *"I'm gaining weight; these pants don't fit!"* Here again, the subconscious mind takes everything literally and accepts these statements, even though this isn't what you want. You may find that after making this statement, you seem to gain weight more quickly. Since the subconscious mind takes things literally, it accepts your statement that you are gaining weight. Oh, no! Let's learn to rephrase this! Instead, you should make a comment like, *"Good, I'm getting closer to getting into these pants. I must be losing weight."* Doesn't that sound more positive?

No matter if it is a statement that you say out loud, or a thought that you just think to yourself, remember to focus on what you *do* want in order to get the desired results.

Direct vs. Indirect Suggestions

When a parent or child wants to change the behavior created by the imprint, we can alter these behaviors using suggestions delivered in a waking or a hypnotic state. There are many different ways of communicating an idea. For simplicity's sake, we are going to arrange these different types of communications into two categories, ***direct and indirect suggestions***.

With the *direct* approach, the parent delivers a suggestion in such a manner that there is no way for it to be misunderstood. If the parent said, *"Turn off the television"*, this would be a direct suggestion. In using direct suggestions, we may select an authoritarian approach or a more permissive approach. The meaning of the suggestion will stay the same, but the delivery will change. Using the same example, let's examine the suggestion first in the **authoritarian** mode. *"You will turn off the television now"*. It is easy to see that not only did we add a few words to the suggestion, but most likely the tone of voice would have been altered as well. An authoritarian delivery is usually said in a more forceful tone.

In using direct suggestions in a **permissive** manner the suggestion might have been, *"Let's turn the television off"*. The delivery is more relaxed than the authoritarian approach. Most adults respond more readily to a permissive approach rather that an authoritarian delivery. With children it is about fifty/fifty. Some children would not respond at all to a permissive approach.

The parent or hypnotist that has fallen into the habit of delivering suggestions only in a permissive manner may find it difficult to have their suggestions accepted. If this is the case, the parent may find himself or herself raising the notorious, spoiled brat. Delivering suggestions only in an authoritarian manner may destroy all rapport with the child and cause resentment.

Each of these deliveries will work well for you, depending on the situation. Most people find that they can always start with the permissive approach and gradually work up to the authoritarian approach. It is advisable to use a combination of permissive and authoritarian deliveries. The child will encounter both types outside of the home environment.

The ability to deliver **indirect** suggestions in an effective manner can eliminate the possibility of resistance to the suggestion. An indirect suggestion is a suggestion with an implied meaning.

Let's now analyze two questions to see the **difference between direct and indirect** deliveries:

1. **Can I borrow a pen?**
2. **Do you have an extra pen?**

It is easy to see that the second question is an example of an indirect delivery. The analytical part of the mind fills in the missing pieces of the question or suggestion. There are times when people seem to respond without the use of the analytical mind.

A friend of mine relayed an experience she had when in her early twenties:

She was driving to a club to meet some friends when she was pulled over by a police officer. She knew that she wasn't speeding (this time!), so was surprised by the stop. The officer told her that her license plates had expired and that's why he stopped her. She looked surprised and said, "On the renewal form it said to come in at my convenience, and it hasn't been convenient." He couldn't argue with that, so she got off with a warning.

As you can see, indirect suggestions can also come in the form of writing. It is so interesting because that phrase, "At your convenience" doesn't seem to be on the license renewal reminders any longer. It would seem that my friend wasn't the only one who took the phrase literally.

Here is an example of a conversation in which one of the parties is not using his analytical mind:

BOB: *Do you know what time it is?*
TOM: *Yes.*
BOB: *Would you be willing to tell me what time it is?*
TOM: *Sure.*
BOB: *What time is it?*

In the above example, Tom responded only to the questions that were being asked of him. He did not use the analytical part of his mind. If he had used the analytical part of his mind, he would have been able to determine that Bob simply wanted to know what time it was and answered appropriately.

Most family members not only use indirect suggestions, but they are also communicating under the premise that other members of the family must have the ability to read minds. We have all encountered individuals who make statements like, *"Are we going to that place?"* *"Please hand me that thing"*, or *"Do you remember what's her name from school?"*

Although the person asking the questions knows exactly what they are talking about, the person being asked the questions is lost. An individual attempting to communicate in this way is having two conversations at the same time. One of the conversations is not shared with anyone verbally, but rather consists only of mental thoughts. Only portions of this internal conversation are shared with the second person.

The danger with this type of action can be seen through the following case history:

A mother brought her daughter to see me under the premise that her daughter does not listen correctly. The mother gave the following example of how poorly her daughter listens:

MOTHER: *Are you busy?*
DAUGHTER: *No, not really.*
MOTHER: *What are you doing?*
DAUGHTER: *Watching television.*
MOTHER: *Is it a good show?*
DAUGHTER: *Not really, but it is something to do.*
MOTHER: *You are totally useless. You never think of others.*

The mother begins her conversation mentally and thinks that it would be nice to have some help with the dishes. Mother verbally asks her daughter if she is busy. When the daughter replies, "No", the mother mentally thinks, "I ask for help with the dishes and even though she is not busy, she will not help". The mother verbally asked, "What are you doing?" The daughter answers that she is watching television. The mother now mentally thinks, "This had better be the best television program in the world if it is more important than helping me". Mother verbally inquires, "Is it a good program?" When the daughter responds with, "No, but it is something to do", the mother gets furious and thinks mentally, "That spoiled brat. She would rather sit and watch a bad television program than to lift a finger around the house". Mother then verbally assaults her daughter with degrading statements.

The mother and daughter both feel that the other person is at fault. In the mother's mind, any normal individual should have known what she wanted from her daughter. The daughter could not figure out what she had done wrong and, thus, the communication was non-productive.

It should be pointed out that many children use the same effective techniques on adults that are being described in this book.

Around 1987, we moved from the city and built a home in the country. My daughter was twelve-years-old at that time and wanted a pet cat. She knew that her Dad was not a big fan of cats and it would take just the right wording to achieve her ultimate goal of being the proud owner of a cat.

Her first technique was to use logic and indirect suggestions. She began in the following way: "Dad, now that we live in this beautiful house that you built, we wouldn't want to see it destroyed by mice." I looked up from the paperwork and agreed with her. She then went in for the kill. "Dad, I have read that cats are very good at keeping mice away." She still did not directly ask for a cat, but she was trying to get me to think that getting a cat was my idea. It did not work. I told her that if we needed to, we could purchase some mousetraps. Her response to that logical conclusion was to say, "Oh, how cruel to break the poor, little mouse's neck."

I almost felt guilty about my decision as she walked to her room. Then I realized that I wasn't being cruel. Her idea was to have those poor mice eaten alive by a giant cat! I felt very proud of myself for not being taken in by a twelve-year-old. I thought that was the end of the cat issue. Was I ever wrong!

Two weeks later she came into the living room with what appeared to be a small kitten wrapped up in a blanket. Before I could open my mouth to protest, she created two tiny tears. The kind only a daughter can produce. She then told me that she and her mother were visiting our neighbor and they found this poor, deserted kitten hiding under a tractor. I was about to say, "No", when she beat me to the punch with the following request, "Dad, can we save the kitten?"

Although I talk for a living, she had me. I could not come up with a response quick enough. What a line, "Can we save it?" What was I to say? "No, let's drown it?" According to the law of children, when there's no response, it means "Yes". With that my daughter hugged me and told me what a great Dad I was. She and our new kitten quickly disappeared into their bedroom.

Although, I wasn't thrilled with the aspect of a permanent houseguest, I was thrilled with my daughter's ability to communicate effectively. She apparently learned very quickly from her mother, my wife, Brenda.

Brenda likes to collect bears. We had so many of them around the house that I built a shelf to go all around the living room for her to display her proud collection. At 50 bears it was cute. When the total got to 200, it became unbearable!

One day Brenda and I were out, so we stopped at a restaurant to get something to eat. It was one of those places that has a gift shop at the entrance of the building. As we were waiting for our dinner to arrive, Brenda looked at me with her beautiful blue eyes and said, "Did you see the bears in the gift shop?" Of course I had. How could I have missed it? When I saw them, I knew she would want one, so I had already anticipated that we would leave with a new addition to her collection. That was fine, as I always pick up a bear for her in whatever city I'm in when I travel teaching classes. So, I responded, "Would you like one?" Thinking that this would make her happy. She quickly responded, "No, I want two!" When I asked her why she needed two bears she replied, "Well, Don, they're TWINS!" What kind of an ogre would break up a family? To this day, I still think that I just bought two bears that looked alike.

Throughout the years in teaching pediatric hypnosis, I've been asked about the difference between conducting sessions with young children around the age of five and those with older children. Most want to know what level of vocabulary to use with certain age subjects. I'm not trying to dodge the question, but there are no specific guidelines you can follow on this subject.

Some children as young as five or six can exhibit a maturity level and communication skills far beyond some teens; and there are some adults that have trouble accurately communicating their thoughts, feelings and wishes. Effective communication with a specific child must be determined as you listen to that individual, paying attention to their vocabulary, as well as their maturity level.

Once, when I was at the home of some friends, their young six-year-old was being asked by an older child to dry the dishes. The six-year-old responded that she didn't want to dry the dishes. The older child asked again, trying to get her to help with the dishes. Again the six-year-old said she didn't want to dry the dishes. Exasperated, the older child asked, "Why don't you want to dry the dishes?" to which the younger replied, "Look, someday I'm going to be grown-up and I'm going to have childhood memories. I'd prefer that they be fond memories, rather than memories of drying dishes."

Another time, I got to babysit the children while the parents were out of town, and there was a storm with lightening and thunder. The older child announced, "I love storms," so I said we could go out in the garage and watch with the door open. The older child was enjoying herself and would exclaim, "Oh, that was a good one," while the younger child was quiet and appeared to be a little nervous. Pretty soon she asked, "Don, are you scared?" I replied, "No," to which she answered back, "Well, if you are, you can hold me." Of course, I told her that I was, in fact, a little scared and picked her up. What a brilliant child! How's that for an indirect suggestion? Never underestimate the power of a hug.

Children can be more intelligent than we think. But, every once in a while, the parent wins. A friend of mine shared a story about what her mother did with her younger sister.

Every day around 2:00 PM, the mother and daughter would go into the mother's bedroom to take a nap. Although the child was very good, she didn't want to go to sleep. She still wanted to play. The mother was in her mid-forties at the time, so the down time was essential in order for her to keep up with all of her duties and a young child.

Out of desperation, the mother invented a new game. She told her daughter to draw a picture on her back and she would guess what her daughter drew. Being a very creative little girl, she loved this game. She would draw all kinds of wonderful pictures on her mother's back. The mother would try to guess what it was, but always seemed to guess wrong. When she didn't get the right answer, the mother instructed the daughter to erase the picture and draw it again.

It took the little girl a few years to realize that this was a very clever way for her mother to get her to scratch her back!

In the next chapter, I will be talking about the importance of establishing rapport with a child before conducting a hypnosis session. One of the best ways to determine what level of communication will be most effective with any given child is to listen and watch how they communicate.

Creating Positive Anchors

This may be easier to do than you can imagine. **An *anchor* is a cue that is developed to create a response.** This can happen consciously or subconsciously; it can be positive or negative. An anchor can be something that we see, hear, touch, smell, taste or feel. An anchor is what elicits the imprint.

A man I know is excellent at creating positive anchors with his children. Let's see how easy it is to do:

My friend has learned to establish positive anchors while his children are relaxed and happy. When his daughters are watching one of their favorite programs on television that makes them laugh or smile, he will touch their shoulder as he passes by and say something positive to them, like, "You are very intelligent." Or "You are wonderful."

Then, if there is a time when they are studying for a big test or feeling a little down, all he has to do is touch their shoulder as he did the previous times. Their minds will repeat the message that he told them every time that he touched their shoulder before.

When something happens and is followed by the same thing repeatedly, the mind automatically will fill in the blanks. The father touches child's shoulder when they are relaxed and happy. The father says something positive to the child. The more times that this sequence is performed, the more it will be ingrained in the child's mind. In the future, whenever the father would touch the child's shoulder, the child will automatically replay the words in their own mind, even if the father says nothing at all.

From Sleep To Hypnosis

Another technique that has been beneficial for children reaching goals is when the parent turns sleep into hypnosis. This may sound complicated, but it isn't.

Many times children fall asleep in our arms, on the living room couch, in the car; you name it! They know what their bodies need and it happens automatically. Wouldn't it be great if we could lie down and go to sleep whenever we felt the urge? Children can get away with it, but adults can't.

Many parents read bedtime stories to their children as a nighttime ritual. This is a wonderful habit to get into. As your child is comfortable in their bed, feeling safe and secure with you reading to them, you will notice when their facial expression starts to change. You will know when they are starting to drift off to sleep. **Before they actually fall asleep**, this is the time for you to deliver positive suggestions to help them to reach their goal. Whether it is to do better in school, stop bedwetting or whatever concern you have about the child, positive suggestions are always a benefit.

Keep in mind that the state just prior to falling asleep, and in the morning just as they are waking up, but aren't quite there yet, this is the time to deliver positive suggestions and have the best chance of someone accepting them.

If you find yourself in a situation where your child has fallen asleep, you can give the suggestion that they can hear and understand what you are suggesting.

> **PARENT:** *You can hear what I'm saying; yet you stay asleep. You are asleep, but you can understand what I am saying. If you can hear what I am saying, lift up one of the fingers on your right hand.* (Wait for response.)

If you **do not get a response**, you may need to lighten their sleep state. You can do this by gently touching their shoulder and giving suggestions that they are coming up just enough to hear and understand what you are saying, and still stay asleep.

If they *did lift up a finger* on their right hand, give the positive suggestions to help them to reach their goal.

> **PARENT:** *In the morning, you feel so good waking up in your bed with dry sheets.*

CHAPTER 4

Hypnosis Session With Child

Thus far, we have been learning about how important effective communication is in our daily lives. It is now time to master the ability of conducting a hypnosis session with the child.

The hypnotic process with children is much simpler than with an adult. Children are in an altered state of consciousness most of the time anyway! It is easier for them to go into hypnosis because it feels so natural to them. They have not established the fears and misconceptions that many adults face surrounding hypnosis, so they have no preconceived expectations of what will transpire during the session. As long as they know that they are not going to get a shot, they're happy.

When taking your child to a hypnotist, he/she will actually be conducting two types of sessions, one with the parents and the other with the child. A hypnotist could accomplish wonderful changes within the child during the session, only to have it destroyed, unknowingly, by one of the parents. The parents must be given a crash course on correct suggestions in order to reinforce the positive changes that were created during the hypnotic session.

In this book, we give you the information so that the parent knows what takes place during a session. This will also affirm with hypnotists what needs to be done when they are conducting pediatric sessions in their office.

The parents using this book have already discovered how important it is to use correct suggestions in the normal waking state. This knowledge will prove invaluable in creating positive, permanent changes within your child.

There are *eight steps* to a hypnosis session that are needed in order to achieve success for adults, as well as children.

1. THE PRELIMINARY
2. THE BODY SCAN
3. THE INDUCTION
4. THE DEEPENING
5. TESTS AND CHALLENGES
6. THE PRESCRIPTION
7. POST-HYPNOTIC SUGGESTIONS
8. EXITING

Working with children is easy and fun. The procedure is different than when working with adults because a child's attention span is shorter. It is easier because children don't have the fears about hypnosis that some adults may have. It is fun because you can play games, do magic and allow yourself to be a kid again for that period of time.

When working with a child, the hypnosis session may be about two or three mini sessions in one. Since they have short attention spans, it is not realistic to expect a child to sit still for thirty minutes. The child may squirm and move about during the session. This is fine; it is to be expected. If the child moves, scratches their nose, or coughs during the session it will not interfere with the process.

In order to do a session with a child, follow the above *eight steps* in the order given. We have broken down each step to explain what needs to be done. Once you've completed that step, go directly to the next step. It is that easy!

The Preliminary

The preliminary session should be conducted with the child regardless of whether the session is being conducted by the parent or the hypnotist. The preliminary is one of the most important steps in a hypnosis session because it is here that we get the information needed in order to help the child to reach their goal. It is necessary for the child to feel comfortable with the person doing the session. The child should feel safe and relaxed..

The following *six requirements* must be met in order for the preliminary to be classified as a success:

> *1. TRUST MUST BE ESTABLISHED*
> *2. MUST BE AN ENJOYABLE EXPERIENCE*
> *3. CREATE POSITIVE EXPECTATIONS*
> *4. CREATE BELIEF IN REACHING GOAL*
> *5. REMOVE FEARS*
> *6. EXPLAIN HOW THEY WILL FEEL*

1. *Trust Must Be Established*

For the parent using hypnosis, normally the trust is already established between the child and the parent. The hypnotist seeing a child for the first time will not have this luxury of established trust.

There are several *effective techniques* that will either *establish or increase* trust.

Three F's

The first technique is through *verbal suggestions*. The procedure is using the *Three F's - feel, felt, found.* These three words could prove to be the three most powerful words for creating trust in a child or an adult.

If we were dealing with the issue of failing in school, the *Three F's* could be used in the following way:

"I know how you feel. I have felt the same way in the past. I used to have great

*difficulty in school, especially in math class, but **I found** that when I used some of the tricks that I am going to be teaching you today, my grades went up quickly. Would you like to find out about these tricks?"*

Regardless of the problem, using the words, *"I know how you **feel"**, "I have **felt** that way before"* and *"I **found**"* will create an instant rapport. All people tend to trust other people they can relate to.

For years, some parents have used a portion of the **Three F's**. *"I know how you feel, but you need to pull yourself up by your bootstraps. It is not easy for anyone."* The parent using this technique came close to establishing an honest rapport, but fell short by not having a valid answer to the dilemma.

PACING

The second way of developing rapport and trust is through the technique called **Pacing**. We tend to like and trust people who are like us. There may have been occasions when you met someone and immediately did not like that person. If someone were to ask you why you did not like person, you might be hard pressed to come up with any specific reasons. It was not anything that they said, nor was it anything that they did. You simply did not take to them. The exact opposite can also occur when you meet someone and you immediately like that person. Once again, it was nothing that they said or did. You simply liked that person.

Within the first three minutes of meeting someone, your subconscious mind is recording hundreds of different responses from that person. After recording these different responses, the mind then analyzes whether this person is similar to you or dramatically different. The mind tends to view people who seem most similar to you as the ones that you are attracted to. The people who are dramatically different than you are the ones that you feel most uncomfortable around.

Children and adults alike have this built-in computer that interprets all the actions of another person and comes back with a conclusion. We have all met individuals that seem to be accepted by almost everyone. People who are instantly liked by everyone they meet. They have either subconsciously or intentionally mastered the technique of **Pacing**. There are people who automatically learn to use pacing techniques without ever being aware of what they are doing. Don't despair if you are not one of those few that have automatically mastered the art of **Pacing**. It is a technique that can be learned easily.

Listed below are the **four** most common avenues to pace:

1. *VOICE*
2. *GESTURES*
3. *BREATHING*
4. *VOCABULARY*

There are dozens of other possible avenues that could be paced, but for working with children, the above four will be adequate. In simple terms, **Pacing is the ability for one individual to respond in the same or like manner of another. The voice is a very easy element to pace.** With the voice we have tone, speed and volume. If the child speaks slightly louder than normal, the parent or hypnotist should **match** the volume of the child. If the child speaks slower than normal, we should slow down our speed of delivery. The tone of voice changes, depending on the conversation. For tone, we might experience excitement, a whine, anger or disgust.

If the child said, *"I hate school"* with a tone of disgust and anger, the parent could respond with, *"I know how you feel"*, with a slight amount of disgust in their voice. The key to **Pacing** is not to mimic, but rather to alter our behavior to become closer to that of the child's. If the child becomes aware of you pacing him, he will feel that you are making fun of him and you will lose all trust and rapport. **Pacing should only be sensed at a subconscious, not a conscious, level.**

When **Pacing gestures**, we have to be especially careful not to look as though we are imitating or mocking the child. Rather than duplicating the child's gestures, it is advisable to first determine the type of gestures the child makes. For parents of a hyperactive child it may seem hard to believe, but some children do not make any type of gestures. If the child does not use his hands in a conversation, it is advisable for the hypnotist to refrain from using gestures. Within just a few moments, the hypnotist should know if the child uses gestures.

If so, does he use the right hand, left hand or both. The parent or hypnotist will not need to use the same type of gestures, but rather simply make his own gestures while using the same hand that the child used. If the child used both hands, the hypnotist should follow suit.

Pacing the breathing rate of the child is one sure way of establishing a subconscious rapport without the possibility of conscious detection. The parent or hypnotist will simply align their breathing with that of the child. If the child's breathing became more rapid during the preliminary session, the parent or hypnotist should allow their breathing to become more rapid. For the child that would occasionally let out a deep sigh, this behavior may also be paced. Associated with breathing are items such as a light cough, clearing the throat or exaggerated swallowing.

We have saved the vocabulary for last since it has the most potential of creating the desired effect. Using the technique of **Pacing through vocabulary** is extremely easy with children, as opposed to adults. The first element is to listen for words that are unusual, words that are unique. Children and teens seem to have their own entire language. It would be impossible not to hear words that are unique.

After the parent or hypnotist has made the decision which words they are going to use during the **Pacing**, they must simply look for an appropriate time to use these new words. It is imperative that the parent or hypnotist knows the correct usage of the word. An occupational hazard of working with children and teens is that you tend to automatically pick-up some of their terminology.

I was giving a lecture to a group of nurses when out of my mouth came, *"It was radical"*. I knew immediately that I had become the victim of my own environment. The nurses, being the kind sort that they are, simply smiled and pretended not to notice. This example shows that we are creatures of our environment; in the same way that an adult may pick-up sayings and actions from children, children will surely pick-up the same from adults.

I have seen three-year-olds who used profanity with every other word out of their mouth. They surely did not learn this mode of communication in their local preschool. It came from imitating the parents. At the age of three, the parents might think it is cute that their young son or daughter is using profanity and does not even understand the meaning of his words, but when the time comes to cancel out these words, the child will be confused.

A hypnotist may develop *trust* **more rapidly by demonstrating trust in the child.** If the child feels that you have trust in him/her they will have trust in you. We have discovered two simple ways for the hypnotist to demonstrate their trust in the child.

TRUST THE CHILD

The first is to **select an item**, such as a special pen, stuffed animal or a framed photo, then tell the child how important this item is to you and that you would not allow even a grown-up to hold it. Pause for a moment and tell the child that you feel as though you can trust him/her and hand them the item. You will notice an instant smile on their face. Please **do not select** a priceless, fragile, family heirloom for this technique!

The second technique for developing trust is through the use of a **secret**. To whom would a child confide their secrets? The answer is only a close friend. The secret might be as simple as where you are going to go for vacation. It is not important that the child feel that the secret is important to them. Your willingness to share the secret means that they must be your friend.

2. MUST BE AN ENJOYABLE EXPERIENCE

After trust has been established between the hypnotist and the child, the hypnotist must make certain that the entire session is enjoyable. If the session turns into a lecture from another adult, the rapport that was initially established will be destroyed. The hypnotist is faced with the task of making what the parents want to also be what the child wants. Many times this task is easier said than done.

It has been mentioned in an earlier chapter that a hypnotized person can never be made to do something against their will. Many of the parents that I have seen over the years are disappointed to learn this fact. Some had the preconceived notion that they would forcibly drag their child into my office, and I would take over their mind.

During the preliminary session with the child, the hypnotist will be asking many questions. This is the part of the session where the hypnotist must demonstrate their great amount of patience. There was a time in my career when I felt that all of the children of the world must have congregated together to come up with a universal answer to questions from adults. The answer that I constantly hear is, *"I don't know."*

Here is a typical conversation between a child and a hypnotist:

HYPNOTIST:	*Do you feel that you can do better in school?*
CHILD:	*I don't know.*
HYPNOTIST:	*Would you like to do better in school?*
CHILD:	*I don't know.*
HYPNOTIST:	*Would your parents like you to do better?*
CHILD:	*I don't know.*
HYPNOTIST:	*Would your teacher like you to do better?*
CHILD:	*I don't know.*

I think you get the picture. This would not be a very productive preliminary session. If the hypnotist does not quickly put an end to the *"I don't know"* response, they may ask the question, *"What is your name?"* and get the response of "I don't know". To overcome this common problem, we have invented the *"I DON'T KNOW" GAME.*

"I DON'T KNOW" GAME

Here is how the game works. The moment the hypnotist realizes that they are dealing with a child that is going to use the *"I don't know"* response, they should proceed in the following manner:

We're going to play a game; it is called the "I Don't Know" game. The way it works is, I am going to ask you questions and each time you answer the question you get a point. Every time you say "I don't know", I get a point. The person with the most points wins the game.

The first question is, "How old are you?" The child responds with the answer and the hypnotist says, "You got that one. Have you ever played this game before? I'll get you on the next one. What day of the week is it?" The child once again answers the question and the hypnotist makes a comment of how well the child is doing, and that the child is going to win the game. Now the hypnotist asks a pertinent question such as, "Could you do better in school if you really wanted to?" As the child answers the question with a "Yes" response, the hypnotist continues complimenting on how well the child is playing the game, while asking crucial questions.

The second way of handling the *"I don't know"* response is to ask the child to take a guess. Many children are so fearful of making a mistake that they have discovered that no response is a safe response. When the hypnotist asks a question and the child says, *"I don't know"*, the hypnotist responds with, *"I know that you don't know, but just take a guess anyway"*. For many children, taking a guess does not constitute a true answer, thus there is no way for them to be wrong. It benefits both the child and the hypnotist to avoid turning the preliminary session into a frustrating situation. If the preliminary session is viewed as an unpleasant experience, the actual hypnotic session may be viewed in the same manner. **A few extra moments spent during the preliminary can dramatically increase the benefits from the session.**

THE "ADD-ON

A successful technique to get the child to want what the parents want is called, the *"Add-on"*. The hypnotist would find out several of the child's interests from the parent. If the parent wanted to see the child spend more time on his homework, but the child was not in favor of the change, the session would be a failure. The *"Add-on"* works in the following way.

The hypnotist tells the child, "We can do hypnosis for many different things today. Your mother said something about spending a little more time on your homework. That would be very easy to do. I'll tell you some of the other things that we use hypnosis for and, if ,you would like any of them also, let me know. We do hypnosis to stop smoking; I know that you don't smoke. We do hypnosis to help people who play golf; I guess you don't play golf. We use hypnosis to help people become better at soccer."

If soccer was the item that the parent shared with you earlier, the child will immediately respond to the thought of improving his soccer game.

Now it is time to do a sales presentation to the child. "Do you really want to improve your soccer game while we are working on spending more time on your homework?" The child will always respond with a "Yes" answer. "I have not talked with your mother about improving your soccer. She might think we should not be doing both at the same time. She may think that if we improve the soccer you won't also spend more time on your homework. Do you think that you can do both? Do you want to do both? Are you ready to work real hard on soccer and your homework?"

Once the hypnotist has achieved the commitment to put forth effort on the primary reason for the session and the *"Add-on"*, he is ready to continue on with the session. It is rare to fail to find an *"Add-on"* that can be used with children. The *"Add-on"* might be related to videogames, sports, dance, swimming, bike riding or drawing. It doesn't really matter what type of sport or hobby it is, as long as it is of interest to the child.

Once the hypnotist has agreed to work with the child on the *"Add-on"*, he must follow through and deliver suggestions for each of the situations that he has agreed to. Sometimes the list of possible *"Add-ons"* is extremely large. There may be ten or more *"Add-ons"* to select from.

A second way of handling the *"Add-ons"* is with a version of the ***"Pin The Tail On The Donkey"*** game.

PIN THE TAIL ON THE DONKEY

During the preliminary session, the hypnotist is writing on index cards all of the things that the child and parents would like to see changed. The list may include items such as, better grades, baseball, videogames, better skateboarding, keeping room clean and reading more. After each of these items has been written on a separate index card, we advise the child that there are just too many things to choose from.

Advise the child that we could do two of the items, and you have an idea on how to select which two we work on. "I am going to place all of the cards on the wall.

In a moment I am going to put a blindfold on you. I will then hand you a pin with a small flag on it. While blindfolded, you will get to stick the pin into one of the cards. We will then do the same thing again, and select the second item that we will hypnotize you for. Whatever two items are picked, will you promise to work hard on improving them?" The child will make the commitment.

Blindfold the child, hand him the pin with the flag in it and aim him at the wall with the index cards. As he sticks the first pin in, tell him that he has picked one of the items, but you are not going to tell him what it is until he does the second one.

*Repeat the same procedure. After the second pin has been stuck, advise the child that he has now picked two items. Once again before taking off the blindfold ask him to commit to working hard on both items. You now remove his blindfold to discover that he has selected better grades and better baseball. (**NOTE: Insure that one of the child's wishes and one of the parent's wishes was chosen.**)*

When I'm working with young children, I love to use my ***magic finger***. I tell the child that when I touch my nose with my magic finger, they will smile. I say, *"Even if that finger sneaks up there, you won't be able to help yourself; you will smile!"* and then I pretend that my hand is sneaking up to my nose. If I would see these children as much as a year later, I could make them smile by touching my nose. It makes them happy and I enjoy making people happy.

3. CREATE POSITIVE EXPECTATIONS

Creating the correct expectations in children is a very simple task. Children and adults tend to experience what they expect to happen. If the child is expecting failure from the hypnotic session, then he will surely experience failure. Many years ago I heard a story that illustrates how much expectations can influence our lives.

MR. DISEASE

In this story, a man was walking down a road leading out of a major city. The man came upon a very ominous looking creature. This strange creature identified himself as Mr. Disease. He stated that he was on his way to the city from which the man had just departed. Mr. Disease was traveling to that city in order to kill one thousand people. The man was very thankful that he was departing the city, rather than preparing to enter it. Mr. Disease and the man proceeded in opposite directions.

*A few months later, the man once again met Mr. Disease. The man reminded Mr. Disease that they had met on a previous occasion and that he was told that Mr. Disease was going to kill one thousand people. Mr. Disease remembered the conversation and said yes, he did kill one thousand people. The man remarked, that ten thousand people had died; you must have lied to me. Mr. Disease laughed and said, "I did not lie. I only killed one thousand people. The other nine thousand people died because they **expected** to get the disease."*

Although this is simply a fictitious story, there is a certain amount of truth to it. People do become ill through high expectations. Individuals can succeed or fail, depending on what they expect to take place.

When my daughter started first grade, I would make a point to drive her to school each morning. On one particular morning, I told her that something wonderful was going to happen to her that day. She wanted to know what it was going to be. I advised her that it was a surprise and when I came home that afternoon, she could tell me all about it. The moment I came home from work, she ran to the front door saying, "You were right! Guess who was chosen to clean the erasers today?" She was expecting something wonderful to happen, so she found it.

The amazing part of expectations is that it works in either a positive or a negative way. If I would have told her that something bad was going to happen, her response that evening might have been, *"Dad you were right. I had to clean those dumb erasers."* **A few selected words can create the right type of expectations for a child.**

LEARNING MODES

We normally only think of delivering suggestions verbally in order to create positive expectations. **People have three distinct learning modes : *visual (seeing), auditory (hearing) and kinesthetic (feeling).*** Although we may use all of these modes, people have a tendency to prefer one over the others.

If a person is *visual*, use words that *show* the child they can reach their goal. They need to be able to see it in order to be successful. Use the child's ability to *visualize*. Hypnotists use *visualization* techniques during a hypnotic session with great results. The same technique may also be incorporated in the preliminary session in order to create an *image* of the correct expectations. Many successful athletes use *visualization* in order to excel in their sports.

The *auditory* child needs to *hear* how they are going to reach their goal. Their goals can be accomplished by delivering *verbal* suggestions to them. There is an old saying that one picture is worth a thousand words. For the *auditory* learning mode, they need to *hear* those words, while the **visual child needs to see the picture.** Think of the positive expectations that can be created if we *told* the child all of the things that they can achieve. Using words that create *sound* is the best way to communicate with this type of individual. They will *listen* to what you have to say.

The *kinesthetic* child needs to *touch* or *do* something. It needs to *feel* right to them. Use words that evoke *textures, temperatures, action or physical sensations*. For these individuals to achieve, they need to *handle* the situation. When teaching them, show them what to do as *they are doing it*. This person learns from practical experience. They need *hands-on* training.

The following is an *example* for a child that is going to use hypnosis to end *bedwetting*.

I know that you are excited about the idea of never wetting the bed again. Before we actually get you to stop wetting the bed, I want to make sure that this will make you happy. Close your eyes and you will get to see a very special movie. This movie is special because you will be in it.

The movie is starting now. You can see yourself in the movie. You are getting ready for bed. As you see the movie, shake your head "Yes". Good. Now it is a movie of you sleeping. As you see the movie with you sleeping, shake your head "Yes". You are doing super. Now the movie is about you waking up in the morning. There you are waking up in the morning, you're stretching your arms. Now you're rubbing your eyes. You now notice that your bed is dry. Yes, your bed is dry! You jump up and down because you are so happy! You say out loud, "My bed is dry!" You clap your hands and say it again. Everyone is so proud of you. How do you like the end of this movie?

This is almost as good as having the child watch his or her own actual videotape. As you can see, we have incorporated all three learning modes in this scenario. This is a great exercise for the child to do during the preliminary and to do on their own, or with their parent(s)'s guidance, at home. After this exercise, the child will have the right type of expectations.

There have been cases that simply using visualization and a child's excellent imagination have accomplished the desired change without a formal hypnotic session. Many parents use this technique of creating positive expectations on a nightly basis to reinforce the changes within the child.

In the same way that our mind records everything that we have ever seen or heard, it also records every feeling that we have ever experienced. For many children feelings or sensations will have more of an impact than spoken words or visual images.

The parent or hypnotist can allow the child to have a **"*sneak preview*"** of how they will be feeling in the future. The technique works in the following way:

I want to see how good you are at telling me about different kinds of feelings. Now, close your eyes for a couple of moments. I am going to have you think about either something fun that you have done before or about something that you are excited about doing soon. As you think about these times, you will feel the same fun that you felt in the past or the excitement that you feel when you think about what you will be doing soon. How do you feel when you think about these happy times?

Now, I would like you to think about a special party that you're going to. It can be a birthday party or maybe even a Christmas party. Think about all of the fun that you are having at this party. Now I want you to feel the same way that you feel when you are at a fun party. How do you feel?

I want you now to think about getting a special present. It could be a toy that you really, really wanted or it can be a big, wonderful surprise; something that you really like. Now, I want you to feel the same way that you feel when you open up this special gift. How do you feel?

Now, I want you to think about getting good grades on your next report card. Just think about all of the exciting things you have learned. You enjoy learning because it is fun to know new things. I want you to feel the way that you will feel when you do get those good grades. How do you feel?

By using the various learning modes of visual, auditory or kinesthetic, either individually or in a combination, the child will be anticipating the changes that are in store for him. We all have the ability to learn by seeing, hearing, or feeling.

Most people tend to lean more towards one of these three learning modes as their prominent learning mode. By conducting a test, using all three of the learning modes, the adult will be able to ascertain which is the dominant learning mode for the child.

Described below is a *test*, using the same technique with *all three learning modes:*

I would like you now to pretend as though we had a time machine. With this time machine we can travel forward or back in time. We are going to try out the time machine by going forward in time.

Close your eyes and take in a deep breath. I am going to count from three down to one. As I count, the time machine is going to be taking you to the future. We are going to travel through time to the moment when you get your next report card.

Three, *we are turning on the time machine.*

Two, *here we go, forward in time.*

One, *we are now at the time when you receive your new report card.*

You are able to see, hear, and feel the way that you will in the future. You are now seeing your great report card for the first time.

What are the grades that you are seeing on that report card? How do you feel? We are now going to the time when your parents are seeing this report card. What are they saying?

At this point the adult may ask questions about visual images. Inquiring about what the child is wearing, which room he is in or questions about colors or sizes will aid the adult in determining how well the child learns through seeing. Any statements about what was being said will help in determining how the child responds to hearing as a prime-learning mode. Discovering how this child feels physically and emotionally will give clues to the child's ability to learn by feelings.

Review this transcript of an actual case history, and then determine which would be the primary learning mode for the child:

HYPNOTIST:	*We are going to play a game. In this game let's pretend that we have a time machine that will allow us to travel forward in time. Would you like to try this with me?*
CHILD:	**Like back to the future movie, can I drive?**
HYPNOTIST:	*I think that would be fun. Close your eyes and pretend that you are starting up the time machine. I am going to count from three down to one and you are driving the time machine forward in time to a time when you are playing baseball better than ever before. Three, here we go. Two, you are able to hear everything. You are able to see everything. One, you are now able to feel the way that you feel in the future. What are you seeing?*
CHILD:	**I see myself playing first base in the World Series.**
HYPNOTIST:	*Are you grown up?*
CHILD:	**Yes, and I'm doing good.**

HYPNOTIST:	*That is good, but I think we went too far into the future. Let's now go back to your first ball game after our session. You drive and I will count from three down to one and this time we go to your first ball game after our session. You are still eleven years old. Three, two, one. Now, what do you see?*
CHILD:	I see myself at the plate getting ready to bat.
HYPNOTIST:	*What color is your uniform?*
CHILD:	Blue and white.
HYPNOTIST:	*What color is the pitcher wearing?*
CHILD:	He is in red.
HYPNOTIST:	*Is your Mom or Dad at this game?*
CHILD:	Yeah, Mom is here.
HYPNOTIST:	*What is she wearing?*
CHILD:	She has on her shirt she got in Florida.
HYPNOTIST:	*What are you hearing?*
CHILD:	Nothing.
HYPNOTIST:	*How are you feeling?*
CHILD:	OK.
HYPNOTIST:	*We are now going to the time of the pitch. What is happening?*
CHILD:	I hit the ball so far that you can hardly see it.
HYPNOTIST:	*How did it sound when the ball hit the bat?*
CHILD:	I don't know.
HYPNOTIST:	*Are people cheering for you?*
CHILD:	I think so.
HYPNOTIST:	*How did you feel when you hit that ball?*
CHILD:	Good.
HYPNOTIST:	*How did the bat feel in your hands, as you hit the ball?*
CHILD:	Just like a bat.
HYPNOTIST:	*Now, you just listen, watch, and feel what is going on.* (Pause for 2 minutes) *Tell me about everything.*
CHILD:	I see everyone clapping as I run around the bases. I win the game and it was neat when everyone throws their hats up into the air.

From the above case, which would you select as the child's primary learning mode? If you made the determination that the **child is primarily visually oriented**, you are correct. All cases are not as easy to determine. If this is the case, the adult may add the following as a last question to the child:

HYPNOTIST:	*Sometimes the time machine might need some work. It should allow you to see, hear, and feel everything. Could you see, hear, and feel everything?*
CHILD:	I could see it just as though I was really there. I knew

**people were cheering for me because I could see them
smiling with their mouths open, but I didn't really hear
it. It felt like fun.**

As we move on to the next element of the hypnotic session, creating belief, the
adult will be able to utilize much of the information of the child's learning mode
to assist him or her. It is not at all unusual for a child to have the ability to use all
three of the learning modes XE "learning modes" equally well.

4. <u>CREATE BELIEF IN REACHING GOAL</u>

There is a major difference between creating belief and creating expectations.
The adult is now faced with the task of creating belief in the child's ability to be
hypnotized.

Every person is capable of being hypnotized. Earlier examples of bypassing the
critical part of the mind show that individuals tend to go in and out of a hypnotic
state each day. It is common to hear from an adult, *"I don't believe in hypnosis"*.
What he is actually saying is that they believe in hypnosis on someone else, but
they do not believe that they could be hypnotized. This is a very common thought.

I have hypnotized over fifty thousand people and have never seen a person that
could not be hypnotized. If I relied upon the very few individuals that come into
my office saying, *"I know that I can be hypnotized"*, I would be out of business.
Most people are naturally skeptical when it comes to hypnosis. This skepticism
can usually be traced back to misinformation from television and movies. If hypnosis was the way that it has been portrayed in the movies, I would also have
trouble accepting it as a reality.

*My first experience with hypnosis was in 1972. I was in the Marine Corps, sta-
tioned in Japan. I attended a hypnosis demonstration and was very suspicious of
what I was seeing. I was born and raised in Missouri, which is known as the
"Show Me State". The man conducting the demonstration noticed my skepticism.
I was invited to participate in a demonstration.*

*The presenter went through his hypnotic patter and in about ten minutes he had
me open my eyes; the demonstration was over. Being a young Marine, and
slightly outspoken, I advised him that I had not been hypnotized. This gentleman
assured me that I had been hypnotized and, in fact, was a very good hypnotic subject.*

*Not wanting to cause a disturbance, I mumbled something like, "If you say so",
and started back towards my seat. Realizing that I was still not convinced, he
said, "Let's do it again". I told him he was welcome to try again, but I didn't feel
that he did anything the first time. Just as a few moments earlier, he had me
relaxed.*

*This time he proceeded to give suggestions that my right arm was becoming
very numb. He continued on with suggestions about anesthesia. He then had me
open my eyes and ran a needle through a part of my arm. The gentleman asked if
I thought I was hypnotized now and I stated that I must be.*

In reality, I still had my doubts, but I was a little fearful of what he might do next to convince me! This thing that they call "hypnosis" was one hundred percent different than everything that I had ever heard about it before.

I hadn't been asleep or unconscious. I knew everything that was going on around me. I was not in his power and, certainly, did not feel out of control. However, I could not deny that I did feel the numbing sensation that he had suggested. I saw the effect of the suggestions for anesthesia. I left the demonstration with many more questions than I had come in with. From that first experience, I believed that hypnosis was real and had true potential for helping other people.

If that demonstration of numbness had been accomplished in his first demonstration with me, my belief would have changed the outcome. I would not have come out of the hypnotic state feeling that nothing had happened.

We are *not* going to be running needles through the arms of children to create belief. We are, however, going to learn how to use the *power of suggestion* before beginning the hypnotic session.

THE POWER OF SUGGESTION

Many adults have confused the idea of being suggestible with being gullible. They are not one and the same.

Regardless of age, all human beings are suggestible, with the ability to accept or reject suggestions. It is important that the reader understands the power of suggestion prior to proceeding with the concentration tests.

Let's examine *three hypothetical situations* where suggestions could have changed an individual's responses. The first example shows *how a verbal and nonverbal suggestion could cause a physical change:*

Mary is a newly appointed vice-president of a large corporation. The annual board meeting is coming up in two weeks and Mary wanted to make a good impression. She decided to purchase a new outfit for the meeting. Mary used good judgment in purchasing just the right dress and shoes. Mary once again made the right decision to wear the new shoes a few days before the meeting. She knew that new shoes could be uncomfortable the first few days.

On the first day of wearing the new shoes, Mary's secretary remarked on how silly her new shoes looked. Mary concluded that a very immature and uneducated person made the statement. She was not going to allow someone to influence her. She convinced herself that the shoes were fine.

Later that same day, Mary was walking down the hall when she passed by two other executives of the firm. As she walked by, she noticed that both of them had turned around and apparently were looking at her shoes. Once again Mary mentally convinced herself that the shoes were all right. They were not overly conservative, nor were they a new fad style. They were just shoes.

Mary made a firm decision that the shoes were perfect and she was going to wear them to the board meeting. She also decided that one day was enough to break them in.

On the morning of the board meeting, Mary got dressed and started to put on the new shoes. Somehow, her feet had swollen so much that she could not wear the new shoes. Without being consciously aware of it, Mary had responded to both verbal and nonverbal suggestions.

In the second example, you will discover **how one simple suggestion can cause an intelligent adult to alter the way he feels about his car:**

John had always wanted a Chevy Corvette. He recently purchased a 1976 red Corvette. The car looked showroom new. Within the first two weeks, John was wondering if he had made the right decision. He experienced problems with the exhaust system and it cost him hundreds of dollars to replace it. Next, he discovered that the transmission was slipping. John's pride in his corvette was slipping away.

He drove to the corner store to pick a loaf of bread. John was frowning and mentally thinking about what a piece of junk he had purchased as he traveled down the road. When he arrived at the store, he parked next to a new Mercedes convertible. He turned the car off and thought, "With my luck, this lemon probably won't start when I come out."

John went into the store, still depressed over the car. As he came out with the loaf of bread, the driver of the Mercedes said, "That sure is a beauty." John said, "Yes, it is nice isn't it."

As John drove home, he was smiling from ear to ear. He had forgotten about the problems with the car. His entire attitude had been changed with a few words from a stranger.

The third example has taken place many times. *A **verbal suggestion can actually change our physical wellbeing:***

Bob and Tom decided to play a little joke on one of their co-workers. They selected Bruce since he was always calling in sick for work. When Bruce arrived at work, Tom asked Bruce if he was feeling all right. Bruce said, "Sure, why do you ask?" Tom said, "It's probably just the light in here."

A few moments later, Bob came into the break room extending greetings to Tom and Bruce. Bob then looked seriously at Bruce and said, "Are you feeling bad? You look sort of flushed." Bruce once again said that he was fine. Tom and Bob then proceeded to talk about a flu that they heard was going around. Tom said, "The people who have it look flushed". Bob joined in with, "And they tend to swallow more often." With that, Bruce noticed himself swallowing. Soon Bruce was reaching up feeling his forehead.

The three left the break room to start work. On the way to his workstation, Bruce stopped by the office. Later that day Tom and Bob found out that Bruce went home with the flu. Bruce may have experienced physical discomfort from the suggestions of two practical jokers.

CONCENTRATION TESTS

These concentration tests will show both the child and the adult how powerful the mind is. In order for the child to respond to suggestions, he must understand the words that are being delivered. Imagine an eight-year-old child attempting to respond to the following suggestions:

I am requesting that you think of me as your mentor and listen to the inflections in my voice. There is no need for you to articulate back to me. You will compre-hend my dialog with your subconscious mind. You will respond to subsequent sug-gestions as you allow your respiratory system to function in an involuntary manner. You are now experiencing a heavy, lethargic sensation. Now, allow every muscle, ligament and tendon to feel slumberous.

It should come as no surprise that the eight-year-old would have difficulty responding to the above set of suggestions. To be certain that our words are being received and interpreted correctly, we should become very descriptive in our delivery and use age-appropriate vocabulary.

Keep your words at a level that is matched with the child's. There are nine-year-old children that have a vocabulary larger than that of most twelve-year-olds. Listen to the child during the preliminary part of the session to determine the vocabulary that would be understood and accepted by the child.

HEAVY ARM TEST

We are going to be doing some fun tests. I want you to stand up and stretch your arms straight out in front of you. Close your eyes and listen to what I say. Your arms are feeling heavy. Your right arm and your left arm are feeling heavier and heavier. Pretend as though there was the handle of a bucket around your wrists. **(Lightly touch each wrist.)** *It is a bright, red bucket. It is the kind of bucket that people might take to the beach and play with in the sand.*

Now it feels like I am pouring wet sand into the buckets. The buckets are really heavy now. The sand is almost to the top of the buckets and your arms are pulling down, down, down. Feel it getting heavier and heavier. Feel them going down and down. Your arms are shaking as they go down more and more.

I am going to count from three down to one. As I count, your arms keep going down. You are doing very well at this. **Three**, *those buckets are filling all the way up with that heavy sand.* **Two**, *the sand is overflowing the top of the buckets.* **One**, *the arms are going down, down, down.*

Do not move your arms but open your eyes and see where your hands and arms are. You did very well at that game. Your arms got really heavy. What made your arms heavy?

As you say the words *"heavy"* and *"down"*, emphasize the deepness with the tone of your voice. Using a deeper tone of voice reinforces the thought of heavi-ness. Drawing out the word *"h-e-a-v-y"* as you say it will increase the physical changes.

By using descriptive terms, such as the color of the bucket or wet sand, the child will begin to create a vivid image of the buckets and the sand. When asked, *"What made your arms become heavy"*, the response is almost always, *"The sand."*

The thing that made the arms become heavy was the child's ability to create a visual image in his mind. He imagined the heavy buckets and it became a reality. Now that you have an understanding of how the concentration tests work, let's examine several other tests:

LIGHT ARM TEST

I want you to extend both of your arms out in front of you. Close your eyes and pretend as though I was tying a helium balloon on each of your wrists. (**Lightly touch each wrist.**) *These are the kind of balloons that you might have seen at a circus, zoo or carnival. These are the balloons that float up in the air. These balloons are now making your arms float up into the air. Feel your arms are getting lighter and lighter.*

The first balloon is a red one. I am now going to tie a blue balloon on each wrist. They're even bigger than the red one. (**Lightly touch each wrist.**) *You now have two balloons on each wrist. Your arms are beginning to float higher and higher into the air. It is now time to add the third balloon. It is bigger than the others. I am now tying this big, yellow balloon on each wrist.* (**Lightly touch each wrist.**) *The red balloon started making your arms float. The bigger, blue balloon helped out. The giant, yellow balloon is now making both of your arms float, lift and move higher and higher. Moving up, up, up into the air.*

As I count from three down to one, the three balloons keep floating up. **Three,** *there they go up.* **Two,** *floating in the air, light as a feather.* **One,** *all the way up, up now. Do not move your arms, but open your eyes and see where your arms are.* (**Tell the child that he/she did well.**)

The next test uses a combination of the light and heavy arms in a single test. It is normal for one of the experiences to be more noticeable than the other:

LIGHT AND HEAVY ARM

Extend both your arms straight out in front your eyes. Listen to the sound of my voice. I am tying a pretend balloon on your right wrist. (**Lightly touch right wrist.**) *This is a helium balloon, the kind of balloon that floats up into the air. I want you to pretend that you can see this light balloon on your right wrist. What color is the balloon?* (**Wait for a response.**) *That's right, and it is getting lighter and lighter. Your right arm is beginning to float up into the air.*

On your left wrist, pretend that I am putting the handle of a very, heavy bucket. (**Lightly touch left wrist.**) *The left arm is now getting heavy. I want you to see this heavy bucket on your left wrist. What color is the bucket?* (**Wait for a response.**) *You are doing great. How does the bucket make your left arm feel?*

How does the balloon make your right arm feel? You're right. Your right arm is getting lighter and lighter and beginning to float up. Your left arm is getting heavier and heavier. As your left arm goes down and down, your right arm goes up and up. As your right arm keeps going up higher, your left arm is going down lower. Which way is your right arm going with the balloon on it? Which way is your left arm going with the bucket on it?

I am going to count from three down to one. Each time I say a number, a change will happen. **Three,** *the left arm is going down further, and further down.* **Two,** *the right arm is floating up higher and higher.* **One,** *feel the difference. Your right arm floats, your left arm sinks. Without moving your arms, I want you to open your eyes and see where your arms are now.*

The light and heavy arm test is using opposite responses. As one arm rises, the other lowers. Using this technique, the adult will not be concerned with which arm moves first. Once the child realizes that one of the arms is moving, he will then concentrate on the other arm.

For most children the heavy arm moves to a larger degree. We tend to call upon past memories in order to respond to suggestions; the majority of children have encountered something heavy more often than they have encountered something light. The suggestions did not directly tell the child to search through his memory bank for sensations of heavy or light feelings. The words *"heavy"* and *"light"* were enough to create the memory of items associated with these feelings.

The child may think, mentally regress, to a time when he was carrying several heavy books. The word *"light"* may bring back an image of a feather. If the child had never experienced a heavy or light sensation, he would have difficulty in responding to the suggestions in this test.

The use of touch was also included. As the suggestion of the balloon or bucket was being delivered, the hypnotist lightly touched the appropriate wrist. By lightly touching the wrist, we are helping the child to create feelings to go along with his visual images.

The visualization the child experienced was enhanced by having the child state what color the balloon and the bucket were. When the child was asked which way his right arm was going, he mentally created an image of the arm going up as he answered the question. The same was true when the child was asked which way his left arm was going. The light and heavy arm test is one of the few concentration tests that allow the adult and the child to verbally communicate while the test is being conducted. The wording provided with each of these tests is to be used as a guideline.

There may be times when the child responds almost instantly. With the first mention of a balloon, the child's arm could be high in the air. Mentioning the bucket once could cause the child's other arm to lower. In the same manner that the child could respond quicker than the adult expected, he may also be responding slower than was expected. The key is to deliver suggestions based on how the child is responding.

THE FALL BACK TEST

(A Special Note: Prior to conducting this test, read through the entire dialog of "The Fall Back Test".)

I would like you to stand facing the wall. I am going to stand right behind you. **(Lightly touch the child's shoulders to assure him/her that you are there.)** *Put both feet together, tilt your head back and close your eyes. In just a moment you will feel yourself beginning to rock forward and backwards. Think about this for a moment.*

Think of yourself rocking forward and backwards. Good. You are beginning to rock and sway. You are now noticing that it is feeling as if there was something beginning to pull you back and over; think about something pulling you back and over. You will not fall; I am right behind you and I will catch you. **(Touch child's**

shoulders.)

*As I count from three down to one, you will be falling back and over, back and over. **Three**, it feels as if someone was lightly pushing on your shoulders; picture or think of someone pushing you back. **Two**, you are starting to fall back, back, back. **One**, let go. You are coming all the way back and over. Falling, falling, falling back, back, back.*

SPECIAL NOTE: **Although we are directing the child to fall back, there may be a time when the child tends to lose his balance and falls forward. This can easily be avoided if the adult keeps each of his hands near the child's shoulders. By placing your hands a couple of inches from the child's shoulders, you will be in the position to catch the child regardless of which way he may begin to fall.**

The moment that he begins to lose his balance, place each of your hands on the center of his back and help him stand up straight, while advising him to open his eyes. *"The Fall Back Test"* will allow the adult to learn several different things about the child.

The first is whether or not you have gained the child's trust. Most people have a natural fear of falling. By judging how much the child let himself go, you will also be able to see how much trust has been established. Some children will literally collapse into your arms, while others may start to lose their balance and then catch themselves before they would fall. Still other children may not actually fall back, but will simply sway forward and backwards.

The second discovery with this test is that the child may actually go into hypnosis with this test. If after catching the child, he seems slightly disoriented for a few seconds, he has gone into a hypnotic state. The child will bring himself to an alert state within seconds. There is no need to bring the child out of this light state.

There are several rapid hypnotic inductions that are used on adults to induce hypnosis instantly. These techniques to rapidly induce hypnosis are using portions of *"The Fall Back Test"*. Many Evangelists who walk from person to person and yell, *"You are healed"*, while lightly pushing the individual back, are also using a form of hypnosis.

In the section on inducing hypnosis, we will describe how to use *"The Fall Back Test"* as a hypnotic induction for children. At this point, these concentration tests are designed to increase the child's belief that he/she is capable of being hypnotized. The children find these tests amazing, and that ensures the session is viewed as enjoyable as well.

THE HAND LOCKED TEST

I want you to lace your fingers together so that you can squeeze your hands together, tighter than ever before. I am going to count from five down to one. As I count back, I want you to keep squeezing your hands together.

***Five**, squeeze them tight.*

***Four**, look at them as you squeeze them tighter, and tighter.*

***Three**, they are now beginning to feel as though they were becoming glued* *together. Yes, they are locking, gluing together.*

__Two__, so tight that they no longer want to come apart. So tight that they will not come apart.

__One__, they are now stuck together.

They __will not__ come apart. Try to pull them apart. The harder you pull, the more they stick together. Your hands are now stuck together. (**Allow the child a few seconds to attempt to separate their hands.**)

I am going to clap my hands together. As I clap my hands, I want you to take in a deep breath, then you will be able to slowly pull your hands apart. (**Clap your hands together.**) *Now, you can pull your hands apart. Relax and pull your hands apart easily now. That was the best I have ever seen!*

The above test is delivered in more of an *__authoritarian__* manner. This is the only test that cannot be delivered in a permissive approach. In this test, you are giving suggestions that sound more like commands. If the adult would try this test saying, *"Allow your hands to lock together. Let them become stuck. They may not want to separate"*, most children would instantly separate their hands.

"The Hand Locked Test" is also delivering dual suggestions. *"The harder that you try to pull your hands apart, the tighter they stick together."* With these words, the child is reinforcing that the hands are stuck together each time he attempts to pull them apart. By observing how the child responds to this authoritarian test, the adult will know prior to inducing the hypnotic state which type of delivery will work better for the child.

There are *__three important elements__* to keep in mind when conducting concentration tests. The first is that **we may not always succeed, but we never fail**. With these tests, there is not a pass or fail status. Every child will respond differently to each test. On some tests, there may be only a slight physical movement, but the child may have experienced the sensation mentally. For the child who responded modestly to the *"Heavy And Light Arm Test"*, the following question should be asked, *__"Was the heavy or light feeling more noticeable to you?"__*

Once the child selects either the light or heavy feeling, he has realized that something did take place. He may not know what that something is, but he will believe that something will take place during the hypnotic session.

For the child that swayed a small amount during *"The Fall Back Test"*, the following suggestion will aid in his belief pattern. *__"Did you feel that you were leaning more forward or backwards?"__* Once again, after the child chooses between front and back, the belief has been instilled. This technique, wording suggestions in such a manner that all responses are acceptable, is known as a double bind. The *__double bind__* technique will be explained in more detail later.

Another element to keep in mind is to **always give the credit to the child**. Concentration tests were not designed for the adult to take bows for successful responses. Once the adult begins to take credit for the child's ability to concentrate, rapport will begin to diminish. Always tell the child how well he/she has done. This praise will lead to additional positive responses from the child. Children need and want the approval of adults. If the adult criticizes the child's responses, the child will lose his belief in hypnosis and possibly himself.

The third element is for the adult. **The concentration tests are the perfect way to practice your delivery of suggestions**. I have been training individuals in hypnosis for over twenty-five years. Everyone that begins using hypnosis tends to pass through three separate phases.

At first they run out of things to say. They find themselves at a loss for words. They find it hard to believe that they will ever be proficient at delivering suggestions.

The second phase is when they have increased their knowledge and experience to such a level that they now do not know when to quit talking! They could go on for hours and hours delivering positive, well-worded suggestions.

The third phase is the one for which we are ultimately searching. It is a happy medium between the first and the second phase. The suggestions are positive, well worded and yet, we know when to quit.

I have seen sales people who fall into the same categories. The first doesn't know enough about the product or how to convey the message that the customer should buy the item. The second is extremely knowledgeable and has the customer ready to make the purchase, but he doesn't stop talking. If he talks long enough, he is bound to say something that will change the customer's mind about making the purchase. The third says what is needed, in a way that is needed, to make the sale. Nothing more; nothing less.

5. *REMOVE FEARS*

A child's fears can be quite different from an adult's. The adult may have the fear of losing control. The child realizes that he is seldom in control anyway! His parents, teachers or older brothers and sisters are always in control of him. For most children, the fear of losing control is not an issue. Adults also may experience a fear of not exiting the hypnotic state because they associate hypnosis with a general anesthetic during surgery. Children have not yet developed these fears of not waking up. Children will always have more of a fear of going to sleep, rather than a fear of not waking.

To understand what a child may be frightened of, it is important to realize that most fears are not founded upon logic:

Many years ago I experienced a fear of bees. I would attempt to remove this fear with logic. I would say to myself, "I am bigger than that bee. I am quicker than that bee. I could swat him and he would be gone". Could I now walk into the room where the bee was? No.

When I was working on the police department there was a call about a man with a gun inside a house. The supervisor said we would go in the front door. I looked up at the front door and there were several bees flying around it. I told the supervisor that I could not go through the front door; I would go in the back way. We got the man with the gun out of the house.

Later that day the supervisor and I were having a cup of coffee and discussing the earlier situation. He said that he could not understand this fear. "You could enter a house where a man had a gun, but you couldn't pass by several bees?"

Fears do not have to make sense in order for them to be present. Later on I used hypnosis and overcame my fear.

Listen to what makes the child fearful. It does not matter if you feel the fear is justified. If the child feels it, then it is real.

Ask the child what he/she thinks being hypnotized is like. This will give you an insight into possible fears that the child may be experiencing. Inquire if the child has any questions about hypnosis.

The *fifteen* most common fears that a child may have about being hypnotized are:

1. **The fear that the hypnotist will tell the parents what he said during the session.**
2. **The fear that he will be given a shot.**
3. **The fear that he will not be hypnotized and then disappoint the hypnotist.**
4. **The fear of what his friends will think of him for being hypnotized.**
5. **The fear of failing to make the appropriate change.**
6. **The fear that he will not know the answers to questions that may be asked of him.**
7. **The fear that the hypnotist might give suggestions that was not discussed with him.**
8. **The fear of losing attention that he has been receiving.**
9. **The fear that the improvement will be only temporary rather than permanent.**
10. **The fear that the hypnotic procedure will hurt in some way.**
11. **The fear that he will not remember what took place while under hypnosis.**
12. **The fear that he might fall asleep.**
13. **The fear of being punished if the session is not a success.**
14. **The fear of divulging secrets about his parents or other adults.**
15. **The fear of looking foolish while in a hypnotic state.**

This list is only the most common fears that children have related to me over the years. The adult should be prepared to address any of these or other types of apprehensions that the child may be experiencing.

The only thing that could stop a willing subject from entering a hypnotic state is a conscious or a subconscious fear.

6. *EXPLAIN HOW THEY WILL FEEL*

The last stage of the preliminary session is to explain to the child how he will feel when he is hypnotized. The explanation procedure will accomplish two specific goals. First, it will *remove any lingering fears* that the child may still be experiencing. Secondly, it will *eliminate the possibility of internally rejecting the suggestions.*

This internal rejection of suggestions can occur when an individual does not realize they are in a hypnotic state. The child may hear the positive suggestions, and mentally think, *"That sounds wonderful, but it will not work since I am not hypnotized."*

If the child was told how he would feel when he was hypnotized, this could eliminate the possibility of rejecting suggestions. Listed below is an ***example of a normal explanation procedure:***

I want to tell you how you will be feeling once you are hypnotized. You are going to feel very relaxed. It will feel like your whole body is asleep, but you will still hear everything that I say to you. If there were a noise outside, you would be able to hear it. You will also remember everything that happens. When you go to sleep at night you will dream.

Sometimes you don't remember all of the dreams when you wake up the next morning. Here, you will remember everything. There may be a few moments when you feel as though you're not listening to me. There may be a time when you are thinking about something different than what I am saying; it happens to everyone. You might feel so relaxed that you feel as though you are almost ready to fall asleep. You won't fall asleep. You will just feel relaxed.

There may be a time when you are wondering if you are hypnotized or just relaxed. Do me a favor and just wait and see. Sometime during or after our session, I will ask you if you thought you were hypnotized. Let's see how smart you are. I am going to ask you a few questions about being hypnotized. Will you be able to hear me when you are hypnotized? Will you hear other sounds when you are hypnotized? Will you remember what happens while you are hypnotized? Will you fall asleep while you are hypnotized? Could you be thinking of something other than what I am saying while you're hypnotized?

The questions that are asked of the child after the explanation procedure are the key points that should be included in your explanation as to how he/she will feel. By asking these simple questions the adult will be certain that the child has the correct expectations.

The Body Scan

The purpose of this part of the session is to get your child to feel relaxed. We want them to be able to let go of all of their thoughts and concerns. Have your child sit in a **comfortable chair**, favorably a recliner. Some like to sit in the straight-up position, and some may want to recline all of the way back. Whichever way they feel comfortable is the right way. We do suggest that they **do not** lie down because they may have a tendency to fall asleep. If they do fall asleep, the session will not be effective.

If the child starts to fall asleep as you are doing the session, you will have to bring them up to a lighter state by gently shaking their shoulders, telling them that they remain in hypnosis, but can hear and understand everything that you say. Confirm that they acknowledge you by asking them to nod their head *"Yes"*.

If your child likes **music**, you may want to play something peaceful in the background. Whatever music you play, it should not be something that they can sing to or tap their foot to as it is playing. Some people like to use the nature sounds

CDs that have birds singing or the sounds of the ocean. Sometimes, children don't want any music at all. Whatever they choose is the right way to proceed.

Lighting can be helpful for your child to feel more relaxed. If you have a comfortable place for them to sit where you can turn the lights down, it may help them to relax easier.

Peaceful colors like blue, green and lavender help in the soothing process. If you have a room that is one of these tranquil hues and you have a comfortable chair in that room, this may be the perfect place to conduct your hypnosis session with your child.

The **temperature** of the room should be between 70 and 76 degrees. When a person is hypnotized, their temperature goes down, so they may feel a slight chill. We have an afghan in the office so that if they want the comfort of a blanket, we can accommodate them.

After you have all of the information that you need from the preliminary and your peaceful environment is ready for your child to relax, the actual hypnosis part of the session begins!

Ask your child to sit comfortably in the chair, close their eyes and just relax. You are now going to deliver relaxing suggestions to your child. We want to relax them from the tip of their toes to the top of their head.

When we do a body scan, or progressive relaxation, we like to start at their feet and work up to their head. Some people prefer to do it in the reverse order. The reason that we like to start at the feet is because whenever someone carries stress or tension in their body, it is usually in their neck, face, jaw and shoulders. If you started in the area that has the most stress, it will be harder to relax. If you start at the feet where it is already more relaxed, the rest of the body has a chance to catch-up. When you are relaxing the feet and legs, the head, face, jaw and shoulders are also getting more relaxed. By the time you reach that part of the body, it is more relaxed than it was when you started.

The body gives you the information that you need in order to do a body scan. With a soothing voice, give relaxing suggestions for your child to relax each part of their body, starting at the feet and working up to their head. Use words that they understand. If you call their stomach their *"tummy"*, then by all means use that word.

A body scan is scanning the body to create relaxation. If you want to tell them to wiggle their toes and then the toes feel relaxed, that is just fine. Look at their body and go to the next part, giving suggestions for that to relax.

As an example, you may use the following body scan, or make up one of your own:

As you sit nice and comfortable in the chair, let yourself relax. Go ahead and close your eyes. You may feel just like you do when you are getting ready to fall asleep at night. That feels so good, doesn't it?

As you relax even more, you may find that your feet and ankles are relaxed. Wiggle your toes and feel just how wonderful it is to be this comfortable. This wonderful feeling moves slowly up your legs and across your knees. This feels to good. You are more comfortable with each breath that you take.

Your tummy is so relaxed. This peaceful feeling of comfort and relaxation move up to your chest. Take in a nice, deep breath and just relax. You feel so good. You may find that your back and shoulders feel so wonderful. You are letting yourself enjoy this quiet time for you.

Move your neck from side to side just one time to help you relax even more. This wonderful and soothing feeling goes down your arms and into your hands and fingers. Wiggle your fingers to feel even better.. Good. You might even feel a little, tingly feeling in your fingers, as you get even more relaxed.

This peaceful feeling moves again into your back, shoulders, neck and into your face. Feel your cheeks and mouth relax. You are feeling so comfortable. Even the top of your head is relaxed. Your eyes are relaxed. Your forehead is relaxed. Your hair is even relaxed. From the very top of your head all the way down to the bottom of your feet, you feel so good and comfortable.

As I count from five down to one, you feel better with each number that I say.

***Five**, you are learning how to relax and feel really good.*

***Four**, as you listen to me talk to you, you feel more comfortable.*

***Three**, you feel better than ever before.*

***Two**, feels kind of like when you are just ready to go to sleep. You are not going to sleep right now. You can hear everything that I say to you.*

***One**, there you go. All relaxed and comfortable. You feel so good.*

There is no need to get **too** detailed on body parts. There is no need to relax each finger and each toe. That would take forever! You don't really need to tell them to relax their derriere! Just use whatever words you would say to your child to comfort and relax them. You will get the hang of this very quickly. The more you do it, the easier it gets.

If you want to change any of the words, go ahead! If you want to make it shorter, that's fine, too. You know your child better than anyone else, so do what works for you. The main goal is to help your child relax. Go with your instincts.

Some children may not be able to relax in the above manner. If this is the case, you may want to have them tighten their muscles and then allow them to relax. As an example, you may tell them to *"Tighten up all of the muscles in their arms. That's right! Tighter and tighter. Now, just let go and allow your arms to just relax."* If they prefer to relax in this manner, go through the body, starting at their feet, giving suggestions to tighten and then relax the muscles.

The Induction

Before you actually begin a hypnosis session, you must make sure you have achieved the following requirements: **You must have established a desire for change, a belief in the ability to make that change and a reward for the child's efforts.** The **vocabulary** skills of the child must be determined in order to communicate effectively. You must be prepared to conduct the session in a **span of time that holds the child's attention**. Most importantly, the hypnotic session should be fun! You will achieve the greatest results if you and the child enjoy this time together.

In order to get a commitment of effort to create a change, the reward must exceed the amount of effort involved. We previously discussed using an *"Add-on"* benefit to the child. If the parent wants the child to concentrate more on his schoolwork, perhaps the *"Add-on"* could be better videogame scores. **It's important to stress the benefits that the child will receive by making the choice to change a certain behavior.** The hypnosis session should not begin until the child is convinced that he will receive more than he will be giving to reach the goal. If the reward is not greater than the effort involved, then the change will be temporary at best.

When working with children, age alone will not dictate their language skills. I've known children with a larger vocabulary than some adults. The simplest way to determine if the child will understand your suggestions is to summarize your script and deliver a portion of it to the child during the preliminary part of the session. Ask the child what was meant in that portion. In a matter of minutes, you will know the level of the child's vocabulary. Remember, just as with adults, we don't want to talk down to the child, but we do want to be certain that the suggestions are understood and received.

When a child is the subject, the most important element of hypnosis is **short sessions.** The lack of concentration on the part of most children is more than made up by their tendency to readily accept constructive suggestions.

Positive changes in behavior can be achieved in a short amount of time. If more time is needed, it's better to conduct several short sessions by bringing the child out of hypnosis and re-inducing the state. Despite their short attention span, children are the best subjects for hypnosis . Children tend to be in an altered state of consciousness most of the time anyway.

There are many ways to induce hypnosis in children . This first induction allows the child to go into the hypnotic state *gradually as they relax their body:*

INDUCTION #1

Today you are going to go to sleep in a new way. Now, normally when you go to bed at night and you go to sleep, you don't hear anything. But this is a special kind of sleep where your body will feel like it is asleep, but what will happen is you will still be able to hear what I say to you. So now I want you to close your eyes and get ready to go into this special, this fun kind of sleep. OK?

Now keep your eyes closed and I'm going to touch the bottom of your right foot. As I touch the bottom of your right foot, let that foot go to sleep. Good night right foot. Now, I am touching the bottom of your left foot. Let that left foot go to sleep. Good night left foot. Now, feel both of your legs. Your right and left legs are going to sleep. Oh, they feel kind of heavy as they go to sleep. Good night legs.

Now, let your tummy go to sleep. Good night tummy. Now let your chest go to sleep. Good night chest. Now, I am going to touch your right hand and, as I do, let that right hand go to sleep. Good night right hand. Now, I'll touch your left hand and, as I do, let the left hand go to sleep. Good night left hand. In fact, let the right arm and the left arm go to sleep, too. Good night arms.

I'm going to lift up the arms and as I let go, they just flop right back down to the chair because they are sound asleep. Get ready. I'm lifting up the right arm.

I'm letting it go. Let it flop. Good. Right back down to the arm of the chair. Now, I am going to lift up the left arm. As I lift it up, let it go. Let it just kind of flop to the arm of the chair. Good night arms.

And now, your neck is going to sleep. The top of your head is going to sleep. Even your hair is going to sleep. Your eyes are going to sleep. Your nose is going to sleep. Your mouth is going to sleep. In fact, everything is going to sleep, except your ears. Your ears are staying awake so you can hear me. Now the whole body is going to sleep, everything except your ears. Your ears are staying awake so you can hear me. Now the whole body is going to sleep, everything except your ears. Goodnight body.

The next induction is a form of a ***rapid induction*** and it's based on a "The Fall Back Test":

INDUCTION #2
I want you to stand up. That's right. Put your feet together and your hands at your sides. In just a moment, I am going to have you close your eyes and, when you have your eyes closed, you are going to find that your whole body starts rocking forward and backward. Forward and backward. In just a couple of moments, you're going to keep going back, back. You will actually be falling over backwards. When you fall over backwards, your whole body is going to go into a special kind of sleep. Now, don't worry, I'll be right behind you so I'll be able to catch you when your whole body goes to sleep. I'm going to set you in this nice, comfortable chair, and you will be able to hear me even though you will be asleep. We will have a lot of fun.

So now, I want you to close your eyes. That's right. Your body is starting to rock forward and backward, forward and backward. Don't worry. You won't fall. Now there is something kind of pulling you back. Pulling you back, pulling you back. You know what happens when you fall over. The whole body goes to sleep. Get ready. You are coming back and back and back and falling over. And <u>sleep</u>!

The next induction really is a lot of fun. I came up with this induction on the spur of the moment and kids really enjoy it. It's based on what's called a ***fixed-eye induction***. It is also an ideo-motor response. An ***ideo-motor response*** is a physical reaction given as a subconscious reply, bypassing the conscious mind.

INDUCTION #3
We're going to do something that is really a lot of fun. I have here what we call a pendulum. It has a little ball and there is a chain. This is kind of magical. Watch how this works.

If you hold it between your finger and thumb and you ask it a question and the answer is "Yes", the pendulum goes back and forth towards you. But, if you ask it a question and the answer is "No", it will go back and forth across you.

Let's try it out. I'll hold the pendulum first. Are there two of us in the room right now? There it goes back and forth towards you. That means "Yes". Let's try another question. Are there a hundred people in the room? It went very quickly, back and forth across you. That means "No". So the pendulum is kind of a way of talking without ever saying anything. Would you like to try it? Good.

Now hold it up in front of you and I want you to watch it. Let's see what the pendulum has to say. I'll ask the question and you get to watch it move. Are you really smart? "Yes." That's good. Would you like to be hypnotized and feel good? "Yes." Can the pendulum help you go into hypnosis? "Yes."

Now I know from working with other people, just before someone goes into hypnosis, the pendulum starts turning around in a circle. It doesn't go back and forth. It doesn't go across you. You just watch it. You will know when you are going into hypnosis because the pendulum will start going around and around and around. Once it starts going around and around, your eyes will close. You will go into deep hypnosis. There they go! They eyes are closing now, closing all the way down. Good.

Now, I am coming over and taking the pendulum out of your hand, lowering your hand back to the arm of the chair. You can relax more.

The following is another version of that type of induction. A lot of children have a natural fascination with flashlights and this induction uses a ***small flashlight or penlight***.

INDUCTION #4

In just a moment I am going to have you open your eyes. I am going to be holding a little flashlight right above your head and I want you to look right at that light.

As you start to look and watch that light, you are going to find that something amazing is going to happen. Your eyes are going to feel really heavy. It will become almost impossible to hold them open. So, I want you to go ahead and open your eyes for a moment.

Look right at that flashlight and as I start moving that flashlight down towards your forehead very slowly, the eyes are beginning to blink. They are starting to water and tear. It's getting harder and harder to hold the eyes open. They are feeling so heavy and as they begin to close, they seal shut. They won't want to open anymore until I ask them to open.

There they go. Closing down, closing all the way down and just locking shut, staying closed. There. Now that they are closed, relax even more.

No list of inductions would be complete without my favorite. Hypnotizing children should be a fun experience for you and the child and I find this one exceptionally enjoyable. This induction calls for the use of a ***puppet*** .

Our puppet's name is *Dr. Moody*. He looks like a doctor. You can use any puppet that you like. If you don't have a puppet, you can use a stuffed animal.

INDUCTION #5

Look right into Dr. Moody's eyes. When you look into Dr. Moody's eyes you will go to sleep. Oops! You made Dr. Moody go to sleep! Wake him up for me. Ok. Now this time, Dr. Moody, you put her to sleep. Uh-oh, you did it again. You hypnotized Dr. Moody! Wake him up for me again.

Dr. Moody, if you don't hypnotize _____ (Say Child's Name) for me this time, I'm going to be mad at you. I know, you're sorry. Maybe when we try this again, _____ will go to sleep instead of you, Dr. Moody. Ok, look into Dr. Moody's eyes and as you do, your eyes will close down, down and down.

This induction works wonderfully. It is a *rapid induction*. The puppet, *Dr. Moody* in this case, actually demonstrates to the child what is expected of him or her. There is also the implied message that, if the child doesn't go to sleep, I'll only be mad at *Dr. Moody*. The child doesn't want *Dr. Moody* to be in trouble and complies.

The Deepening
Children go into hypnosis quite easily, but sometimes we need to deepen the level. The type of deepening we would use with a child is the same as an adult, but they are shorter in length. These are delivered at a slower pace than the induction, similar to the pace you would use when telling a story. There are several different types of deepening. Here are just a few examples of the many types of deepenings that can be used.

A deepening can be worded to bring to mind a *visual scene*. Within this next scene are many indirect suggestions. For an example, there are subliminal messages to encourage the child to make the effort to change his or her behavior. Perhaps, you will find some others as well.

DEEPENING #1
I want you to imagine yourself walking down a beautiful beach. This beach is different from any other beach. As you imagine walking down this beach, you see that somebody, a younger kid, wrote the numbers 5 down to 1 in the sand. It was like this kid had taken a stick and wrote the numbers in the sand.

You go up to the number 5 and slide your foot across the number and, as you do, the number 5 just disappears. Oh, and you get to relax further. You go on down to the number 4 and as you slide your foot across the number, you are not sure how this even happens, but you relax even further as the number 4 fades away. Now it is kind of like, maybe, you have discovered the secret, so you go down to the number 3 and, as you get ready to slide your foot across the number, water comes in, just barely touching your toes. It's cool and refreshing. The water helps you erase the number 3 and, as it does, you relax further and deeper again. You look back at where the numbers 5, 4 and 3 once were, and now the sand is smooth and flat. But you feel as if you've done things only half way, and that's not your style. You don't want to do anything half way. You want to complete everything you begin.

You go down to the number 2 and, this time, the water comes in covering your toes. The water does most of the work for you. The number 2 fades away and you relax even further, even deeper again. And now you feel so good, so wonderful, so great that you go down to the number 1. This time, before you can even begin to slide your foot across that number 1, the water comes in all the way up to your ankles. It's cool, refreshing and wonderful. The water does all the work for you. The number 1 just fades away and you relax even deeper and further again.

You look back and remember how on the number 5 you put forth the first effort, but you didn't stop there just because it was going to take a little work. You went on to the number 4 and put forth the effort needed. By the time you reached the number 3, the water came in and did some of the work for you. By the time you reached the number 2, the water was doing most of the work for you. Finally, when you reached the number 1, the water was doing all the work for you.

It's kind of amazing. That's how things are our whole life; we begin the work and it keeps getting easier and easier for us.

Counting can be an effective way to deepen the hypnotic level. Depending on the age of the child, you may start at 10 or more; or you may want to start as low as four for a younger child.

DEEPENING #2

In just a moment, I am going to have you begin to count back from ten down to one. Now, each time you say a number, I want you to become twice as relaxed. You will be able to relax so far, so totally, that before you even reach the number five you will lose track of all the numbers. You won't be able to find any other numbers.

So begin counting back for me out loud, very slowly, from ten down. That's right. The numbers are beginning to fade away. That's it. You are relaxing even more, becoming kind of sleepy. You're almost done. As they fade away, feel good, all the way. The numbers are disappearing. Once they are totally gone, shake your head "Yes". That's it. Shake your head "Yes". Relax all the way down now.
(NOTE: You are giving these suggestions at the same time that the child is counting. Whey they say a number, you give one of the relaxing suggestions in-between each number they say.)

This next deepening uses the closing and opening of the eyes. Each time the child goes under, they go deeper. Years ago they believed that an individual had to be hypnotized many times in order to achieve deeper states of hypnosis. This technique is simply a quicker way to attain that deeper level of hypnosis.

DEEPENING #3

I know that you are feeling relaxed, kind of sleepy, really nice. But, you know in your own mind that you are still able to relax even more. In just a moment, I am going to have you try to open those heavy, heavy eyes. It is going to seem hard to get them open because they are so heavy. But the wonderful part is, when I ask you to close your eyes again, you will be able to close them and you will then become twice as relaxed as you are right now. So get ready!

I want you to go ahead and try to open those eyes. They are so heavy! Now close them and become twice as relaxed. What a nice feeling.

Now we are going to do the same thing again. I am going to have you try to open those heavy eyes, but when I tell you to close them, you will be able to close them and become twice as relaxed as you are right now. Go ahead. Try, attempt to get your eyes open. A little more, all the way. Close your eyes and become twice as relaxed again. What a nice feeling that is.

Now we are going to do the same thing one more time. But this time when I tell you to close your eyes, you are going to relax further than anyone has ever relaxed before. Go ahead. Try, attempt to open them. Just a little more. Good.

Tests and Challenges

Tests and challenges are simply a way to confirm in the mind of an individual that they were indeed under hypnosis. Children tend to respond to these with exuberance far beyond that of most adults. There are many, many different ones and I've found that most children really enjoy this part of the hypnosis session. You can have a lot of fun with this. Eventually, you will find yourself coming up with many creative tests of your own.

LIGHT HAND

I'm going to come over and touch your right hand. And as I touch your right hand, we are going to do some magic together. As I touch your right hand, your right hand is going to feel light as a feather. Get ready. I'm touching your right hand and as I do, all the weight, all the heavy feeling is leaving your right hand. In fact, your right hand is becoming so light, now it is starting to feel as though there is a string tied around your wrist and on the other end of that string is a big, helium balloon. It's the kind of balloon that, maybe, we would see at a circus, carnival or fair. The kind of balloon that just kind of floats up, up into the air.

Think about a second balloon being added, and you can feel the hand start to float up. If we add a third balloon, it floats even higher. We add a fourth balloon and it is starting to rise up and up. We add a fifth balloon and you hand is becoming lighter than anything in the world. One more is all it ever takes. We add a sixth balloon, six big, beautiful balloons floating and lifting your hand up into the air. Your hand has lifted from the arm of the chair and is floating high in the air. Your hand is so light.

Now we're going to have fun. If I try to push your hand back down, watch what happens. I push your hand down. Oops! There it goes! Your hand floats up again! Wow! Your hand feels so light!

Now, just let your hand and arm relax on the arm of the chair. Whew! You feel very relaxed and comfortable after all of this.

AMNESIA

Now, we all know that we can remember things and we all know that we can forget things too. We are going to do a bit of magic now. You are starting to forget the number that goes between five and seven. The number that goes between five and seven is just fading away.

In fact, it has faded away so much that I am going to teach you a new way of counting. The new way of counting will be one, two, three, four, five, seven, eight, nine and ten. That's right. The new way of counting is one, two, three, four, five, seven, eight, nine and ten. Counting backwards it would be ten, nine, eight, seven, five, four, three, two and one. This is a new way of counting because the number between five and seven isn't there anymore. We can't think about it. We can't say it. So I want you to count the new way from one to ten for me. (**Wait for response.**) *Good. This is going to be the new way of counting for right now.*

You know that there is something missing, isn't there? But you can't think of it. I'm going to touch your forehead and as I do, you will know what that missing number is. Get ready. Touching your forehead, what is the missing number? (**Wait for response.**) *That's right. It is six. Now you can count and you can use the number six. Go ahead and count from one to ten using the number six now. The numbers are all back to normal, back to normal. You are relaxing even more.*

REVOLVING HAND

In just a moment, I am going to come over and lift up your right hand. I am going to turn your hand around and around in a circle. Now, the magical thing that will happen is, even when I let go of your hand, it is going to go around and around in a circle. The other really great thing is that each time it goes around in a circle, you are going to relax more.

Now I am lifting your right hand. I am starting to move it around and around in a circle. Feel it going around and around. I am letting go of your hand, but it keeps going around and around. As I let go of your hand now, the hand is going around and around and around. It keeps going around and around and each time it goes around, you relax more. In fact, it is going around a little faster. As it keeps going faster, you get to relax more. You are having fun. In fact, it is going around so much, so fast now, that you can't even stop it.

I want you to go ahead and try to stop your hand. You will find that the harder you try to stop it, the faster it goes. Go ahead and try. There it goes! It's going around faster and faster. Good.

Now as I touch your hand, it is slowing down. As I touch your hand now, it stops moving. Allow your hand and arm to totally relax. You are now relaxed and comfortable.

EYES LOCKED

Now you have been letting your whole body relax further and further. But, now I want you to really think about relaxing the muscles in and around your eyes. I am going to count from five down to one and, as I count back, feel your eyes getting heavier and heavier.

Five, even though they are closed, your eyes tend to be feeling heavier and heavier.

Four, they are feeling so heavy that your eyes just don't want to open anymore.

Three, feeling so heavy, almost like they are kind of glued shut. They don't want to open now.

Two, there they are. Your eyes are so heavy now that they just won't open.

One, once you have your eyes so heavy that they don't want to open, I want you to test them. Make sure that they will not open. Make sure that your eyes will not open. Go ahead. Try to open your eyes, but they won't open. There. Now you are sure your eyes won't open. Just relax, relax.

The following is one of the most fun tests that can be conducted with a child while in the hypnotic state. This type of test originated from stage shows, but serves a useful purpose when working with children.

LAUGHTER

I want you to pretend that you are at the movies with me. You can see that movie screen with your eyes closed, can't you? (**Wait for response.**) *Good! I am going to count from three down to one. On the count of one, you will begin to see and think about one of the funniest movies in the world. It will be so funny that you will start to laugh out loud.*

Three, the movie is about to start. The laughter is already wanting to slip out, isn't it? Two, get ready for that funny, funny movie. One, there it is, the funniest movie in the world! It makes you laugh more and more. It is getting funnier and funnier. That's it! Enjoy the movie. (***NOTE: As you are giving suggestions that the movie is funny, laugh a little or chuckle yourself as you are counting down.***)

Now allow that movie to fade away, and allow yourself to relax even deeper.

There are two ways of using fantasy as a test and challenge. You can change something that is there, creating an illusion. Or you can create something that is not there; that is a hallucination.

ILLUSION

(**NOTE: When the child opens their eyes, hold a pen in your hand. Hold it up so that the child can see it.**)

As you relax even further, your mind is relaxing , too. As your mind is relaxing, all kinds of thoughts are entering your mind. You are very creative. You can think of so many things. On the count of one, you will open your eyes and look at what I'm holding in my hand.

Three, you are feeling relaxed and at ease. Two, as you open your eyes, you will see a beautiful flower in my hand. One, open your eyes and see the beautiful flower. Isn't it pretty?

Now, close your eyes and relax even deeper. The flower is all gone. There is no more flower.

HALLUCINATION

You may not know this, but I have a yellow canary in this room. Even with your eyes closed, you can see him flying around the room. Watch the bird with your eyes closed as he flies all around the room.

In just a moment, you're going to be able to open your eyes and see the yellow canary. Won't that be nice? Go ahead and open your eyes. Now, if you hold out one of your fingers, he'll land right on it. Here it comes! It's landing on your finger! The canary really likes you!

Now it's time for you to relax even more. Close your eyes and relax deeper. The canary is going back to where he lives. The canary went back to its home.

The Prescription

This is the part of the session when you give positive suggestions to your child to help them in reaching their goal. The last chapter in this book gives you an abundance of topics for which your child may need assistance.

Everything is written out for you so that you know exactly what to say. The scripts are worded as if a hypnotist were conducting the session, but by changing a few words or phrases, it works equally as well for the parent.

Just follow the step-by-step instructions on how to conduct a hypnosis session with your child, and you'll have it made! You may want to organize your notes in the order that you will do them (**The eight steps for the session**) so everything will flow easily.

Remember to word suggestions so that they are age-appropriate for your child. It is advisable for you to read over everything **_before_** you do the session. When you are familiar with the wording, you will feel more comfortable and so will your child. Also, you'll be able to change any wording that may need to be altered for your child.

Post-Hypnotic Suggestions

Post-hypnotic suggestions can be very effective in *reinforcing the behavioral changes* brought about during the hypnosis session. They can also create positive expectations regarding the ongoing improvement. That is definitely a good thing!

This post-hypnotic suggestion will give the *parents first-hand proof* that something positive happened during the session. The following post-hypnotic suggestion is one of my favorites to use with children:

POST-HYPNOTIC #1

*We have had a real good time today. When I bring you out of this wonderful, magical kind of sleep, you're going to feel great. When you walk back out front, where your mom (**and/or dad**) are waiting for you, the first thing that you are going to want to do is give her/him a big hug and a kiss. Tell them "Thanks" for bringing you here because you know that you are going to do better. If you understand this, nod your head "Yes".* (**Wait for response.**) *Good.*

*I am going to count from five down to one. On the count of one, you will open your eyes and be wide-awake. When you walk out front, you will give your mom (**and/or dad**) a big hug and kiss. Tell them "Thanks" for bringing you here today because you're going to do better.*

*Five, now we have really had fun today. Four, some of the feeling is coming back into your feet, your legs, hands and arms. There it is! Three, breathing a little heavier, a little easier. Now you've got it. Two, coming all the way back and feeling happy. Getting ready to go out and give your mom (**and/or dad**) a big hug and kiss and tell them "Thanks" for bringing you here. One, open your eyes all the way, wide awake. What a nice feeling. Let's go now to see your mom (**and/or dad**).*

Sometimes, you may wish to *induce hypnosis rapidly* in an individual. An effective way to accomplish this is with a *re-induction using keywords:*

POST-HYPNOTIC #2

You have done very, very good today and, if I ever get to hypnotize you again, you'll find that you will just go into this wonderful kind of sleep even easier than before. In fact, I'm going to give you a secret word that will allow you to go back into this wonderful sleep, real quick and easy.

The secret words are "Yaba Daba Do". You know, like the Flintstone's would say. So, in a moment, I'm going to count from three down to one. On the count of one, you will open your eyes and be wide-awake, but when I say "Yaba Daba Do", your eyes will close. You will never be able to put yourself to sleep this way, only me. When I say "Yaba Daba Do", your eyes will close and you will go back to sleep. Will that be okay with you? (**Wait for response.**) *Good.*

Three, starting to breathe a little bit easier. Two, that's right, coming back up and up. All the way back; all the way up. One, take in a deep breath, let your eyes open all the way, all the way awake. That was fun. You liked that, didn't you? (**Wait for response.**)

Would you like to do that again? (**Wait for response.**) *You would? Ok. This time, we are going to do it real quick. Get ready. "Yaba Daba Do". There goes your eyes, closing all the way down. You're going back into that good sleep. You will remember from now on that any time that I, and only I say the words "Yaba Daba Do", your eyes will close and you will go back into hypnosis much, much deeper. I am the only person who can make this work. I'm going to count from five to one and on the count of one, you will feel great.*

Five, feeling better with each breath that you take. Four, realizing that you are reaching your goal easily. Three, you know that you can do it! I'm so proud of how wonderful you are today! Two, you can do anything you put your mind to. One, gently open your eyes, feeling great! Knowing that you are now reaching your goal.

This next post-hypnotic suggestion includes a test and challenge and gets the child to make a verbal commitment to make the effort needed to bring about his or her change in behavior. What a wonderful thing!

POST-HYPNOTIC #3

In just a moment, I'm going to bring you out of this wonderful, beautiful sleep. I am going to count from five down to one. On the count of one, you will be awake, fully alert. You will get up from the chair and walk toward the door. On your second step, your right foot is going to become stuck to the floor. It will become stuck to the floor and you won't be able to move it until you say, "I am going to do better". As soon as you say, "I am going to do better", you will be able to move your foot again.

I am now counting from five down to one. Five, you are starting to breathe easier. Four, coming out of this wonderful sleep. Three, beginning to move a little bit more. **Two,** *hearing sounds around you, almost there. Soon, as you are wide-awake, you are going to get up, walk toward the door and, on your second step, your foot will become stuck to the floor.* **One,** *you are wide-awake and feeling good.*

That's it. Do you want to get up? (**Wait for response.**) *Ok, you can get up and try to go toward the door. Now your foot is stuck! You can't lift it. Go ahead and try to pull it. It won't move. Do you know what you need to do so that you can get your foot unstuck?* (**Wait for response.**) *Sure. What is it that you need to say?* (**Wait for response.**) *You are right.* **"I am going to do better".** *Now you can move your foot. You know that you are going to do better.*

If you really want to make an impression on the parent, you can word the suggestion so that the child's foot gets stuck right before they get to mom (**and/or dad**) in the waiting room. It is quite an effective realization for the parent when the child's foot gets stuck and then is released after making the verbal commitment to do better, right there in front of the parent(s).

Exiting
When guiding an individual from hypnosis to an alert state of consciousness, it is advantageous to use some form of counting. If an individual progresses to a conscious state too quickly, they may experience a momentary disorientation or headache.

The Wording For Exiting
In just a moment, I am going to count from five down to one. As I count, you feel wonderful. All of the suggestions and instructions begin to work for you <u>*now*</u>*.*

Five, *you are feeling very well. You know that you can do anything that you set your mind to do. You are becoming more aware of the outside sounds and noises.*

Four, *slowly, gradually some of the feelings are coming back into your feet and legs. You are taking control of your own life. You are a winner.*

Three, *becoming more and more aware of everything around you. Becoming more and more aware of your own abilities and talents.*

Two, *coming all the way back to an alert state where you are in control of your own life. Feeling happy, wonderful and confident.*

One, *take your time. As you are ready to, take in an easy breath and, as you breathe out, let your eyes open. Allow your eyes to open at your own pace. There's no need to rush.*

CHAPTER 5

The Transformation Process

Prior to inducing the hypnotic state, the adult should understand what types of changes are possible when using hypnosis. Over the years, I have heard hundreds of different complex clinical explanations as to what transpires during a hypnotic session. In 1988, I had the privilege to attend a lecture by Ormond McGill .

Ormond McGill is the author of several books on hypnosis and has more years of professional experience with hypnotism than any other person in the world today. As I eagerly awaited his in-depth interpretation of what takes place in a hypnotic state, I was shocked to hear such a simple description. Mr. McGill stated that what a hypnotist does is to help another person *"change their mind"*.

This definition is so simple that it is actually profound. You will be doing exactly what Ormond said. You will be helping children change their minds. Throughout our entire lives, we have changed our minds on the way we think, respond and act.

We can change our minds on many different issues. We can change our minds on how we respond to a situation, person or an object. This simple definition, once again, reinforces the fact that hypnosis is a safe, natural way of helping ourselves and others. Knowing that we can change the way a child perceives a given thought, situation, person, object or feeling allows us to help the child in a multitude of ways.

FIVE CATEGORIES FOR A HYPNOSIS SESSION

Types of hypnotic sessions can be divided into *five basic categories*, which apply to different behaviors. They are not intended to be a guideline to the origin of the problem. Instead, by determining which category a behavior falls into, gives you information on how to work with the situation.

1. HABIT PATTERNS

Habit patterns consist of behaviors, such as bedwetting, nail biting, overeating, sleep patterns and thumb sucking.

2. FEARS

Common fears for children are animals, being left alone, darkness, doctors, monsters, needles, storms and tests.

3. *BEHAVIORS*
Behaviors consist of conduct, throwing fits, lying, sportsmanship, stealing and talking back.

4. *PERFORMANCE*
Performance relates to cleaning their room, grades, reading, completing homework and sports.

5. *SELF-IMAGE*
The category of self-image includes guilt feeling, happiness, nightmares, self-confidence, self-esteem, stuttering and tics.

It is easy to see that many situations may overlap from one category to another. A child that is disruptive in school or at home, may be doing so simply out of habit. The behavior may have begun initially due to a poor self-image problem. It could be related to a fear of school or a test. At home, it could be to get attention from parents or jealousy of a new sibling.

1. *HABIT PATTERNS*
When we examine habits, they should be classified as conscious, subconscious or a combination of both. This classification will aid the adult in removing the unwanted habits. There will be different techniques in removing subconscious habits, as opposed to conscious habits.

A subconscious habit is one that the child is responding to automatically. The child may not be aware that he/she is doing a certain action. Nail biting is an example of a subconscious habit. Most children do not look at the nails deciding to take a bite from them. Children that bite their nails are doing so without being aware of the action.

When working in the area of weight loss, the adult may experience a combination of both conscious and subconscious habits working at the same time. Let us review two examples of overeating and then classify which of the examples was subconscious and which one was conscious:

EXAMPLE #1
Johnny has been out playing all day. He comes home for the evening meal and feels starved. He eats a normal size helping and then asks for a second helping. His father knows that Johnny is trying to lose weight and inquires, *"Are you still truly hungry?"* Johnny then has a second helping of each item from the table.

EXAMPLE #2
Johnny has been out playing all day. He comes home for the evening meal and feels starved. He eats a normal size helping. After the meal is over, Johnny watches television and grabs a few potato chips from the bag that was sitting on

the table between him and his brother. Johnny reaches for chips several times during the television program. At the end of the program, Johnny walks into the kitchen to get a drink of water. On his way out of the kitchen, he takes a handful of candy from a dish on the counter.

If you selected Example #2 as being the subconscious habit, you are right. In the first example, Johnny finished his first helping and still felt hungry. With the help of his father, he consciously decided that he was honestly still hungry and chose to have a second helping.

In Example #2, Johnny ate his evening meal and, without being aware of what he was doing, he reached for potato chips. He began to eat subconsciously. After the television program, he consciously went to the kitchen for a glass of water. As he was leaving the kitchen, he subconsciously reached for the candy dish.

Eating is just one of the many habits that we can learn to perform subconsciously. To help you determine if a behavior is conscious, subconscious or a combination of the two, examine an adult who smokes cigarettes . The average smoker smokes approximate one and a half packs of cigarettes each day. That is a total of thirty cigarettes. If the smoker thought, *"Do I really want this cigarette?"* He would never smoke thirty cigarettes a day. There would be times when his response to that thought would be *"Yes."* There would be other times that the answer would be *"No"*.

If you could ask the child, *"Do you really want to do that?"* and his answer was always *"No"*, this would indicate the habit is subconscious. If the child answered *"Yes"* then the habit would be conscious. If the adult received a mixture of *"Yes"* and *"No"* responses, then the adult is dealing with a combination of conscious and subconscious habits.

2. *FEARS*

The category of fear encompasses many of the problems that a child usually faces. The fears are either of an internal or an external nature. Internal fears are apprehensions that the child has that cannot be identified with a specific item, place or person. External fears deal with issues relating to a specific item, place or person.

Examples of internal fears are when a child experiences the fear of being left alone, darkness, being kidnapped, monsters or entering sleep. These fears are not related to anything tangible. They are thoughts of things that could happen to the child. Although most adults have not seen or touched a monster that lurks behind the closed doors of children's closets, most children have *"seen"* or at least *"heard"* them many times. This is in their imagination, so it is not tangible.

After hearing a television newscast of a child being kidnapped, the child could create an internal fear of some person trying to hurt them. The child would not be identifying this fear with any specific person. Instead, he would be experiencing fear and anxiety over the possibility of an upcoming event that would be harmful to him. Any item or event that creates fear in the child but cannot be seen or heard, is an internal fear. Internal fears will require an internal solution to resolve them.

External fears are items such as animals, cars, doctors, needles and storms. These are all items that can be seen, touched or heard.

It is always easier to help a child to become free of an external fear. The item, place or person that is the cause of the fear was initially viewed in a different manner at one time or another in the child's life. Children are not born with a fear of doctors, monsters or storms. These fears are learned through experiences that they have had at some time in their lives. Some children have a terrible fear of clowns, while other children love them. Fears are formed through the combination of sights, sounds and emotions. The case history below is an *example of how a fear can be created*:

The Story Of Tina

Tina was a bright ten-year-old that was experiencing an unnatural fear of turtles. Her mother stated that they had a weekend cabin in the country. If Tina saw a turtle, she would be petrified for the entire weekend. Her mother further explained that this fear started for no apparent reason about two years ago. The mother went on to explain that the fear had now escalated to the point that even a cartoon character of a turtle created anxiety for her daughter.

Under hypnosis, Tina recalled a time at the age of eight when she was going down into the basement of their family home. As she reached the bottom step of the stairs, her older brother was hiding around the corner. He was holding his pet turtle in his hands. Her brother jumped out from around the corner and held the turtle just a few inches from her face while making a growling sound. Tina screamed at the top of her lungs and ran terrified up the stairs. This was the origin of her external fears of turtles. It created a phobia of turtles through the combination of seeing, hearing and feeling. Tina saw the turtle in a different manner than usual. She had never been in a position of having a turtle mere inches from her face before. Although the turtle did not growl at Tina, her mind associated the growling sound from her brother as coming from the turtle.

The kinesthetic sensation was that of shock at being surprised when her brother jumped from his hiding place. The next time Tina saw the turtle, her mind instantly associated the turtle with the feeling of fear. From that moment on, she began to compound the fear of turtles each time she thought of one. This compounding effect worked to reinforce the fear of turtles.

Many children encounter situations or objects that they view as frightening and, yet, do not necessarily develop a phobic reaction. To understand how a child could experience a fearful situation that would not turn into a phobia, let's review the following hypothetical situation:

The child is sitting in her yard on a blanket. Her parents are nearby at a picnic table. A large, black snake slithers across the child's leg. The child jumps up and screams with terror. The snake quickly disappears from sight. A few days after the event with the snake, the child is in the yard and thinks of the past experience with the snake. The mind then recalls past events of seeing snakes at the zoo. The child does not view the zoo or the snakes at the zoo in a fearful manner. The traumatic event of the snake in the yard is no longer dwelled upon. This child will not be associating the fear that she experienced with a fear of snakes. This child would not develop a phobia of snakes.

Phobias are not normally formed by a frightening encounter. The phobia begins after the frightening encounter when the mind looks back on the situation and views the experience as one to never confront again, like feeling fearful of a surprise like a growling turtle in your face. This reviewing process is how the mind defines positive and negative reactions. The child spends the day at a picnic with her parents. The family has a wonderful time. At a later date, the mind reviews the event of the picnic and concludes that picnics are pleasurable.

3. *BEHAVIORS*

Behavioral problems are normally a result of the subconscious mind choosing an inappropriate way of responding. The subconscious mind does only what it believes to be in the best interest of the child. By realizing that the subconscious will only generate thoughts that it feels will benefit the child makes understanding some behaviors easier.

The drawback of the subconscious mind is that it does not have the ability to analyze, but rather takes information on a literal basis. Children tend to use more of their subconscious mind than adults. As adults, we review the information that is presented to us. We then examine past experiences and come to a decision of how to respond. A child normally has little to no past experiences to review and, thus, relies more on his subconscious mind to direct his actions.

A young child may hear his parents saying that they wish they could have their car painted. The young child, wanting to please his Mom and Dad, takes his finger paints out to the garage where the car is parked. He then proceeds to use his artistic ability and paint his parent's automobile with every color imaginable. The child's behavior is not acceptable, but his intentions are understandable.

The behavior is not always designed to benefit another person. The behavior may benefit the child. One type of behavior that every child has experienced is that of lying. Regardless of why the child began the cycle of lying, if it is not stopped, it may become an automatic habit. The child will begin lying without realizing that he is doing so. Lying is a learned behavior that can either be encouraged or discouraged by the adults.

Yes, adults have a tendency to encourage a child to lie to them without meaning to do so. There are two ways in which an adult can unwillingly encourage lying.

The first is by asking the child questions when the answer is obvious. The child is the only person sitting at the kitchen table. The child's mother turns her back and hears a noise. She looks at the table and sees that the bowl of cereal that the child was eating is now spilled on the kitchen floor. The mother asks the child, *"Did you spill that"?* The mother knew the answer to the question before she ever asked it.

She unnecessarily established a situation that could encourage the child to lie to her. The reason for asking questions is to gain information that we do not already have. The information that the mother was seeking was *how* did this happen, rather than who did it.

The second way that adults encourage lying is to conceive a plan that would make lying the lesser of two evils. Imagine a child that has never lied to a parent before. The child was told that if he plays with the ball in the house, he would be grounded to his room for the entire summer. The child plays with the ball in the house and breaks one of the lamps. The father comes home and asks the child, *"Were you playing with the ball in the house?"* The child instantly says, *"No"*. If the adult establishes a punishment that is too severe for the child's behavior, they will be encouraging the child to lie.

As adults, we would respond in the same way. Imagine if the punishment for speeding was a fine of $50,000.00 and five years in prison. You were speeding, but there was no proof of it. A police officer asked you if you were speeding, your response would be, *"No"*. You might lie to avoid an unjust punishment for a minor offense.

Adults have a tendency of sending out mixed messages to children. In the heat of anger the adult may say that the child may never watch television again. A few days later the child is allowed to watch television. The child is happy that he is allowed to watch television, but not sure when to believe a statement made by the adult. These false statements from adults cause the child to establish the theory that adults do not actually mean what they say. The child will test this theory of his by constantly asking to be allowed to do something that he was told he could not do. If the adult eventually gives in to the child's numerous requests, then the child's theory has been validated.

A child comes into the house and requests a cookie. The father says, *"No"*. The child goes back outdoors and plays, only to return in a few moments to ask again if she could have a cookie. The father once again replies with a "No" response. The child comes in a third time and says, *"Dad you are the best father in the world, could I have a cookie?"* The father still says, *"No"*. If the child came in a fourth time, her response might be, *"Dad, never mind"*. She would not ask the fourth time because she would know what the response would be.

The father had just created what is known as a *"No" set*. The only types of thoughts that enter our minds are things that we might say *"Yes"* to or achieve a *"Yes"* response from another person. If the answer would be definitely *"No"*, there would be no reason to ask or think about it. As a child or an adult changes their behavior patterns, they are creating a *"No" set*.

The person that makes a decision to stop eating chocolate may mentally go through situations similar to that of the child asking for a cookie. The mind may generate the thought of a piece of chocolate and the person says, *"No"* to that thought. For most people the thought will return. One piece of chocolate would be all right. The person again refuses the temptation and says, *"No"*. The mind may become more creative. You have worked extremely hard; you deserve a small piece of chocolate. As before, the person does not give in to the thought. In a short period of time the subconscious mind will respond in the same way as the child asking for the cookie. The mind will no longer generate the thought of chocolate because the answer has already been determined to be *"No"*.

The only types of thoughts that the mind will bring up are things that we might say *"Yes"* to. If the answer is a definite *"No"*, the mind will not waste time generating the thought. If on the second or third request the answer suddenly changed from a *"No"* response to a *"Yes"* response, the lesson would be to not give up; keep generating the thoughts to have chocolate or asking for a cookie and eventually you will get a *"Yes"* response.

Another type of unwanted behavior in children is back talk XE "back talk". Along with back talk comes slamming of doors, storming out of the house and the all-too-familiar rolling of the eyes. Most parents want to stop that behavior, but not everyone realizes how easy it is to alter. Once you understand that from the child's point of view, it's a display of frustration, it's easy to see that we simply need to help the child learn a new, more appropriate way to communicate that frustration.

A simple change of phrase can make all the difference in the world. A frustrated child who responds with, *"I am not happy about this"* instead of, *"I hate you"* is still venting their frustration, but in a more acceptable way. The added bonus of teaching them to use words that describe their emotions when angry or upset is that they will be more effective in expressing themselves in all aspects of their lives.

Some children throw fits or tantrums and the parents are usually advised to try to ignore this behavior. Most of us find this almost impossible. An alternative that works wonders is what we discussed earlier. The tantrum is a way of saying, *"Look at me, I'm totally and completely, physically, mentally and emotionally out of control!"* If the child has to do something first (**like putting her left shoe on top of the TV**), it's virtually impossible to go back into that tantrum mode. They lost their momentum. It takes all the fun out of it.

The idea is to make any behavior a conscious decision. You are also teaching the child to be in control of a situation, instead feeling as if the situation is controlling them.

If you were hammering a nail and missed the nail and hit your thumb instead, you might be tempted to say a few bad words, throw the hammer and kick the wall. However, if you had to make a conscious decision about it, you might weigh your options. *"Let's see. I can say two, maybe three, curse words and then throw the hammer across the room, followed up with a good kick against the wall. Or, I could go run some cold water on my thumb."* Most of us, if we had to stop and think about it would probably decide to run the cold water on our thumb, right?

4. *PERFORMANCE*

Most children love the idea of getting better at video games or their favorite sport. Often times we can tie that desire together with improving school work or completing chores at home. The child may not jump at the chance to get better grades in school, but if she can also improve her video game playing, the interest level is greatly increased.

We can also help the child to establish a habit of turning a task into a game. Once the child enjoys the behavior, she will duplicate the new behavior until it becomes part of their lives.

Many parents have trouble getting a child to clean her room. We suggest playing the "Sherlock Holmes Game" with them. Purchase a large magnifying glass and tell her that Sherlock Holmes is going to come look for clues. (**Things that need to be done.**) It won't take long before the child will want to change places with the adult and look through the magnifying glass. The idea here is to use the child's own creative imagination to get her enthusiastic about the game. Not only will the child clean the room, but she will also enjoy hunting for those *"clues"* until the room is really done. The game becomes a pattern of behavior that is part of their daily lives.

You can get a young child into the habit of dressing more quickly for school or other time-sensitive activities by having him pretend to be a *fireman*. Instead of yelling at him to hurry, the parent rings a bell to signify a fire alarm going off, and the child sees how quickly he can get dressed and be ready to put out the fire.

Slowing a child's eating habits can be as simple as having everyone at the table pretend they're astronauts out in space where everything they do is in *really slow motion*. A child's imagination offers an excellent opportunity to improve performance. Children use their imaginations every day anyway, why not use it in a constructive way!

Bob's Story

Bob was trying to convey the importance of good communication to his youngest daughter, so he related the following story:

*Suppose someone was trying to get a $20 donation from an individual. **Now, keep in mind that the goal is the $20 donation.** They start by asking the individual if they would be willing to take a large group of juvenile delinquents into their home for a month. The individual replies, "Absolutely not!" Then, they ask if they would be willing to take at least some of them for two weeks. After being turned down again, they ask if just a few (the ones that were not convicted of arson) could spend the weekend. Finally, they ask if they are willing to make a $20 donation in order for someone else to take the delinquents. The $20 donation was quickly and gratefully given.*

Well, this young child with an active and productive imagination turned the story around on her own Dad. Sometime later, she found her Dad busy with something and asked him if he would help her bake a cake. He replied that he didn't know the first thing about baking cakes, so she suggested making homemade ice cream. Again, he exclaimed that he didn't know how to make homemade ice cream. "Well then," she sighed, "Can I at least have two or three cookies?" He quickly agreed.

She certainly learned how to use her creative imagination and the art of getting what she wanted on her unsuspecting Dad. How's that for a fast learner?

5. SELF-IMAGE

The one thing that is universal about self-esteem is that you won't find an individual who says, *"I already have enough and don't want any more, thank you."* A poor self-image can manifest itself in the form of stuttering, tics, nightmares and shyness, among many other problem areas. Even behavioral problems can be a symptom of a poor self-image.

Sometimes parents damage a child's self-image without ever realizing it. The following illustration shows the importance of proper communication:

The Glass Of Milk

A child sits at the dinner table and accidentally spills her cup of milk. Now the parent could shout a number of things. "How can you be so clumsy!" sends the message to the child that clumsy is who she is. "How many times have I told you to put your glass further from the edge of the table?" implies the child isn't capable of learning. When it happened with my daughter, I said, "Angie, someday you are going to be graceful!" Now, she knew from my tone of voice I wasn't happy about the spilled milk, but the subconscious XE "subconscious" part of the mind doesn't pick up sarcasm, as it is very literal. She knew I wasn't happy about the spilled milk, but the implied message was that she would get better as time passed.

A child's self-image can be shaky at best when she doesn't trust what the parent says to be true. A parent who grounds a child for a month, and then allows her to go out with her friends just days later, is actually doing that child no favor. Parents also send out mixed messages when they throw out extreme threats. If the parent threatens to make them stay in her room until she's 55-years-old, the parent is basically saying, *"Look, I'm telling you something, but you can't believe me"*.

We came up with something very simple. If I tell my daughter, *"I promise"*, it will never be a lie. Therefore, if she were to come to me to ask to go to the show and I say, *"No, Angie, I promise, you won't be going to the show"*, she knows that no matter what happens, I won't change my mind. It became almost enjoyable as time went on. I would say, *"No, Ang, you're not going to spend the night over at your friend's house"*. And she would say, *"Okay, Dad, but don't promise. This way, you have some flexibility to change your mind later, if you'd like"*. This also allows for some humor. If I did say, *"You're never watching TV again for the rest of your life"*; she would just laugh and think to herself, *"He didn't promise!"*

This is also a *"No"* set. It is useful on cutting down on whining and begging, as well. What we're striving to have the parent and the child learn is that, if you word things in the right way, the child is going to be able to understand and behave in a more appropriate manner.

Therapeutic Techniques

Amazingly enough, we can modify behavior in children fairly simply and quickly. There are many methods to facilitate these changes. We will go over some of the common techniques, like Ideo-motor Response, Changing Sides, The Hero, The Talking Puppet, NLP, Reframing, Automatic Writing, *"Reject"*, Rehearsing and Regression.

IDEO-MOTOR RESPONSE

We know from previously in this book that an **ideo-motor response is a physical reaction given as a subconscious reply, bypassing the conscious mind.** One of the ways that we created the ideo-motor response was to establish a finger response. We established that the index finger is the *"Yes"* response and the little or baby finger is the *"No"* response. When we use the fingers, we specify that the little or baby finger means *"No, N-O"*. We spell it out so that the subconscious mind doesn't confuse that response with *"Know"*.

We ask a few test questions before asking the questions necessary for assisting the child in reaching their goal. We want to see how the *"Yes"* and the *"No"* fingers respond so that when we ask our questions, we are familiar with the way or the amount of movement the fingers will make.

In a previous induction, we used a swinging pendulum as a way for the child to respond subconsciously. When they would hold the pendulum between their finger and thumb and asked a question, if the answer is *"Yes"*, the pendulum goes back and forth towards you. But, if you ask it a question and the answer is *"No"*, it will go back and forth across you.

Even nodding the head up and down for *"Yes"* or shaking the head to the right and then left for *"No"* can be used as an ideo-motor response with children, as well as adults. The suggestion can be made to the child that they will not even be aware of the nod or shake of their head as they respond. We have found that we cannot get the head response beyond the conscious awareness of most adults, but it is very easy to do with children.

Some hypnotists use a floating left hand for *"Yes"* and a floating right hand for *"No"*. There are so many creative ways to implement an ideo-motor response. The only limitation is the practitioner's imagination.

Establish which ideo-motor response you are using prior to asking questions. There is not one that is necessarily better than the others. Whatever is easiest for the child to respond to is the one that you want to use.

As we all know, there are times when we realize that there's a part of the mind that can work against us, making our efforts feel as if we're taking one step forward and three steps back. When a child is trying but still failing at school or having trouble overcoming a fear, we often think it would be nice if we could get the part of the mind that is working against the child to change sides.

CHANGING SIDES

Changing sides is done using an ideo-motor response. Ideo-motor response techniques are wonderfully effective when used to overcome an irrational fear.

Tell the child that you will be asking them some questions. Support the child's hand under their wrist with one of your hands. With your other hand, lift their index finger and release it, while telling them that if the answer to a question is *"Yes"*, you want them to lift the index finger, the pointer finger next to their thumb. If the answer to a question is *"No, N-O"*, tell them to lift their little or baby finger. Again, you demonstrate this by lifting and then releasing the little finger.

This is the time for you to ask a couple of test questions. The goal is to ask a question that you already know that the answer will be *"Yes"*, and then ask another question that you know the answer will be *"No"*. By doing this, you will see the way the child responds, whether their fingers move greatly or a slight amount. The child now understands what is expected of them.

Here is an example of the wording that may be used in a session:

I want to speak with that part of Mary's mind that has been making her afraid of cats. Would that part of Mary be willing to talk with me now? (**Wait for response.**) *Good.*

I know that you are a very smart part of Mary, isn't that right? (**Wait for response.**) *You have been making Mary afraid of cats for a long time now.*

Would you be willing to trade sides and start to be on Mary's side? (**Wait for response.**) *Good.*

If you are now going to change sides and be on her side, can you now see a cat without being afraid? (**Wait for response.**)

You may want to conduct a **visualization** afterwards to show that the sight of a cat is no longer frightening.

If anyone were to ask me what was my favorite therapeutic technique to use with children, I would have to say the following, *The Hero*. This technique can be used for bad habits like nail biting; fears such as fear of sleeping in their own bed and many, many others.

THE HERO

As you continue to relax, I am going to count from three down to one. On the count of one, even with your eyes closed, you are going to get to watch your favorite cartoon.

Three, *it is going to be really clear. You are going to do some real magic today.*

Two, *almost there. Get ready. And . . .*

One, *as soon as you begin to see your favorite cartoon, I want you to shake your head "Yes" for me.* (**Wait for response.**) *That's good.*

Now, I want you to tell me who your favorite character is. (**Wait for response.**) *That's good. "Papa Smurf".* (**Or whatever character your child says.**) *Now, using magic, you can talk to him. Ask "Papa Smurf" if he likes you. What did he say?* (**Wait for response.**) *"Yes", I thought he did. Now ask "Papa Smurf" if he would be willing to help you.* (**Wait for response.**) *From this moment on, if you start to bite or chew on your fingernails, "Papa Smurf" will whisper in your ear, "No, don't do that!" And you will be able to move your hands away.*

Let's try it out. OK. Bring your hands up to your mouth like you are going to bite on your fingernails. Listen. What happened? (**Wait for response.**) *That is right. "Papa Smurf" told you not to do that because he is pretty smart and he is going to help you from now on. So, from now on if you start to bite your finger-nails, "Papa Smurf" is going to be there to help you out. We can trust him, can't we?* (**Wait for response.**) *Good.*

Sometimes you will have difficulty getting the child to talk to you about his or her problem. I have found that a useful tool for getting the child to open up is a puppet. It doesn't matter the size of the puppet, or whether or not you can open and close it's mouth. You don't need to be a ventriloquist to use a puppet when helping children. You can let the child play with the puppet. Tell them they can use the puppet to tell you about the problem. (If you don't have a puppet, you can use a stuffed animal and get the same results.)

It can be much less intimidating to have the puppet do the talking for them. A child that doesn't want to talk about a problem will often be willing to make the puppet talk for them. You can use the puppet in the following manner:

THE TALKING PUPPET

Sometimes there are things we want to say to a grown-up that we know we just can't say. In just a moment, I am going to have you open your eyes and I am going to give you a puppet. I'm going to have a puppet, too. My puppet is going to be the grown-up. Your puppet can be anyone you want. I don't know who my puppet is. The only thing I know is that it is a grown-up. This is going to be your chance to tell that grown-up whatever you want. Whether it is a teacher, Mom or Dad, a relative or a neighbor, you are going to be able to tell that puppet, that grown-up, anything you want to tell him. I am going to count to three. On the count of three, this is your chance.

One, two, three. Go ahead. Now, here is your puppet and here is a grown-up puppet, the one you really wanted to say something to. Who is that grown-up puppet? (**Wait for response.**)

Continued asking the child questions, making sure that they feel safe and secure.

The following therapeutic technique utilizes Neuro-Linguistic Programming, or NLP, to trigger the change in behavior. NLP is based on the way people internalize information. Everyone sorts, stores and retrieves information received through the senses and, over time, tends to develop a preference for one mode: visual, auditory or kinesthetic. Children with irrational fears respond very quickly to this technique.

NLP

I want you to begin to think of one of the happiest times in your life. I am going to touch your right shoulder. As I touch your shoulder, you are going to remember one of the best times of your life; a really happy time when you felt great.

I am touching your right shoulder. As you begin to feel those wonderful feelings that you felt at one of the happiest times of your life, I would like you to nod your head "Yes" and relax even more. As you think of this happy time in your life, I'd like you to tell me what it was. (**Wait for response.**) *You got a red bicycle for your birthday?* (**Or, whatever happytime your child recalls.**) *That is wonderful.*

Now as I take my hand away from your shoulder, let those wonderful feelings leave. Now when I touch your right shoulder again, let those feelings come back. Isn't that wonderful? (**Wait for response.**) *Yes!*

Now I'm going to touch your left shoulder and when I do, I want you to think back and remember one of the last times you were kind of afraid of grasshoppers.

(Or, whatever fear your child has.) *Ok, as I take my hand away, those bad feelings all leave. As I touch your left shoulder again, you feel just a tiny little bit of that fear. As I take my hand away, those bad feelings leave.*

Now I want you to think about the future, thinking about seeing grasshoppers. Only now the feelings are all confused. **(Alternate touching the left and then the right shoulders over and over while continuing to talk.)** *Wait a minute. Things are changing. There's all kinds of thoughts going on in your mind. Now when you think about grasshoppers, you find that you are feeling this way* **(Touch the right shoulder.)** *That's right. You're thinking about grasshoppers, but you're feeling this way.* **(Touch the right shoulder.)**

(At this point, you can even challenge the fear.) *I want you to think about grasshoppers and try to remember the fear.* **(Touch the right shoulder.)** *Instead, you feel the same way you did when you* **got the red bike.** **(Or whatever their happytime was.)** *Right?* **(Wait for response.)** *Right!*

Don't worry, we've never had a child run out into a field and start collecting grasshoppers like they were red bicycles after one of these types of sessions! Keep in mind. We retain every sensation we have ever encountered, stored in our mind, both positive and negative. We can bring these feelings back and use them to get rid of irrational fears. It is so rewarding to be able to help children remove their fears.

Adults and children alike have a tendency to resist being told what to do. When we try to change behaviors on a conscious level, we are basically attempting to tell the subconscious what to do. The subconscious level of the mind always tries to do what's best for the individual. Sometimes the subconscious mind has been conditioned to respond in a way that, in reality, is not in the individual's best interest.

A person that has been given food repeatedly as a reward or to make them *"feel better"* will learn to respond to emotions with food. For that person, simply saying over and over not to eat sweets will not be an effective way to overcome that conditioning. *"Do not eat any candy, do not eat any candy"*. It's easy to see why this is not effective. With reframing, we are actually enlisting the help of the subconscious mind to come up with safe, positive, healthy alternatives, replacing the negative behavior. This technique is conducted with an ideo-motor response.

VISUALIZATION EXERCISE
NOTE: Do this exercise after the preliminary <u>before</u> going into hypnosis.

Just sit back, get comfortable and close your eyes. I want you to imagine, just think about the way things are going right now in your life. You came in here today to make some changes. Think about what it is that you want to change. Think about how things are not going the way you would like them to be.

When you have this image in your mind of things not going the way you would like, are you looking through your own eyes, or can you see yourself in the image? **(If they are looking through their own eyes, change it to seeing themselves in the image.)** *When you look at this picture, is it in color or black and white?* **(If**

in color, change it to black and white.) *Is this image near or far away? (If near, change it to far away.)*

You can see yourself in this black and white image. It's kind of grainy and defocused, kind of fuzzy looking. It's impossible to make out what it is that you're looking at. Now push that picture farther away until it becomes a little black dot. Then tuck it into the lower right or left hand corner of your vision. Release it. Let it go.

Take in a nice, deep, easy breath. Hold it for a moment. Release it easily. That's it. I wonder if the weather will be the same tomorrow as it is today.

Take in another deep, easy breath and exhale slowly, easily. Now, I want you to imagine that everything is going exactly the way you want it to be. Picture, imagine in your mind what it is that you want. When you get this thought or idea in your mind, are you looking through your own eyes, or can you see yourself in the image? **(If they can see themselves, change it so that they are looking through their own eyes.)**

As you look through your own eyes, is everything in color or is it in black and white? **(If it is black and white, change it to color.)**

Is this image near or far away? **(If far away, change it to being near.)** *You are now looking through your own eyes. Everything is in bright, vivid colors. It is close up as you look through your eyes. Now put some positive, excited feelings and emotions with this image. You may even smile, right now, smile! That's it! Let your body feel the excited emotions that are present as you reach your goal. Pump some positive feelings into this image. Get excited! Feel it! You are now reaching your goals! You have achieved it. That's it!*

Now take in a nice, deep easy breath. Hold it for a moment. Release it. Now, open your eyes and come back into the room.

REFRAMING

Would the smart part of Billy be willing to help him stop getting into fights? **(Wait for response.)** *Good! Would that smart part of Billy now be willing to come up with five, new ways of doing things, instead of getting into fights?* **(Wait for response.)**

Are any of these five, new ways of doing things bad? **(Wait for response.)** *Good! Will your mom and dad like all of the five, new ways of doing things?* **(Wait for response.)** *Good! Can you begin to start these five, new ways of doing things right away and stop all the fighting?* **((Wait for response.)**

It is not expected or desired for the individual to remember what those five, new ways of responding are going to be. There cannot be interference on a conscious level if there is no memory of the new responses.

We use this technique often with adults for weight loss. I had a client that came back in for an appointment and announced, *"I know what one of the new ways of responding is. My husband pointed it out to me. During commercials, I would go to the mailbox and check for mail, instead of going into the refrigerator checking for food!"* If we had come up with that suggestion as a new way to respond, chances are she would have rejected it completely, or done it once or twice and then stopped, thinking it was silly. Since her own subconscious mind came up with it as a new way to respond, she did not resist the idea.

We use this next technique, automatic writing, most often with children. Some adults associate the concept of automatic writing with the occult. Actually, this procedure is simply another method to gain a response without the interference of the conscious part of the mind. To begin, you must establish whether the child is right or left-handed. We do the technique with a pad of paper and a pencil in the following manner:

AUTOMATIC WRITING

As you continue to sit there nice and relaxed, in just a moment, I'm going to put a pencil in your hand. Underneath the pencil I'm going to put a pad of paper. We are going to do some real magic. In just a moment, as I put that pencil in your hand, you are going to find that without even knowing how, your hand is going to start moving.

You are not going to have to make it move, but it is going to happen all by itself. As the hand begins to move, it is going to write out a word, maybe one, two, maybe three words. But, it is going to be a word. It's going to be the secret that has been causing you to hold onto these fears, to be afraid of things.

So, I'm going to put the pencil in your hand now and, as I do, don't try to make it move. Don't try to make it write anything. But, all by itself, the pencil is beginning to move. It is writing out a word, maybe two words, or maybe three words. It is beginning to write out the reason that you have been having all of these fears. Get ready. You can feel your hand starting to move. That's right, you can feel your arm starting to move. Now the pencil is beginning to move across the page. It is writing out a word. Writing it out. That's right.

Once the reason you have had all these fears is written out, you will find the pencil slips right out of your hand, and you relax even more. You get to relax even deeper. Let it keep going until the word or words are all written out, and then the pencil just slips right out of your hand. There, the pencil has slipped out of your hand. You relax even more, even deeper.

Most of the time, the child's handwriting will be illegible. It would be impossible to read what the child has written, so we tell the child that on the count of three, they will open their eyes and be able to read what they have written on the paper. This is a wonderful way to initiate a message directly from the subconscious mind.

Anything a child mentally rehearses; he or she will have a tendency of duplicating. Just like the example we gave you earlier when we were talking about visualization. Remember the three groups of students trying to shoot the most basketballs? Many professional athletes use visualization to improve their sports performance. If it works with sports, doesn't it make sense that it can work with anything that we can imagine?

There are many instances where the rehearsing, or visualization technique, would be a very effective method for changing a behavior. A child trying to improve their conduct, whether they are at school, at home or trying to overcome bad sportsmanship would benefit from the following dialogue:

REHEARSING

I want you to think about someone who is on television. This person has to practice what he is going to say and what he is going to do. He practices over and over again until he gets it just right. With your eyes closed, you can now be like that person on TV. You can practice and make sure you get it just right.

I want you to practice how you will respond when you don't get your way. What you will say and what you will do. You know what your parents (teacher, coach, etc) would like you to say or do, right? (**Wait for response.**) *Right! Now you are going to practice doing things that make you feel good about yourself. People like you more because you are nicer to everyone. You do the right thing. You are a good sport.*

You can then go through a visualization of an example of the problem behavior and help them practice an acceptable response. As I stated before, anything a child mentally rehearses, he or she will have a tendency of duplicating.

Regression has to be one of the most amazing elements of hypnosis. There are many types of regressions that can be used when working with children. The **Ideo-motor Response** is a type of regression. There is also a regression called **Restoring the Memory**, which is simply bringing back a memory, thought or sensation that we haven't recalled on a conscious level. A **Visual Regression** allows the child to view the memory as if watching a movie without experiencing any of the sensations associated with the memory. And, there is a **Reliving Regression**, which involves actually experiencing the event as it happened.

REGRESSION WITH AN IDEO-MOTOR RESPONSE

In just a moment, I am going to lift up your right hand. We are going to be talking in a whole new way. If I ask you a question and the answer is "Yes", your index finger, the one I am touching next to your thumb, is going to rise up into the air and it will stay there until I push it back down. But, if I ask you a question and the answer is "No, <u>No</u>", the small, the little finger is going to rise up into the air and it will stay there until I push it back down.

Let's try this out. Today, right now, are you living in the United States of America? (**Wait for response.**) *Yes. Good. I'm pushing the "Yes" finger down. Now, have you ever lived in China?* (**Note: Make sure this question is a definite "No" response before asking it.**) (**Wait for response.**) *No. Good. I'm pushing the "No" finger back down.*

At this point, you can begin to ask *"Yes"* or *"No"* type of questions to determine the past memory of an event or feeling relating to the problem area. It cannot be stressed strongly enough that, when regressing individuals, especially children, care must be taken with the questions asked. False memories can easily be implanted by careless questions. Questions that lead the subconscious part of the mind to create a response, rather than recall an actual experience, can cause more harm than good.

RESTORING THE MEMORY REGRESSION

You are nine-years-old. In a moment, I am going to begin counting from age one up to your present age of nine. Each time I say one of the years, your mind is going to look through that whole year and see if there are any feelings that happened at that age that are causing you the problems that you are having today. You will be able to tell because you will feel those same feelings again. Once you start feeling those same feelings, if you start experiencing those feelings, I want you to lift up one of your fingers on your right hand for me.

*Age one, age two, age **three**, age **four**.* (**Watch for a response.**) *That's right. You are lifting up one of your fingers now. I am going to come over and touch your right hand. I want you to tell me what kind of feelings those were and what was happening. Back at age four. You are secure. You are comfortable. You are here with me. I am touching your hand. Tell me about those feelings now.*

The following is an example of a Visual Regression. We are having the child imagine watching a television with a remote control. Most children know how to use the remote control for their television.

VISUAL REGRESSION

I want you to pretend you're sitting in front of a big TV set and that you've got the remote control for that TV in your hand. I'm going to count from three down to one. As I count back, you are going to see a kind of movie on this TV. It's going to be a movie of a time in your life about the age of five-years-old.

***Three**, the movie is starting. Get ready.*

***Two**, it's going to be really clear. One of the happiest times of your life around the age of five. And . . .*

***One**, there it is. There is a movie, a movie of you at about five years of age.*

As soon as you start to see that movie of yourself at about age five, nod your head "Yes". (**Wait for response.**) *Good. Now, think about pushing the volume control button on the remote control so you can also hear what is happening. As you start to have not only the picture of the movie, but also the sound of the movie, nod your head "Yes" for me again.* (**Wait for response.**) *Good. If you want to, you can stop this movie. You can speed it up or go backwards. Whatever you want. Now, tell me. What happened in the movie?* (**Wait for response.**)

With this technique, the child is simply recreating the image or thought and does not experience, or relive the event as it occurred. You can turn this into a **reliving regression** in the following way:

In just a moment, I'm going to touch your hand and when I do, you will look down and tell me what you are wearing at this time when you are five years of age. (**Wait for response.**)

The child will actually respond with the information of the clothes they were wearing during that event. This type of regression brings back the emotions with the memory, so we want to make sure it is a positive memory.

Next is an example of a reliving regression:

RELIVING REGRESSION

Anything you have ever seen, anything you have ever heard, and anything you have ever felt before in your life is stored within your own mind. That's right. Anything that we have stored in our own minds, we can bring back. Now, I am going to count from three down to one. As I count back, you are going to actually get to travel back in time. You are going to travel all the way back in time to the age of five. You will be five-years-old again. Get ready.

Three, feel yourself as you are becoming younger and smaller, getting younger and smaller. Going back, back to the age five.

Two, that's right. All the way back to five-years-old. There you are. Almost there. Get ready. And . . .

One, you're back. Five-years-old. Five-years-old and happy.

As soon as you are back to five years old, I want you to nod your head "Yes" for me. (**Wait for response.**) *Good. Now, five-years-old is so different from the age you were before. Even with your eyes still closed, I want you to look down at your feet and tell me what you are wearing on your feet now that you are five years old.* (**Wait for response.**) *That's good. Now tell me what else you are wearing. Five-years-old; happy time.* (**Wait for response.**)

Homework For The Child

We want the child, as well as the adult, to become aware of the improvements the child is making as time goes on. There are several ways to accomplish this realization for the child. The homework that the child does works superbly to reinforce the work accomplished during the session.

Here are the things we want the child to do and to focus on:

    1. VISUALIZATION
    2. LOG BOOKS AND CHARTS
    3. TAPES
    4. KEY WORD(S)
    5. REJECT NEGATIVE THOUGHTS

1. *VISUALIZATION*

Visualization is one thing the child can do on his or her own at any time. Each night before going to sleep, a child can visualize sleeping through the night and getting up to discover their bed is dry. If the goal is to overcome an irrational fear, the child can visualize their improved reaction to the object or situation that previously caused that fear. As they find it easier and easier to visualize their own success, the child recognizes his or her own improved abilities and talents.

2. *LOG BOOKS AND CHARTS*

This does not have to be complicated or complex. It's important to have the child involved in the design and method of keeping track of his/her progress. Schools have used this method with great success for many years. The reward can often be as simple as a star, smiley face or even a check mark. This is a very positive way of reinforcing the positive behavioral changes made by the child.

Even if there is not total success in reaching the desired goal, it is very important to show improvement. Some changes may require multiple sessions. This should not discourage the child from continuing to make the effort to improve. Logbooks and charts can be brought to subsequent sessions, discussed with the hypnotist and used as ongoing encouragement for the child.

3. _TAPES_

You may use a tape recorder to record the session and then give it to the child to play whenever they have time. When they listen to the session tape, they should do it at a time when they are able to close their eyes and relax without interruptions.

It can also be effective to use a recording on CD or tape cassette that has positive statements relating to the desired behavior change. This would be an affirmation tape. The child could listen to this type of recording at any time, while riding in the car, at night before bedtime or while playing.

4. _KEY WORD(S)_

A key word is any word or words that the child will verbally or mentally say to reinforce a certain behavior. It is advisable to reinforce the use of a key word after the session has been completed.

The following is an example of a **key word** that will help a child **slow down their speaking**:

I am going to tell you a couple of magic words. These words are "Slow Talk". Any time you find yourself beginning to speak rapidly, I want you to say the words, "Slow Talk" to yourself. As you say "Slow Talk" to yourself, you begin to talk slower.

These wonderful, magic words work for you from this moment on. You easily remember the words, _"Slow Talk"._

5. _REJECT NEGATIVE THOUGHTS_

It is a wonderful thing to show a child that they have the ability to reject negative thoughts. After a child is back home, sometimes a parent or sibling may make statements or behave in a way that could undermine the improvement made by the child during the session.

When a child is in a negative environment, it could be at home or at school, it can affect their self-esteem. If someone would call the child names or if they are always told something negative about themselves, we use this next technique to make them stronger.

We can show the child how to **reject** any **negative influences** they may encounter with the following script:

"REJECT"

As you close your eyes and get comfortable, I want to tell you about a Super

Hero. Now, you may or may not have heard of him before. His name is Superman. He came from another planet and is very, very strong. This Super Hero is a good guy. He helps people when they're in trouble. He helps the police to catch the bad guys. Sounds pretty exciting, doesn't it? (**Wait for response.**)

Now, Superman is a very special Super Hero. He can do all kinds of neat things. He can fly faster than an airplane. He can jump from one tall building onto another one. Superman is so strong. He can even bend steel. One of his Super Human Strengths is that if someone shoots him with a gun, the bullets bounce right off of him! It is so cool!

The bad guys are always surprised when they try to shoot Superman, but he stands there strong and confident.

Sometimes people say things that can be bad or hurtful to us, can't they? If anyone ever says anything negative to you, you will be just like Superman. Those bad words or negative things that people say will bounce right off of you, just like the bullets bounce off of Superman's chest when the bad guys are after him.

I am now going to give you a very special, secret word that you can use so those hurtful things just bounce off of you like bullets bounce off of Superman. This special word is **"Reject"**. *Say this word several times to yourself.* **"Reject,"** **"Reject"**, **"Reject"**, **"Reject"**.

From this moment on, any time someone says something mean or cruel to you, you just say this special, secret word, **"Reject"**, *and it will make those hurtful things just bounce off of you.*

Starting today, right now, you think about positive things. You think about what you do want. You have a very powerful mind, so it doesn't matter if someone calls you a name you don't like, or if they say something mean, it will bounce right off of you! You are positive! You are confident! You are wonderful!

Homework For The Parents

Most parents are interested in doing whatever they can to help their child achieve success. We are going to cover a few of the many things they can do to ensure that success. Some of these may seem obvious, but parents often have such hectic schedules that it's advantageous to outline these details:

> *1. LOG BOOKS AND CHARTS*
> *2. USE POSITIVE TERMS*
> *3. TALK OF THE FUTURE*
> *4. BE SUPPORTIVE*
> *5. USE THE "TIME OUT" GAME*

1. *LOG BOOKS AND CHARTS*

The parent may want to keep their own log book or chart so they can keep track of the child's accomplishments to reward or encourage the child's progress. This may be the place where the parent would choose to keep track of special treats or rewards the child can earn at different high points of their progress. A parent may offer a new book of bedtime stories or inexpensive toy for the first grader that goes from an "F" to a "C", for a clean room or for a dry bed two nights in a row.

2. *USE POSITIVE TERMS*

A parent can help the child immeasurably by showing appropriate appreciation for any improvements. This sounds simple, but sometimes a parent has the inclination to point out or comment on the behaviors that still need work.

It is essential for adults to remember to use positive terms and statements when dealing with children. Tell your child what you want them to do, instead of what you want them *not* to do. We want to help the parent learn to be the most effective they can be in their efforts to encourage the child.

3. *TALK OF THE FUTURE*

When discussing their progress, you may want to tell your child how good they are doing. Then make a statement like, *"Since you are doing so well today, just think how great you will be doing next week!"* Let them be aware that their progress will continue to progress as time goes on.

4. *BE SUPPORTIVE*

Again, while this may seem obvious, it cannot be overly stressed that the child's ongoing progress can be hindered or aided by those around him or her. The child can only benefit from feeling that he/she has a team around him or her that is supportive.

5. *USE THE "TIME OUT" GAME*

The *"Time Out"* game has been proven to be a very effective way of handling a negative behavior with the use of negative suggestions. The parents simply uses the words *"Time Out"*, which the child recognizes as a sign that the behavior is not acceptable for the situation.

There should be a pre-determined place where the child may go during the *"Time Out"* period. It should be a place that has no stimulation. This is not designed as a punishment, but rather to reinforce the idea that this behavior is not welcome.

The amount of time for this period is determined by the age of the child. The standard is one minute for each year of age. (Example: three minutes for a three-year-old child.)

The child may request a *"Time Out"* when he or she is having difficulty handling a situation. They may come to appreciate having this quiet time.

The *"Time Out"* is very similar to the technique that many adults use when they count from one to ten. It allows the person time to think. By having the time to think out the situation, the child will now interact, rather than react.

CHAPTER 6

How To Handle Different Topics

There are many different types of sessions that have been conducted success-fully with children. Included in this chapter are the actual scripts used to bring about the desired changes in behavior. These positive changes can often take effect immediately. Sometimes the change is progressive, with gradual, yet steady improvement of behavior.

Read through the scripts **before** doing the session. You may need or want to re-phrase or re-word some suggestions so that they are age-appropriate for your child. Remember to talk with them in their language. If you try to use a larger vocabulary than what they are prepared, the session will be meaningless because they will not understand what you said. Always talk with children at their level of comprehension.

ADD & ADHD

Remember when working with children with ADD/ADHD, they often have trouble with change. They need consistency in their lives. They feel more com-fortable in a routine.

When giving them suggestions, make sure that they are direct and easy to understand. Keep them simple. Children with this disorder take things literally, so it is important that you tell them **exactly** what you want.

Any of the following scripts may be used for whichever topic you need for chil-dren with ADD/ADHD. You may, however, need to re-write some suggestions to change them from indirect or metaphors to direct suggestions. Sometimes it is just a matter of changing a few words. Although we do have direct suggestions in the following scripts, it is the indirect suggestions and metaphors that are also in the scripts that need to be changed for your ADD/ADHD child.

You may choose to word the script in a way that it fits into your child's daily routine that they already have. Since they like routine, it would make sense to incorporate the desired action with activities that they are already familiar with doing.

As you can see, it would be impossible for us to write each script that would be appropriate for each ADD/ADHD child. There are so many variables. But, by you having the insight to your child and a script that is already written, it will be easy for you to adjust the wording so that your child achieves the desired results.

Attitude

Attitude is everything. When a person is positive and puts all of their effort into what they are doing, they accomplish so much more. We want our children to be healthy, happy and successful in their lives. We want them to fit into society and enjoy all that life has to offer. When a child feels loved, safe and secure, they are comfortable to be themselves. Each person is unique with their own set of skills and abilities. With the right attitude, they can do anything!

Sometimes, our children don't realize their own potential. They may want to be noticed, but not know how to go about it in a positive way. Since their brains are not fully developed, their reasoning factors aren't totally in gear! They make bad decisions. Here's some help in this area:

CONDUCT PROBLEMS

This type of session gets an immediate, positive response from the child, however it can be temporary. In improving a child's conduct, we are breaking a cycle of reacting in a negative way to an order or request from a parent, teacher, coach, etc. For this to become a permanent change, it is often necessary for the adult to change their reaction to the child, as well.

You need to be consistent. If you say that you are going to do something, then you need to follow through. If your child misbehaves and you tell them that they are not going to watch TV for the rest of the night if they continue this behavior, if they act up, you need to enforce your statement. There will be no TV for that child for the rest of the night. *No exceptions!* Immediate, short-term consequences are necessary in order to be effective. When you take a stand, don't give in. If your child knows that you will cave in with a certain amount of their begging, crying or throwing a tantrum, you've lost your leverage.

Children reflect the parents' actions. If you yell, children will yell. If you spank them, they will be physical by hitting. We know that we cannot *reason* with a two-year-old. They don't understand what we are saying. But, children do learn by our actions. You may think that they don't notice, but they see and hear everything that you do. You are their role model, the example to them of how they should act. The same sex parent is the most influential person in a child's life. Give them a good example to live up to.

Change affects children. If the family moves to a new neighborhood or if there is a new baby in the home, the child may feel insecure. When children start school, or go into a higher grade, they may feel apprehensive. We need to create a feeling of acceptance and belonging for the child to feel safe. The good news is that children are resilient. They do adjust to change.

You may want to set aside a special time for just you and your child do something special together. It could be reading a favorite book, going to the park to swing, going for a walk, listening to music and dancing, playing their favorite game or even baking their favorite cookie. Make it something that just the two of you do together. Do this on a regular basis. It will make them feel very special that you do this particular activity just with them.

You may choose to do this with each of your children. Create a special activity and time just for them. When we make time for our children, this let's them know that they are important. By creating a special activity that you do only with them, they know that they are special. We want each of our children to know that they loved and are truly special. They will remember this for the rest of their lives.

A friend of mine recalled what her parents did when she was growing up. Her father would take her *"mushroom hunting"*, which was basically a good excuse to take a nice walk in the park. They would talk about everyday things. It was a very relaxing time for the two of them. Her mother taught her how to knit and crochet. It was a great way to have one-on-one time by teaching her a skill. This gave her confidence that she is good with her hands. To this day, this activity brings her comfort and relaxation.

Each child is different, so it might require a hug, verbal praise, and/or a special privilege that makes the child want to continue on with this improved behavior. I've found that one of the more effective ways to encourage good behavior in a child is to let them catch you bragging on them to others. Direct praise is nice, but if you're talking about them in a positive way to others, well, that's really something wonderful to a child.

CONDUCT AT HOME

If you are like most kids, even though you really love your mom and dad, it's still fun to fool them sometimes, isn't it? Well, we are going to fool them in a really fun way.

Let's think of how we have done things in the past. Mom or dad would tell you to clean your room and you would say, "No", or you wouldn't do it. They would tell you it was time to go to bed and you would argue.

They would tell you to do something, and you would come up with a hundred reasons why you should do it later. So that's what they know you are going to do. That's no fun. That's not fooling them at all.

From now on, you are going to do the complete opposite of what you have done before. Think of what would happen to your mom if she said, "Clean up your room." She is going to expect you to say, "No", or that you just don't do it. We are going to play a joke on her and we are going to fool her. When she says, "It's time to clean your room", I want you to say, "Ok, mom, I'll do it now." Then, go and clean your room. She will be so confused; you'll fool her so much. She won't even know what's happening. You will be playing a joke on her.

Think about your dad telling you it is time to go to bed. He is all ready for you to argue with him. Instead, you say, "Ok, dad, I'll go right to bed." He'll leave the room and you will be lying in your bed, kind of giggling and laughing to your-self because your dad won't even know what is happening. You will be playing a joke on him.

You will be fooling them all. They won't know why you are doing this. Each time you do the opposite of what they expect, you will fool them again. We are going to have so much fun. You will be able to go into your room, pick up your mess and clean it up, but you will be kind of giggling because you will be fooling everyone. They won't know why you're not arguing.

There may be a time where they will try to find out what you are doing, but you don't have to tell them. It can be your own secret. Do you think you will enjoy fooling them? **(Wait for response.)** *I thought so!*

CONDUCT AT SCHOOL

I would like you now to think of being in school in a whole new way. The time that you are at school really isn't that long. Sometimes it seems like a long time, but you have all the time when you are at home after school. You have all the time in the evening. You have all the time when you are asleep at night. You also have time in the morning before you go to school.

Most of the time you are not really at school. Of course, there are weekends, holidays and vacation when you don't go to school at all. Most of the time you are not even at school.

Let's start thinking about the time that you are in school in the same way we think about playing a video game or a sport. If you are playing a video game, you really have to concentrate on it. If you were playing basketball, you would be thinking about the game. If you were out riding your bike, you would be thinking about riding your bike.

So there seems to be a time for everything. When you are at school, you are going to be thinking about things to do at school. When you are out of school, that's going to be the time to enjoy playing with your friends, cutting up and being kind of silly.

From this moment on, when you are at school and you start thinking about cutting up (doing things you know you shouldn't), you'll stop and think you are only at school for a short time and you can wait. The magical thing that is going to happen is the time that you are at school is going to seem like it just flies by. Before you even realize it, it is going to be time to go to lunch. You'll come back from lunch and, before you know it, it will be time to go home. You are going to find it easier to be good when you are at school.

CONFIDENCE

Sometimes we hear people say that they are confident. What does that mean? Well, it means that they feel good about themselves. It may be that they feel good about themselves when they are playing a game, or when they do something that they like. The more you do something, the better you get at doing it. If it is something that you like, you will do it a lot, so you will be very good at doing whatever you spend your time on.

What do you like to do? **(Wait for response.)** *I bet there are a lot of things that you do very well. I bet that you can do more things than you even think about. Can you tie your shoes? Can you spell your name? I bet that you are a nice person. You are good to your mom and dad. You are smart in school. You do your homework. See. There are many things that you do very well.*

You are now thinking about all of the things that you do very well. Each day, you add more things to your list. You take pride in what you do. You always do your very best. You are a good person.

Each day you feel better about yourself. You are now confident. You like the way that you feel because there are many things that you do well. There are many things that you will do very well in the future. We are always learning. This makes it fun. The more we learn, the more things we can do.

Now you are confident in how you feel about yourself. You know that you are a good person. You learn quickly and easily. You are nice to people. So, not only do you feel confident about all of the things that you do well, you feel confident because of who you are. You are nice. You are happy. You are smart.

You make friends more easily now because you feel confident. You feel good about yourself. You are easy to talk to. You are interested in other people. You like to know what they like to do. You make friends easily. You are happy. You are confident.

ENJOY LIFE

I believe we should all be enjoying life, but above all, kids should be enjoying life to the fullest. We want to set things up to help them to see the fun in things, to look at things as being better. When my daughter was younger, I got a call from her teacher. She wanted to talk about my daughter's attitude. When asked for specifics, the teacher told me that she'd been talking non-stop in class and, when the teacher told her she'd have to stay in for recess, my daughter thought for a minute and replied that that would be okay because she had a book she wanted to read anyway.

The teacher thought she was being a smart aleck when actually, it's just impossible for her to have a bad day. By the end of the year, they had nicknamed her *"The Duck"* because everything just rolls off her back. Recess is good, but reading is too!

ENJOY LIFE

Today you are ready to have some fun and find out that there are fun things everywhere you look. I think that sometimes we don't think about all of the fun things that you can do.

Let's pretend that you are riding in the car. I want you to think of something fun to do. When you think of something fun, nod your head "Yes" and tell me what it is. **(Wait for response.)**

Good, now I want you to pretend that you are sitting in your room at home. When you think of something fun to do, nod your head "Yes" and tell me about it. **(Wait for response.)**

You are beginning to see that there really are fun things everywhere you look. I now want you to think of any place where you can't have fun. Once you realize that you can't think of any place that is not fun, nod your head "Yes" again. **(Wait for response.)**

You now start to have more fun and enjoy life more. You can find fun in everything that you do. Even if the fun is just something that you think about, it is still fun! You have fun every day. Each morning when you wake up, you think, "Today is a fun day!" You are happy and loved. You enjoy life every day.

MOOD SWINGS

There may be times when you feel pretty happy or on top of the world. There may be other times when you feel sad or hopeless. Believe it or not, this is very normal. It's called being a teenager.

Your body is going through many changes at this time. Your nervous system is adjusting to all of the things that you are going through. For some people it is easier than for others. Your hormones are going through a major change. So are your emotions.

Keep in mind that you are in control of the way you respond. Yes, you can allow yourself to be crabby and emotional. That's the easy way out. If you feel like it, do it. But, you can also be aware of when you are starting to feel crabby and emotional and change the way that you respond. Catch yourself and change to a positive response. Do something special for yourself that makes you feel better. It may be reading a book, listening to some relaxing music that you like or soaking in a nice bath or shower.

Begin to look at things in a different way. If you start to feel crabby or sad, you may find that a minute seems like only a second. An hour feels like a minute. A day seems like an hour. A week feels like only a day. The time that you feel crabby or sad seems to be less and less until it drifts away. You replace being crabby or sad with feeling happy and balanced. You choose to feel good. You decide to be positive. You put your thoughts and energy into the wonderful things that you choose to create for your life.

You have a powerful mind. Whatever you focus on is what you create in your life. If you focus on the negative, that's what you get. You deserve to be happy. You deserve the very best. Allow yourself to focus on what you do want. Allow yourself to be happy and balanced.

Each day you feel more balanced and happy. You feel confident and secure. Your moods are even and positive. You are beginning to feel the way you enjoy feeling. You are in control of the way you respond. You now respond in a positive manner. You distract your negative moods by doing something that you enjoy. You are in control. You are centered and balanced. You feel better each and every day. You are now in control.

POSITIVE ATTITUDE

Always focus on what you want. Put your energy into the positive outcome in situations. Look for the good in others and in yourself. When you have a positive attitude, nothing can stop you.

There are some very negative people in this world. Negativity is contagious. Why? Because it is the easy way out. People who are negative don't want to put any effort or energy into getting what they want. They just want to complain that they don't have anything. If they really wanted something, they would go after what would make them happy. Some people are happy to be negative. But, that's not you!

You are a person who is successful. You know what you want and you get it! You *make a plan to follow and you achieve your goals. Your life is very happy and enjoyable because you choose to be positive.*

When you go to school, you enjoy all of your classes because you find something interesting in each one that makes learning more fun. Your grades improve because you are more interested in learning.

You look for the good in others because you like to inspire those around you. People feel good when you're around because they like your positive attitude. When you go to work, your boss and coworkers appreciate you because you make everything more enjoyable with your positive attitude.

Each day you feel happier and better about yourself. You look for the good in every person and in every situation. If you looked for something bad, you would find that too. Isn't it better to focus on the positive?

You are healthier, happier and more successful with your positive attitude. You enjoy life to the fullest. You make friends more easily. People enjoy being with you. You get more things done. Your reach your goals easier. You are an inspiration to those around you. You have a positive attitude. You feel great about who you are. You are comfortable in every situation. You are truly a winner!

BEING MORE RESPECTFUL

You may have heard a saying that whatever you throw into the water comes back to you. In other words, how you treat others indicates how others treat you. If you want to be respected, you need to respect the people in your life. That means that you should be respectful of your parents, siblings, family, friends, teachers, classmates, employers, co-workers, acquaintances, even strangers.

It's the little things that people notice; like holding the door open for the person approaching behind you, saying "Please" and "Thank you". These actions make good impressions on others. As you become an adult, you may find that you can get more of what you want by being considerate of others.

People think more of a person who is respectful. They want to help you when you show that you appreciate their efforts; when you are respectful of them. This can help you in many ways, in many areas of your life. When you are aware of how others feel and treat them with respect, you feel better about yourself.

Respect yourself; respect others. This is very simple to do. You feel so much better when someone thinks about your feelings or what you would like. Do the same for them.

Always do what makes you feel proud. Be the best person that you can be. If someone were to see you and you didn't realize that they were there, wouldn't you feel good if they were to tell someone else what a wonderful person you are? Imagine, just think about a friend of your parents remarking that they saw you when you were out with your friends. You were not aware that this person was even around, but they noticed that you were well mannered and respectful. Wouldn't this feel so good for your parents to hear how wonderful you truly are? Wouldn't you feel proud of yourself for doing the right thing?

No one can always see what you do, but if you act as if they can see you, you never have to think about what is right or wrong. You are always respectful of others and of yourself. You are proud of your actions. You are proud to be you.

SPEAKING UP FOR YOURSELF

You may not want to rock the boat, but if you don't speak up for yourself, who will? You cannot rely on anyone else to make your concerns their priority. If you don't care enough about what happens to you, why should anyone else?

You are finding that it is getting easier for you to express your feelings in a very effective manner. You know what to say and how to say it. You know when to speak up and when to say nothing.

Think about, imagine someone else speaking up for themselves. Do you think badly of them for saying what they want? No. Are they are terrible person because they ask for what they need? No. Just as you don't give it a second thought because they spoke up, no one will care if you do. As a matter of fact, they may respect you more when you do. If you need or want something, you have the right to ask for it. Do this in a respectful way. There's no need to be rude or demanding. If it is something that can be obtained, there is no reason that you shouldn't have it. Ask for it.

There's no guarantee that just because you ask for something you will get it, but if you don't ask, you are sure that you will not get it. Isn't it at least worth a try? You may be surprised how easy it can be to just be honest about what you think and feel. If someone asks for your opinion, they want it. Otherwise, they would not have asked.

You are very effective in expressing yourself. You say what you mean and you mean what you say. You do this in a very respectful manner. People are interested in what you have to say. You are confident and secure. You feel comfortable asking for what you need and want. You express yourself in a positive manner. You are considerate and respectful.

Speaking up for yourself is now something that you do automatically. You take good care of yourself. You are responsible for your own needs. You make decisions easily. You have everything that you need and want. You are effective in your communication.

BAD HABITS

Bad habits can be changed because they are a choice. When a child does something a certain way over and over again, it becomes a habit. This goes for good as well as bad habits. Usually, a bad habit is the easy way out. It is easier to sit and watch TV than it is to exercise. It is easier to throw things on the floor than to clean a room.

The important thing to keep in mind is that you cannot remove a negative habit with negative suggestions. You want to help your child to focus on positive results, instead of negative ones.

Once your child gets in the habit of creating good habits, they begin to feel better about themselves. Some things will be easier for them to change than others. Every child is different. Some children may do better with one change, and a different child may do better changing something else.

We cannot compare children, especially with their siblings. Just because they came from the same gene pool does not mean that they have the same potential. Each child has his/her own gifts, skills and abilities. We need to celebrate each child's uniqueness.

CHEATING

What do you really get when you cheat? You may feel that you got away with something at that moment, but did you really? You are hurting yourself when you cheat because you are telling yourself that you don't think that you can do it. You are underestimating your own abilities.

When we do something well and we win the game, get the prize, pass the test or get the credit, we feel good about ourselves because it is an earned reward. We know that we deserve it. Whenever you put forth your best efforts, you are a winner. Sometimes you may win and other times you may lose. When you know that you did the very best that you could, you feel proud of yourself for your efforts.

If there is something that you want to do well, you practice. Each time that you do it, you get better. As you improve, you feel more confident. Being honest and putting forth your best efforts builds character. Even if you lose once in a while it builds character. It teaches you how to be a good sport. People respect good sportsmanship. No one likes a bad loser or a bad winner.

*When you cheat, you are the only one who thinks that you won. Imagine that you cheated on a test at school. You receive a good grade. What happens in the future when you are **expected** to know that information? If you cheated, you don't know it. If you don't know it, you can't go forward. Who is the real **loser**? **You are!***

*You have now decided that you want to be the true winner that you know you are deep inside. You feel so proud of yourself because you always give your best efforts in everything that you do. One time you may win and one time you may lose. If you lose, it makes you more determined to win the next time. When you win, you have that great feeling that you earned it! You feel so proud and confident. Who is the real **winner** now? **You are!***

DISOBEYING

There are times when your parents or teachers may tell you to do something, but you end up doing exactly what they don't want you to do. Why do you think that is? I guess it may depend on what it is that they are asking you to do. If you don't want to do what they are asking, it would be very easy for you to just ignore them, wouldn't it?

Sometimes adult are talking to us, but, maybe our mind wanders and we're thinking of something else instead of what they're saying. That may be a reason why we don't obey them. We weren't listening. I guess that could create all kinds of problems when we don't listen.

Let's look at this in another way. Imagine that you asked your parents to take you some place where you really wanted to go. It was really important to you. They didn't feel like doing it, so they just ignore you. You wouldn't feel very happy, would you?

That's kind of how your parents feel when you ignore them. It is very important for them when they ask you to do something. When you don't do it, it makes them feel sad that you don't care enough about them to obey.

You now obey your parents and teachers and do what is right. You do your chores around the house. You do your homework. You feel good about yourself because you get things done quickly.

At home, you feel really good that your parents trust you to do the chores. These are important things to get done. They have faith in you because they know that you will do a great job. You feel so good being part of your family. Everyone has his/her jobs to do. You do your chores very well. You are part of the team! What a great feeling!

At school, you turn in your homework on time. You pay attention in class when the teacher is talking. Even if some of your friends like to clown around and be funny in class, you know that doing that is rude. You wouldn't want someone else making fun and joking around when you were trying to say something.

You know how important it is for you to learn. The more you learn, the more things you can do. You want to be successful when you are out of school. The best way to do that is to be successful while you are in school. It's easy for you to learn now because you listen when your teacher is talking. You learn a lot. You are very smart.

You have learned that obeying your parents and teachers helps you to be a better person. You feel better. You learn a lot. They appreciate you more when you obey. You like helping people. You like helping your parents and teachers.

Every day you feel better about yourself when you obey. You are a good person. You are smart. You learn quickly. You get things done. You are a good listener. You are a good friend.

BEING LATE

Sometimes we think that we have more time than we do. If we're playing a game or watching TV, we may be so involved doing that, we may forget that we were suppose to get ready to do something else.

How would you feel if you and a friend were going to a movie that you really wanted to see, but your friend wasn't ready on time? Your friend was suppose to pick you up and take you to the movie. You're at home all ready to go. You are so excited about seeing this movie. Your friend was suppose to pick you up at 1:00 pm. It is now 1:15 PM. You tell yourself that they will be here any moment. You still feel excited about the movie.

Then, it is 1:30 PM. Your friend still hasn't come by. You call your friend to see if anything happened. No one answers the phone. You don't know where your friend is, or if they are even coming by to pick you up. You hate to get to the movie late. You want to see everything in the movie, especially the beginning.

At 2:00 PM, your friend shows up, smiling as if there is nothing wrong. You are feeling a little upset by this time because you know that you already missed the beginning of the movie. You don't say anything because you don't want to upset your friend. When you get to the movie, all of the good seats are taken. You missed the beginning, so you don't really know what is going on. You feel mad, but don't want to show it. You think that they were so rude to you by not being on time, or not calling you to let you know that they would be late.

When you think about this, do you think that other people feel the same way when you are late? Can you understand that it is rude to other people that you are not taking their feelings into consideration?

You now realize what it feels like if someone else wasn't on time for you. It's not a very good feeling. You are now on time for everything. You plan ahead so that you are ready. You now treat people the way that you want to be treated. You are not a rude person, so you are always on time. You are a very nice person and you treat people very well. You like being on time. You may even surprise yourself and find that you are now early. You get ready on time. You feel good about yourself. People respect you because you respect them.

LYING

Lying can become a subconscious habit. Sometimes parents even teach a child to lie. Imagine if you will, a child playing by herself in the living room, with white carpet no less, holding a glass of chocolate milk. The parent comes into the room and sees chocolate milk spilled on that white carpet and hollers, *"Did you spill that chocolate milk?"* The child replies, *"No"*. Now, that parent already knew the answer to that question, but put the child in a situation where she was tempted to lie in order to avoid getting in trouble. Done often enough, and the child will begin to respond in the same manner automatically.

Another way of teaching a child to lie is to make the punishment threat too severe. If the punishment for forgetting to turn out the light in his/her room **ever** again is that the child won't be allowed to go to Disneyland with the family on vacation, there's a good chance that the child will lie if asked if they left it on.

STOP LYING

I don't think that there is a person anywhere in the world that has not told a lie at least once or twice in their life. I also feel that most people, after they told the lie, wished they had told the truth. But, they didn't think far enough ahead. I wonder if, perhaps, there have been times when you told a lie and wished afterwards that you had told the truth. I'm sure that has happened to you, as well.

We are going to make it so that you will never, ever have to tell a lie again. By making it so you will never have to tell a lie again, you will never have to feel bad later. The first secret in becoming free of lying is realizing when you are telling the truth and when you are telling a lie. I am going to ask you three questions. I want you to answer them and tell the truth.

1. Have you ever eaten a cookie? (**Wait for response.**) *That's good. That was the truth.*

2. Have you ever told a lie before? (**Wait for response.**) *Good. That was also the truth.*

3. Do you know how to ride a bicycle? (**Wait for response.**) *Good. That was also the truth.*

So, you know when you are telling the truth. Now, I am going to ask you three more questions. This might be the last time in your life that you ever get to lie. On all three of these questions, I want you to tell me a lie. This is just kind of a game, so it's okay to lie right now. After this, you won't ever have to lie again.

I am going to ask you three questions. Each time you answer, I want you to lie for me. Something magical is going to happen. Each time you lie, your right hand is going to begin to shake a little bit. You will feel it shaking on the arm of the chair.

Let me show you how it is going to work. I'm touching your right hand and I am moving it back and forth. Can you feel it shaking? (**Wait for response.**) *That's right. Of course, you can. I'm going to ask you three questions now. Each time I ask you a question, you are going to tell a lie. As you lie, your right hand is going to start shaking. Get ready.*

1. Have you ever had a glass of water before? (**Wait for response.**) *No, that was a lie. Feel your right hand.*

2. Have you ever watch television? (**Wait for response.**) *No, that was a lie. Feel your right hand getting ready to shake.*

3. Do you go to school? (**Wait for response.**) *No, that was a lie. I can see your right hand starting to shake.*

Now, it is stopping. From this moment on, if you get ready to tell a lie, your right hand is going to shake. It will be a reminder to you that you really don't want to tell a lie. If you get ready to say something that is not true, your right hand will begin to shake and you will realize that you don't want to say that. You want to tell the truth. A lie is going to become something from your past. You will hardly remember it again.

From now on, you tell the truth. You feel so proud of yourself. You feel so much better when you say things that are true.

BAD MANNERS

Table manners seem to be at the top of the list when parents complain about bad manners. When they take their family out to a restaurant or if they are invited to someone's home, some parents cringe at the thought of their children at the dinner table.

Here is a script that will help your children to improve in this area:

PLAYING WITH FOOD

When people are nice to us, it makes us feel good. When people treat us with respect, we like being around them. If someone is rude or mean, no one wants to be around that person.

I know you heard probably hundreds of times, either your Mom or your Dad, telling you to stop playing with your food. I guess they are right. The purpose of having food in front of us is to eat it. Food is what our bodies need to be healthy and strong. When we're healthy, we can do all kinds of fun things. But, we need to eat so that we feel our best.

It would be kind of silly to take our food outside and throw it up in the air and play catch with it. We have baseballs to do that. It would be kind of silly to take one of the biscuits outside and try to play soccer with it. We have soccer balls that are made just for that reason. That would be playing with our food. Of course, you are not doing that. Maybe what you are doing is scooting it around on the plate, picking at it or things like that.

From now on, you are going to think of food the way it is. It is there to eat. You are not going to be moving it around. You are not going to be playing with it. You will find that you will be happy to be able to finish a meal, nice, quick and easy.

If you think about a car or a truck, they need gasoline for their fuel so that they can move and get where they are going. Just like they need fuel, so do we. But, our fuel is food. When we eat the food on our plates, it gives our bodies the fuel that they need so that we have the energy to move around and get to where we are going. Food keeps our bodies healthy and strong.

Our parents know what kind of food we need to be healthy. They know how much food we need so that we have the right amount in our bodies. You are eating the right kind, the right amount of food for you to be healthy and happy.

It takes more time if you scoot and push the food on your plate. If you eat it, then you're done! You can do something else. But, first, you need to eat the food to get the energy that you need.

When you eat, you sit comfortably in your chair. Your legs are down. You sit with good posture. You enjoy eating at the table with your family. When you want someone to pass food to you, you say, "Please." After they have given you the food, you say, "Thank you." It feels good when people enjoy having you around. You have wonderful manners. When you eat, you keep your mouth closed when you are chewing. You are very respectful of the other people sitting at the table with you.

Your parents are so proud of you. You are growing up to be a very polite, respectful person. Everyone likes being with you because you are so nice. You have good manners.

PROCRASTINATION

*Sometimes we have things to do that we don't want to do, so we put them off as long as we can. That's okay at first, but then there is **too much** to do! Whew! We can get tired just thinking about that. Instead of just having to do one little thing, we waited too long and now we have a **lot** of things to do. It's going to take a lot more time to do it now!*

There was this little boy who had to read one page for homework. It didn't seem like it was that much. He thought to himself, "It's only one little page. I can read it later." So he went back to playing his game. The next day the teacher gave them two pages to read. When he got home from school, some friends asked him to play outside. Again, he thought, "It's only two little pages. I can read them later." And went outside to play with his friends.

The teacher told the class that there was going to be a pop quiz on the three pages that they read over the past two days. The little boy was surprised and embarrassed because he still hadn't read his homework. The teacher was very disappointed in his score because she knew that he was a smart boy. She knew he could do better.

You learn very quickly. You don't need to fail a pop quiz to know what you have to do. Whenever you have a chore, homework, or whatever it is that needs to be done, you think to yourself, "It will only take a short time to do it now!" So, you do it! Then, you're done.

You have plenty of time now to do the things that you want to do when you have all of your chores and homework done. If the little boy had read that one little page when he was first told to read it, it would have only taken him a few minutes to finish it.

Sometimes we can take a homework assignment or a chore that we do at home and make a step-by-step plan to get it done more easily. If the boy had taken that one little page that he had to read, he could have made a deal with himself. If he read at least one sentence, then he could play his game. But, when he was finished with that game, he would read at least one more sentence. By reducing the one page to a sentence at a time, it makes it easily to do. You can read just one sentence, can't you? Of course, you can!

If the boy had read that first sentence, he may have gotten interested in what it was about and finished reading the whole page. That would have been even better because his homework would be all done! He could really enjoy playing his game then!

Make a deal with yourself to get things done as soon as you can. When you do, it's over and you can think about the other things that you want to do. It's very easy to take one step at a time to get something done. Try it! I think you may surprise yourself!

Let's practice right now. I want you to think of something that you need to do. It could be homework, or maybe a chore that your parents asked you to do. Can you think of something? (**Wait for response.**) *Okay. Now, if you were going to do only one thing that would help you to do this, what would that one step be?* (**Wait for response, If they don't answer, make a suggestion. Remember, keep it very simple, almost ridiculous on how easy it is.**) *Wow! See how smart you are! I know you can do this now.*

STEALING

Stealing is a behavior that can create conflicting emotions in an individual. On one hand, there could be a feeling of happiness for attaining whatever was stolen but, on the other hand, there could be guilt feelings. The individual could actually have both emotions, feelings, at the same time.

STOP STEALING

I want you to realize that almost everyone has stolen something at some time in his or her life. As they steal, whatever it might be, they thought that it would make them happy. But, at the same time that they were starting to feel happy about having the item, they were also starting to feel bad about taking it without permission.

I want you to understand how we can have both feelings at the same time. I'm going to come over and touch the top of your right arm and, as I do this, you are going to have a kind of happy feeling. Get ready. I'm touching the top of your right arm. As I touch the top of your right arm, here comes that wonderful kind of happy feeling. As you start to feel it, I want you to nod your head "Yes" for me. **(Wait for response.)** *Good.*

Now, I am going to touch the bottom of your right arm. As I touch the bottom of your right arm, you are going to feel kind of bad. It is going to feel kind of rough, almost as if it was a little piece of sandpaper rubbing across the bottom of your arm. Now, I am touching the bottom of your right arm. Feel it, kind of rough and uncomfortable. Yuck! As you feel this, I want you to nod your head "Yes" for me again. **(Wait for response.)** *Good.*

Now get ready. I'm going to touch the top and then the bottom of your arm. You are going to feel a little bit of happiness, but you are also going to feel uncomfortable, kind of bad at the same time. Now, I am touching both the top and the bottom of your arm at the same time. What a really strange feeling.

This is kind of how we feel if we steal something. Part of us may feel a little happy. But, notice how the happy, good feeling fades away. No longer am I touching the top of your right arm and what you are left with is just that bad feeling. So we realize that stealing can't make up happy and can't give us pleasure. It just makes us uncomfortable. So, you will never steal again.

You are learning now about respect. Respect for other people and for their belongings. If it doesn't belong to you, you leave it alone. When you receive a gift or if you buy something, you feel great because you know that it belongs to you.

How would you feel if you had something that you really, really liked. One day, it is missing. You don't know where it is or what happened to it. You would feel very sad that you no longer have your prized possession. That's how other people feel when you take something that belongs to them. Now, you understand. You no longer steal. You are good.

FEARS

It doesn't matter whether or not we understand or share an individual's fear. One child may fear butterflies, while another is afraid of the dark. It's a good idea, however, to make sure the fear is an irrational one before beginning.

An individual came to our office some years ago wanting to be hypnotized for fear of heights. Before we began, I asked him, *"If you stood on a chair, would that cause you to be fearful?"* He replied that it would not. I asked him, *"If you were standing up on a ladder, would that cause you concern?"* Again, he said that it would not. *"Okay"*, I replied, *"How about if you were up on a balcony several stories up?"* The man replied that would not frighten him either. Finally, when I described dangling from a skyscraper, I finally got a positive response from him. Well, that is not an irrational fear. That's self-preservation and we don't want to remove that fear.

If the fear is affecting one's ability to function normally on a daily basis, then we can help overcome that fear in a couple of different ways. One way to overcome an irrational fear is to **change the way we feel about that which we fear**. To do this, use the following script, **FEAR #1**, to accomplish the goal.

Removing fears is much easier than you think. In most cases, one session will remove the fear. We have great success with this type of session because there is no reason for the fear. In the above case, the fear of heights is needed for our protection. Irrational fears serve no purpose.

The most common fears for children are: being left alone, animals, darkness, doctors, monsters, needles, storms and tests.

FEAR #1

In just a moment, I am going to come over and touch your right hand. As I touch your right hand, you are going to feel one of the happiest feelings of your life. It might have been a time when you won a contest or received a gift. It will be a very happy time for you. As I touch your right hand now, you are beginning to remember and create those happy feelings again. As you start to feel those happy feelings, I would like you to nod your head "Yes". **(Wait for response.)** *Good. Now, each time I touch your right hand, feel those happy feelings again. Each time I touch your right hand the happy feelings become stronger.*

*I am now going to touch your left hand. As I touch your left hand, I want you to remember the last time you had a fear of **storms**.* **(Or whatever their fear.)** *As I touch your left hand, I want you to bring back some of those fears of storms again. Think about **storms**. Feel some of the feelings about **storms** as I touch your left hand. You are beginning to feel those feelings, kind of scared, kind of frightened. As you begin to feel those feelings of being afraid of **thunderstorms**, I want you to nod your head "Yes".* **(Wait for response.)** *Each time I touch your left hand, feel the feelings getting stronger. Touching your hand again, that left hand; feelings become stronger. Now, I want you to think about a **thunderstorm** as I touch your left hand. I know that is kind of frightening, isn't it?* **(Wait for response.)**

*Now watch what happens. Imagine that instead of feeling that frightening way when I touch your left hand, it is now feeling this happy way, the way it feels when I touch your right hand. That's right. Feeling like it was back in that happy time. I want you to imagine a **storm**, but now you're beginning to feel this happy way. Isn't that a nice feeling? Nod your head "Yes" when you feel that happy feeling.* **(Wait for response.)** *It puts a smile on your face, doesn't it? Yes, that's right. Feel it growing stronger and stronger.*

(As you give the following suggestions, keep tapping the <u>right</u> hand.) *I want you to try to bring back those scared feelings. You can try harder than that. The* *harder you try, the farther back it goes. Go ahead and try. Think about thunder-storms and try to bring back those feelings. You can't do it, can you? Isn't that a nice feeling?* (**Wait for response.**) *Yes, it is. From now on, anytime you would even think about **thunderstorms**, you will feel this way, this happy, happy way.*

Another way to remove a fear is with a **visual regression** , such as we discussed earlier. With this regression, the child **does not re-live** the event that caused the fear. Instead, they view it as if it were happening to another person. They disso-ciate themselves from the event. We can establish when the child first experi-enced the fear without them having to go through that time again.

FEAR #2

*I am going to count from three down to one. As I count back, you are going to begin to see a movie. It is going to be a movie about the first time you started to be afraid of **dogs**.* (**Or whatever their fear.**) *You won't be afraid, but you will remember the first time that you had that fear.*

*__Three__, you are sitting very comfortably in your chair. __Two__, relaxing even more __One__, you are beginning to remember. There it is, like watching a movie, that first time you had a fear of **dogs**. As that movie becomes clearer, as you begin to remember that, I want you to nod your head "Yes".* (**Wait for response.**)

Now as I touch your right hand, I want you to tell me what is happening and how old you are? (**Wait for response.**) *Okay. You were **four** years old and **a dog bit you**. That was frightening, wasn't it?* (**Wait for response.**) *Yes. Of course it was. Now has **a dog ever bit you since**?* (**Wait for response.**) *No. So, it makes sense to be afraid of **dogs when they bite you**, but there is no need to be afraid of **dogs if they don't bite you**. I am going to count from three down to one again and this time, you are going to see a movie about a time in your life, not far away, when you are not afraid of **dogs**.*

*__Three__, feeling even more relaxed than before. __Two__, take in a nice, deep breath and let it out slowly. __One__, that's it, you are feeling very good. There it is, a movie of you and you are not afraid of **dogs** anymore. Isn't that a nice movie?* (**Wait for response.**) *Yes, and tell me, how old are you in this movie?* (**Wait for response.**) *Oh, you are at the age you are now. You are not afraid of **dogs** anymore, are you?* (**Wait for response.**) *So, it was okay to be afraid when you were **four** because you were a little kid. But now, being **nine**, you don't have to be afraid. When we finish today, you won't be afraid of **dogs** anymore because the movie you are seeing is becoming real.*

*So, I want you to think about yourself. You are out playing and there is a **friendly dog** around, but now you are not afraid, are you?* (**Wait for response.**) *No. I want you to think that you went to someone's house with your Mom and Dad and they had a **dog**. But, now you are not afraid, are you?* (**Wait for response.**) *You won't ever be afraid again, will you?* (**Wait for response.**) *No, I didn't think so.*

We are using the **hero technique** with this next session. We let the child pick his or her own hero as a part of the session. This is particularly effective with younger children because they feel comfortable with a familiar part of their life included, their hero.

If they don't have a hero, it could be a cartoon character, celebrity, athlete, teacher, friend or someone who makes them feel good or safe. Children have great imaginations, so it is very easy for them to think of someone for this type of session.

FEAR #3

Now, with your eyes closed, I want you to think about the bravest person in the whole world. It might be someone real. It might be someone imaginary. It might be a cartoon character, but think of someone that you think is the bravest person in the whole world and, as you begin to know who the bravest person in the whole world is, I want you to nod your head "Yes". **(Wait for response.)** *Good.*

Now I am going to touch your right hand, and as I touch your right hand, I want you to tell me who that person is. I am touching your right hand. Who is that person? Who is the bravest person in the whole world? **(Wait for response.)** ***Batman?*** **(Or whoever they say.)** *Oh,* ***Batman*** *is pretty brave.* ***Batman*** *is probably not afraid of anything, is* ***he?*** **(Wait for response.)** *No, and if you were* ***Batman's*** *friend, if he could be with you, you wouldn't be afraid either, would you?* **(Wait for response.)** *No.*

Let's pretend you could talk to ***Batman*** *and* ***he*** *is not only brave, but* ***he*** *is also smart. Ask* ***Batman*** *who protects people and who's a good* ***guy,*** *if* ***he*** *would be willing to be your friend and protect you. What did* ***he*** *say?* **(Wait for response.)** *He would?*

That's great. Because from now on, if you would ever start to become afraid, all you have to do is close your eyes for a second and you will be able to see ***Batman*** *just like you can now. Can you see* ***him?*** **(Wait for response.)** *Yes. And you will know that* ***he*** *is right there with you and* ***he*** *won't let anything happen to you.*

Now, I want you to think about something that used to cause you to fear. Close your eyes even tighter, and there is ***Batman*** *and you're not afraid anymore, are you?* **(Wait for response.)** *No, because* ***Batman*** *will always do the right thing. So* ***he*** *will protect you. And, as long as* ***Batman*** *is your friend, you won't ever be afraid again, will you?* **(Wait for response.)** *No, I didn't think so. That's good because you and* ***Batman*** *are friends forever. You are always safe and protected.*

HEALTH ISSUES

Health issues can be real or imaginary. We all want our children to be strong, healthy and happy. Sometimes children are very sick and need constant attention. Other times, they want constant attention, so they pretend to be sick. When we learn what our children need, we can give them all of the love and attention without going through the illnesses in order to get it.

It doesn't matter how many children you have, each one is unique. Some children need and love all of the hugs and kisses that you can give them. There are other children who are quiet or would rather be left alone. There is no right or wrong way for your child to respond. Whatever way they do, is right for them. Be aware of their needs so that they are fulfilled.

IMPROVE HEALTH

This next script can be altered to use with children who have cancer, chronic pain or a different illness. The idea is that they can use a **mental ray gun** to zap and get rid of the cancer cells, infection or whatever else is affecting their health.

With your eyes closed, I want you to pretend that you can see two funny-looking little armies. There is a red army, which is the bad one, and then the white army, which is the good one. The red army is the things that sometimes get in our body and make us not feel good. But now, the white army is coming to the rescue. Yeah!

I want you to think about the white army marching in there and looking for the red army. They are starting to get rid of them. One by one, there they go! The white army has ray guns and is shooting the red army until they are all gone. Zap! There goes one. It just disappears, and ZAP! He shoots another one. The white army that is inside of you is shooting up the red army and making them all disappear, until they're not there any more so you won't be sick.

The white army is going to work all day long, all night long, every day making sure none of those nasty red army come back to make you sick. Just zapping the red army with the ray guns is all the white army will do. They are just getting rid of that nasty red army so that you are healthy and strong. You feel so much better. The white army is here to protect you. You are getting stronger, healthier each and every day.

ILLNESS

This next session is designed for the child who misses a lot of school with **supposed illnesses**. This is not targeting the average child with the thought process of, *"I just want to stay at home today."* A child may be brought in because they are worrying about imagined sickness, rather than real illness.

SCHOOL ILLNESS

You told me earlier that there have been a lot of days lately where you felt too sick to go to school. I know sometimes we can honestly be ill, but then there are other times when maybe it's more the idea of going to school, if we are honest.

*Let's see just how honest you are. Has there ever been a time in the past that you stayed at home, kind of pretending to be sick? But, in reality, it was just that you didn't want to go to school? If this has been the case before, nod your head "Yes". Now, be honest. (***Wait for response.***) Good. Thanks for being honest.*

*Sometimes, we are not really sure if we are honestly sick. Or, is it that we didn't really want to go to school? Honestly, we don't know the answer. From now on, if you wake up in the morning and you simply don't feel good, you are going to ask yourself the following question, **"If instead of going to school today, we were going out to an amusement park or going on a picnic or doing something I really like to do, would I feel well enough to do that activity?"** If the answer is "Yes", you know you are well enough to go to school. If the answer is "No, I feel too bad to do anything, no matter how much fun it would be", then you know you are sick enough to stay home.*

This way you'll know for sure. "Am I really sick, or am I just sick of school? You will find that each time you test yourself and you go ahead and go to school, you are going to feel better. You may even surprise yourself and find that you have a great day in school.

Your mother is going to feel better. Your father is going to feel better. Even your teacher is going to feel better. They all feel better when you are healthy and happy. They worry about you when they think that you are sick. They want you to enjoy life as much as you can. You are not able to enjoy life when you are sick. You have even less fun when you <u>pretend</u> to be sick. You cheat yourself out of all of the fun things that you could be doing.

When you stay home and you are not really sick, then you have extra work to make up. So, without fail, you will know when you are truly sick and when, maybe, you just didn't want to go to school. It's going to be kind of fun to be honest with yourself. You are making a very big decision today. You are choosing to be healthy and happy. You want to grow up and be strong and successful. There are many things that you can do when you are healthy. You choose to have fun. You learn quickly and easily. You are healthy and strong. You may even surprise yourself and find that you enjoy school more now because you have a healthy attitude about learning. You like to learn. You like to be healthy and have fun. It is your choice.

PAIN CONTROL

We can remove pain through direct and indirect suggestions. In the first script, we show the child that they can **create numbness through realization, and then move the numbness** to the area in their body that is in pain. In the second script, we show them how to **switch off the painful sensation** whenever they need to. The effectiveness of these suggestions increases dramatically if the individual is currently experiencing pain. People who have chronic pain are very interested in pain control.

Whenever we work on pain control, we **must** have a doctor's written prescription saying that it is approved by the doctor to use hypnosis to decrease or remove pain from the specific part of the body that is afflicted. **No exceptions!** The reason that we do this is because we do not want to camouflage symptoms. Hypnosis works in conjunction with medical treatment, not instead of it.

Imagine that there are two friends. One person is a hypnotist. The other is not. The one person who is not a hypnotist went out partying with his friends all night. The next day, he has a terrible hangover. He calls his friend, the hypnotist, to ask for some help. He tells his friend that he has the worst headache in the world. He knows why he has the headache, because he was out drinking the night before.

If the hypnotist helped his friend to remove the headache, what would happen if the headache wasn't really from the hangover? What if the headache was a signal from the body to let the doctor know that this person has a brain tumor, or some other condition that would have a severe headache as a symptom? If the pain is gone, so is the symptom. The individual, as well as their doctor, would have no way of knowing that something was wrong.

We are very careful when working on this type of session. We want their doctor to be aware that the pain is decreased or removed so that they are not using pain as a barometer for the condition. When the doctor is aware of using hypnosis, it is taken into consideration when examining the patient.

We get many doctor referrals for stop smoking, weight loss, fears, memory, pre and post surgery and many other types of sessions as well as pain control, by having this regulation. Doctors trust us because they know that we are not trying to be something that we are not. We are not doctors. We are not counselors; we are hypnotists. We know our limitations and when we are in an area that is beyond our experience and training. We refer clients to doctors and therapists when a session falls into a category for which we are not equipped.

Hypnosis is very effective in helping people to control pain. We teach them different techniques that are easy to do. As with anything else, the more they do it, the more effective the techniques will be. Distracting the mind is a very effective way to eliminate pain.

Years ago, I happened onto an automobile accident. I went up to a car that had a woman trapped inside and saw that part of the steering wheel was protruding into her knee.

Now, I knew that in order to attain rapport, I would need to be truthful. So I said that that was one of the worst injuries I'd ever seen in my life. Even though that was a negative thing to say, don't you think that she was thinking that very thought? She knew that I understood what was happening to her. We were then on the same wavelength. This established some trust between us.

I then pointed to her other leg, which had a small cut. I remarked that she was injured there, too. Now I have her focused on the less injured leg. By doing this, her mind is getting more relaxed because the injury is very minor on this leg, nothing compared to her other leg.

I said that she had run her nylons, too, and that my wife seems to get a run in her nylons almost every week. By mentioning something so trivial, her mind is now thinking about everyday occurrences.

By the time she received medical attention, I was able to distract her conscious mind enough to help her to feel more comfortable until the medics arrived.

The mind can be distracted from pain spontaneously, as well. I'm sure you've heard of instances where a family is in a car accident and a parent is severely injured. However, they don't even notice or suffer from their own injuries until they've gotten their children to safety.

PAIN CONTROL #1

In just a moment, I'm going to come over and touch the top of your right hand. As I touch the top of your right hand, your right hand is going to become very, very numb. Numb means that you can't feel any pain. Kind of like magic. Get ready. I am touching the top of your right hand and you can kind of feel it tingling there. That's right. As soon as you start to feel that right hand becoming numb where you can't feel any pain, I want you to nod your head "Yes". (**Wait for response.**) *Good.*

Now, I'm going to lift up your right hand and, as I do, it just feels wonderful.

Doesn't that feel nice? (**Wait for response.**) *It sure does. Your hand is feeling very numb. Kind of like it fell asleep.* (**Now pinch hand and keep pinching so when child opens their eyes, they can see you pinching it.**) *Well, in a moment, I'm going to have you open your eyes but, even with your eyes open, you are going to stay in this wonderful sleep. When I ask you to close your eyes again, you will be able to go even deeper into this sleep. Will that be okay?* (**Wait for response.**) *Good.*

So now, I want you to stay in this sleep. I want you to open your eyes for just a moment, and look down at your right hand. Look how hard I have been pinching your hand, but it didn't hurt at all, did it? (**Wait for response.**) *No. Kind of like magic. Ok, now close your eyes and go even deeper.* (**Stop pinching hand.**)

We're going to do some more magic now. You did very good at making your right hand numb. Now, let's see if you can make it move! That's right. Let's have you move that numb feeling from your right hand over to your left hand. That's right. But, as you move that numb, numb feeling into your left hand, it's going to feel even more numb than it was when it was in your right hand. Can you feel the change starting now? (**Wait for response.**) *You are so good at this. Have you done this before?*

Here we go with the magic again. Now we are going to move that numb, numb, numb feeling that is in your left hand over to your right knee. Whew! That numb feeling is really getting around. Let the right knee feel that very numb, numb, numb feeling. This time, it is even more numb than it was when it was in the left hand! Wow! It is really numb! Can you feel it? Kind of like it fell asleep? (**Wait for response.**) *You are very good at this!*

Now, we're going to move it another time. This time we want to move this very, very, numb, numb, numb feeling over to (**Place where child has pain.**) *That feels so good there, doesn't it?* (**Wait for response.**)

Now, let that wonderful, numb feeling help your body to relax and feel comfortable. You have such a powerful mind. Your mind and body are now working together to help you to feel comfortable. That wonderful, numb feeling feels so good. Now, just allow yourself to relax.

Sometimes we don't want to totally remove the pain, but rather turn it down. We can reduce the pain to a manageable level with the **visualization of a switch** that can lessen the pain as it is pulled down, like a dimmer switch.

We can learn a lot from children. I had a child that I was helping with the side effects from chemotherapy and she'd lost her hair. I was feeling emotional about her situation. She picked up on it and said, *"Don, you're worried about my hair."* Now I tried to deny it, but she went on to say, *"Look at it this way. I don't have to get up as early in the morning as my sister because I don't have to wash and comb my hair."* When you hear people worrying about possessions like boats and cars, children like this can sure bring you down to earth.

This technique is great for taking children to the doctor to get shots or other procedures that may be painful. My assistant uses this for her chronic pain. It works wonder!

PAIN CONTROL #2

You and I are going to do something really magical. It might even surprise you. Now, I want you to pretend that there was a magical switch on the wall. If we flipped this switch, what happens? (**Wait for response.**) *It doesn't turn on a light; it doesn't turn off a light. What it does turn off is all the feeling in your right hand, so that you can't feel any pain. You can't feel anything in your hand. It kind of feels like it fell asleep.*

So now, reach up with your left hand. Reach high up into the air. There you go! Start to flip that switch, pull it down, pull it down, pull it down until it's all the way off and you have turned off any pain in your hand. Once you have flipped the switch all the way down and all the pain is gone, I want you to nod your head "Yes". You can't feel anything in your right hand. It feels like it fell asleep. You know how that feels. That's good. That's good.

Now, I'm going to lift up your right hand. It just feels good and you can hardly feel that hand, can you? (**Wait for response.**) *No. Now, I'm going to lift up your right hand and, as I do, it just feels wonderful. Doesn't that feel nice?* (**Wait for response.**) *It sure does. Your hand is feeling very numb. Kind of like it fell asleep.* (**Now pinch hand and keep pinching so when child opens their eyes, they can see you pinching it.**) *Well, in a moment, I'm going to have you open your eyes but, even with your eyes open, you are going to stay in this wonderful sleep. When I ask you to close your eyes again, you will be able to go even deeper into this sleep. Will that be okay?* (**Wait for response.**) *Good.*

You're going to stay in this special sleep, even with your eyes open. I want you to go ahead and open your eyes for a moment. Look at your hand. Look how hard I have been pinching it, but you can't feel anything, can you? Why can't you feel anything in that hand? (**Wait for response.**) *That's right, because you flipped that switch. Good.*

Now I want you to close your eyes again. That's good. (**Stop pinching hand.**) *I'm going to put your hand back down on the arm of the chair and I want you to turn the switch back on so you can feel things in your hand. That's it. Turn it back on so all the feelings are back. Once you have flipped the switch back on, I want you to nod your head "Yes" for me.* (**Wait for response.**) *Good.*

Now, the next time you go to the doctor and he is going to give you a shot, what you are going to do is tell him to wait a minute. Just close your eyes and you will see that switch. You will flip it down and what you are going to do is turn off the pain. All feeling for a shot is gone. It won't bother you at all. Then when he is done, you will turn the switch back on and open your eyes. You can do that, can't you? (**Wait for response.**) *I know you can. You can do anything you put your mind to doing.*

STRESS

The next session uses a technique that relies on key words. The key words in the session on stress are ***"Relax now"*** The child learns that they can use the key words at any time to bring back some of those wonderful, relaxed feelings they had while hypnotized.

This is very easy for the child to do because they can just think about the key words in order for them to work. No one else needs to know what they are doing. It is their own little secret!

RELAX NOW

I want you to realize that you have the ability to feel either relaxed or to feel really tense. To demonstrate this, I am going to come over and touch your right arm. As I touch your right arm, let every muscle, every part of your arm relax. Now your arm feels loose and limp. Feel it now. Loose, limp, relaxed and at ease, like an old rag doll. I'm lifting it up. When I let go of it, it just flops right back down to the arm of the chair. **(Lift up right arm and then let go of it.)** *Now that is what we call being relaxed.*

I am going to come over and touch your left arm. As I touch your left arm, I am extending it straight out in front of you. As I touch your left arm, feel the muscles becoming tighter and tighter. They are feeling very stiff. In fact, the left hand and arm are feeling so rigid that they are beginning to feel as though the left hand and arm are as stiff as a steel beam. Stiff and rigid as a steel beam, so stiff, so rigid that it won't bend any more. I want you to go ahead and try. The more you try, the tighter, stiffer it becomes. Attempt to bend it. It just will not bend. Your arm is stiff and rigid as a steel beam. Now, that is total stress. Tightness.

There is only one person in the world that can make you relax. That person is you. That's right. You have the ability to relax. I am going to give you the key words that will allow you to relax whenever you want, wherever you might be.

I want you now to say the words to yourself, **"Relax now"**. *As you say the words* **"Relax now"** *to yourself, notice that the tension, the tightness in that left arm just disappears and you can bend the arm. It flops back down to the arm of the chair. Say the words* **"Relax now"** *to yourself. Anytime you say the words* **"Relax now"**, *you will be relaxed. These will be your secret words that will work forever.*

PHYSICAL ACTIVITY

Physical activity involves the way we move, get around, sports, well, you get the idea.

By giving positive suggestions, we can assist our children to be the very best that they can be.

COORDINATION

Did you know that there is not a single person anywhere in the world that has not tripped, stumbled, fallen or knocked something over at one time or another in their life? It's part of being human. It's part of growing up. Sometimes, when we go through a stage of being a little clumsy or awkward, we tend to pay more attention to the times we knock something over, bump into something or trip.

But, let's be honest. Most of the time we don't have a problem. That's right. Most days you don't trip, you don't fall. From this moment on, you are going to be thinking more about the days, the hours that go by very easily, perfectly well.

You will be thinking less and less and less about the times when you felt kind of clumsy or awkward in the past.

As you begin to think only about the days that are good, that you are coordinated and in control, you begin to act more coordinated and in control. What you think about is what you get. You always focus on what you want. You are coordinated. You move perfectly, easily.

This is a building process that you find very enjoyable for you. Each day you feel more confident and better about yourself. Every step every movement you make is exactly that you wanted it to be.

Your family, your friends and your teachers are all amazed at the improvement. They are happy for you. You are happy for yourself. You are coordinated. You move the way you want to move. You feel more confident and better about yourself. You are the best!

HYPERACTIVITY

We found that giving the child a magic word or words to use can help them to have more control over their own responses. This helps children to focus on slowing themselves down. This is particularly true of children with ADHD.

Another thing to keep in mind is that when we feel all rushed and excited, our children pick up on this energy. If you want your child to calm down, start with yourself. Make sure that you allow time for yourself each day. Even if you start with just five minutes, find time just for you. When you learn how to relax, you will be a good role model for your children. They will learn from you how to relax. So, **relax**!

HYPERACTIVITY

You know that your mom and dad and your teacher say that you're just too active. You are always on the go, moving a mile a minute. But today, here with me, you're sitting there nice and quiet. Everything is kind of slow.

Through the use of magic, I'm going to give you secret, magic words that if you start getting too excited, start getting too wound-up, you will be able to say these magic words to yourself and you will just become calm and slow down. These magic words will work for you from now on for the rest of your whole life.

*The magic words are going to be **"Slow Down"**. Now, you will say it just that way, real slow, **"Slow Down"**, and you won't be so hyper. You won't be so active, and you will just kind of do what the magic words say. You will **"Slow Down"**.*

*Now, you won't have to say the words out loud because we don't want anyone else to know what the secret words are. But, you will be able to say them to yourself. Let's try it out loud one time. (**Wait for response**.) That was great. **"Slow Down"**. You can feel yourself slowing down and feeling relaxed, can't you? (**Wait for response**.) Good.*

*Now let's try it the secret way where nobody knows. I want you to say the magic words to yourself, not out loud this time. (**Give child a moment to do this**.) Good. You can feel it working, can't you? (**Wait for response**.)*

We won't tell anyone else what the magic words are, but if you find you are kind of getting all hyped and worked-up, all you need to do is say the magic words to yourself **"Slow Down"** *and you will feel nice and relaxed. The fun part is, the teachers won't know the magic words, or your mom or dad. It will be our secret.*

PACE

This is the opposite of hyperactivity. Some children by nature move very slowly. There are times when we want a child to move quickly and times when we want them to move slowly. We need to help our children to find a balance. We can assist our children in learning that they can control their movements and then put that control to good use when it is appropriate.

MOVE QUICKER

There are three different speeds that we all have. One of the speeds is slow. The second is medium. The third is fast. There are times when we need to move at a slow speed. There are times when we need to move at a medium speed. Then there are times when we need to move at a fast speed.

We are going to take a little test today. I am going to ask you some questions. You will answer with one of the following answers: ***Slow, medium or fast****. Okay?* **(Wait for Response.)**

(After asking each question, wait for child to answer.)
If a monster were chasing you, how would you move?
If you were in church, how would you move?
If you were getting dressed in the morning, how would you move?
If you were walking toward the school bus, how would you move?
If you were playing a sport (your favorite game), how would you move?
If you were in a race, how would you move?
If you were going to the dinner table, how would you move?
If you were helping your parents with chores around the house, how would you move?

You are very smart. You know all kinds of different ways to move. You know that sometimes it is best to move slowly. Other times, we need to move at a medium speed. Then there are times when we need to move fast. You now know how to move for each thing that you do. You can keep up with everyone. You learn very quickly.

SPORTS ENHANCEMENT

One way to improve sports performance is have the child begin to feel, hear, experience and even know the sport the same way someone they admire does it. You can ask the child for the name of an athlete they look up to before the session, if you want. It can be a professional athlete, someone on his or her team or another player on a different team. If they don't know of anyone, they can make up a person in their mind who would play the sport perfectly, just the way that they want to play the sport.

SPORTS ENHANCEMENT #1

*You have decided that you want to be a better **ballplayer**. I want you to think about one of the best **ballplayers** that you know. I want you to pick a **ballplayer**, professional or maybe just someone on your own team or maybe on another team that you play against. But, I want you to select a **ballplayer** that you want to be like. Once you have selected that particular **ballplayer**, I want you to nod your head "Yes" for me.* (**Wait for Response.**)

*You are going to begin to play the same way that **selected ballplayer** plays. You are now beginning to see things in exactly the same way that **special ballplayer** sees things. You are starting to hear things in a new way. You are starting to hear the same way that **special ballplayer** hears. You are beginning to feel the way that **special ballplayer** feels–**Confident**! Most of all, you are now beginning to know what that **special ballplayer** already knows. You are becoming just as good as that person. You are becoming a great, great **ballplayer**.*

The following is a **visualization** for sports. This would be a script you would want to use with a child that is very visual. We talked in an earlier chapter about determining in which mode a child operates most frequently. When communicating with anyone, especially our children, it helps to get the message across when we speak with them in their learning mode.

SPORTS ENHANCEMENT #2

*You have said that you want to be a better **baseball player**. This means that you can. This means that you are able to do it. I want you to spend a moment. I want you to create a kind of dream. That's right. A dream of yourself, playing **baseball**. But, in this dream, everything is going to be perfect.*

I would like you to start the dream off with you at bat. You are looking through your own eyes, as if it is really happening. See the bat in your hands. You are looking over the plate. You are getting ready for the pitch. As the pitcher throws the ball, you know exactly what you should do. You hit the ball perfectly. Right on the sweet spot. It's probably one of the best hits of the entire game, maybe the whole season.

You are really, really excited. You run the bases in the fastest time you've ever run. You hit in some other runs, too. Oh, my gosh! You hit a grand slam!! The bases were loaded and you hit a home run! Your team is so excited! Everyone is cheering for you. The fans are on their feet. The crowd is cheering your name!

That is only part of your dream. Now I want you to imagine that you are out on the field. The other team hits the ball. You are making one of the most dynamic catches anyone has ever seen. You are looking through your own eyes as if it is happening right now. I want you to imagine in this dream, no matter what position you are playing, that you are throwing the ball faster and farther than you ever have thrown it before. Your ability to throw is outstanding. The other team didn't think anyone could get them out on this play, but you did. You did it again! You are a fantastic player, both offensively and defensively. Wow! You improve every time you play the game. You are great!

Now I want you to imagine that you are playing the game. You are very alert to the other players. Your instincts are right on target. You may even surprise your-self at how easy it is for you to hit, catch and run. You do everything so perfectly, so easily. It feels second nature to you.

So, go ahead and repeat the whole dream now. Your hitting is perfect. Your ability to throw is outstanding. Your catching ability is wonderful. Your speed around the bases is the best there is. Keep dreaming this new dream.

Whenever you do think about this, you always imagine that you are looking through your own eyes, as if it is happening right now. Every night before you get ready to go to sleep, spend a few moments and have this dream again of you playing better and better.

Before each practice or each game, imagine that you are looking through your own eyes and see everything happening the way you want it to be. The more you do this, the better you get.

Each day your skills are getting better and better. You feel so proud of yourself because you can feel the improvement. You are the very best that you can be.

You are happy to realize that you are now in the process of turning this dream into reality. You are making it become real. You are a great ballplayer.

You can also bring about positive changes by creating positive expectations. With all of these sports enhancement sessions, it helps for you to show your excitement in the tone of your voice and in your delivery. When you do this type of session, it helps if you can imagine that the child is actually doing what you are saying at the same time. This makes it more real for you, as well as the child. When you get excited, the child feels it, too. They begin to believe that you have faith in their ability to achieve this goal. If you believe they can do it, they feel confident that they can do it, too.

SPORTS ENHANCEMENT #3

For any person that has ever played sports, whether they are professional or amateur, there seems to be days when we just know we are going to win. But, then in the past, there seems to have been days when we felt we were going to lose for sure.

It is amazing how on the days when we woke up and really felt like we were going to win, we had the ability to do just that. We did win. However, on those days when we woke up and felt like we would probably lose, we usually did.

From this moment on, before you start to play, you have a winning feeling. You are feeling confident that you are going to win and be the best that you can ever, ever be. If a thought or an idea of losing would come into your mind, you are able to shut it out. You turn it off and think the way a winner thinks. You focus on what you are doing. You focus on winning.

As you practice thinking like a winner, you are becoming a winner. With every day that passes, your abilities, your talents, your motivation is becoming greater and greater. You are becoming the best that you can ever, ever be. You are going to almost forget what it was like to ever lose because you are only thinking in a positive way about winning. You reach your goals! You exceed your goals! There is no stopping you now!

Other teammates and your parents begin to notice a difference. They begin to see you in a whole new way. This winning attitude that you have begins to flow over in all parts of your life. You have a winning attitude not only about sports, but also about your family, friends and school. You are a winner in everything that you do.

RELATIONSHIPS

As children grow up, there relationships change; not only with their parents, siblings and friends, but also with themselves. They begin to feel differently. Their tastes change. The things that they are interested in change. Remember, their brains are not fully developed, so there are all types of changes going on in their lives physically, mentally and emotionally.

DEALING WITH AUTHORITY FIGURES

Parents tell us what to do. Teachers give us homework. It seems that everywhere we go, everything that we want to do, there is someone who is telling us how to do it or that we can't do it at all. If you have a part-time job after school, you have a boss giving you orders. It can feel overwhelming at times.

When you think about it, though, there must be a reason why they are in a position of authority. It may be because they have lived longer than we have and have had many experiences. They, hopefully, have learned from their own mistakes in their past. Who knows; they may be doing us a favor so that we don't repeat something that they did that did not turn out so well. Maybe they are just trying to spare us from going through the same thing.

Allow yourself to keep an open mind when dealing with people in authority. Perhaps, they are right. You may be able to learn from their mistakes or their experiences. After all, they are older than you are. Maybe there is something to this.

You want your own freedom and independence at this time in your life. You may feel like you can't make one move without someone breathing down your neck. When you prove to others that you are capable of making good decisions, they won't have to watch you as they are now.

It may not seem cool, but there are reasons why there are rules. We may not understand some of them, but it may be the best way to prove to others that you are becoming a responsible adult. When you act like an adult, you are treated like one. If you rebel, smart off or disobey the rules, more discipline may be used.

Keep an open mind. Allow yourself to be in control of the way you respond. You are intelligent and you learn quickly. It is better to learn from someone else's mistakes. There is no need for you to repeat the errors that have been made in the past. You are polite and respectful when communicating with your elders and authority figures. You are polite and respectful even with strangers. The better you treat people, the better they treat you.

DEALING WITH A BREAK-UP WITH A TEEN

You are a wonderful, loving person. There are so many things about you that anyone would like. It is important for you to love yourself. Be aware of all of the things about you that are appealing. Once you learn to appreciate yourself and all of your qualities, you realize that you are lovable and capable of having a lasting relationship. Anyone would be lucky to have you in their lives.

When we think about a relationship ending, we think that we will always feel this way. We can't imagine not having them in our life. But, everything changes. This is one thing you can count on.

When you think about this person, you probably imagine all of their wonderful qualities that made you like them. You may focus on the fun times that you had together. This is very normal for you to do. However, keep this down to a minimum. Only allow yourself to think about the good times for about **one minute.** *Then focus on their negative qualities.*

You may be thinking to yourself, "Oh, they didn't have any negative qualities. They were perfect." You know deep down this is not true. Everyone has positive and negatives qualities. It's now time for you to focus on the things that you did not like about this person or the relationship.

Were they controlling? Did they tell you what to do or when to do it? Did they complain a lot? Were they selfish or demanding? Did they put you down or embarrass you? Did they ignore your feelings? Think very carefully about all of these issues. When you look closer into the way things really were, you may find that this person wasn't as wonderful as you once thought.

Each day you are feeling better about yourself. You focus on your own strengths and abilities. You are realizing how you are changing. You take good care of yourself. Allow yourself the time that you need to grieve this relationship. Release it. Let it go. Open your mind and heart to a new, exciting, lasting relationship. You deserve the best. If you focus on the past, you may miss the fantastic person who would be coming into your life. Release the past and get ready for a wonderful future.

HANDLING THE BULLY

NOTE: Before going into hypnosis, do the *"Visualization Exercise"* that is in the *"Therapeutic Techniques"* section of this book. The first image that you are working with is the negative feeling. Have child see that the bully is picking on them and the child feels like they normally would respond. The next image is to have child imagine themselves standing up to the bully with the bully backing down and leaving them alone.

When you realize that the bully is really someone who feels insecure, it makes it easier to deal with them. They may pick on you because you are a nice person and they think that you won't fight back. They may think that you won't say anything or do anything, so they can get away with treating you bad. They are in for a surprise!

You are now learning to stand up for yourself. A bully only picks on you because they think that they can. You are now feeling more confident and better about yourself. You are now able to look your bully in the eyes and let them know that this is not acceptable. You are not someone they can push around.

You are strong, confident and very capable of taking care of yourself. You respect yourself and you respect others. You don't lower yourself to fighting for no reason. That's a waste of time and energy. You are smarter than that.

Once you stand up for yourself, the bully realizes that you are not someone they want to mess with. You may surprise yourself and find that the bully may come to respect you. You may even become friends. It's amazing how people change when the situation changes.

Let others know that you don't have to fight to be strong. You don't need to beat someone up to feel good about yourself. You are not someone who likes to fight. It doesn't prove anything. Bullies fight because they don't know how to communicate. They intimidate people so that others won't see that they are scared and have no social skills.

You are confident. You are capable of taking care of yourself. You stand up for your rights. You are peaceful and effective. You fit in very well with others because you are a good person. You are a winner!

HANDLING DIVORCE

When parents decide to divorce, children often believe that they are the reason the parents are splitting up. Sometimes the parents actually give the child this message without realizing it.

HANDLING DIVORCE

Your mom and dad have decided to get a divorce. That does not mean that they don't love you or that they don't want to be with you. In fact, they both love you very much and want to be with you as much as they possible.

There may have been a time in your life when you had a friend and, as time went by, the two of you weren't close friends. As time went by, the two of you didn't get along. Maybe you didn't like the same things anymore. And, one day, you just decided that you weren't going to play together anymore. It doesn't have to be anyone's fault. People change.

*This is what happens with grown-ups. They start out being friends, then close friends. As time goes by, sometimes they find that they have different interests. It didn't have anything to do with the kids. It was the two of them. If I had a friend and we decided that we weren't going to be together anymore, if surely wouldn't be **your** fault.*

Sometimes people just grow apart. It's not anyone's fault. It happens sometimes. Your mom and your dad each love you in their own way. Your mom still loves you. Your dad still loves you. The same way that you still love your mom and dad, the two of them still love you. Most of all, they are not leaving you. They are not leaving each other because of you.

The three of you will always have a very special relationship. This will go on forever. The love that your mom and dad have for you will last forever.

FITTING IN

It can be very lonely at times, even when there are other people all around you.

Sometimes you may not feel that you quite fit in. This may happen when you are in school, or when you go to school functions. It can happen at different times. Just know that this is very normal. Most people go through this at one time or another.

You are now feeling more comfortable with other people. One reason may be because you stop thinking about yourself. Find out what others like to do. Focus on them. Ask people about things that they are interested in. You may find that they may be interesting to you as well.

Fitting in is just a matter of feeling comfortable. When you feel comfortable with yourself, you are comfortable with others. You are becoming more confident in yourself. You are aware of many qualities and talents that you possess that you feel good about. You focus on the things that are positive about you.

Find one person that you feel comfortable with. Create a friendship with this person. Then, find another person to add to your friendship list. You may find that it is easier to make friends than you ever thought possible. Before you know it, you fit in perfectly!

Everything starts with one thing at a time. Feel good about yourself and who you are. When you appreciate yourself, others will, too. Once you let others get to know you, you get to know yourself better.

You are a wonderful person. You have skills and abilities that you have yet to discover. You are smart, kind, thoughtful and fun to be with. When you think of yourself in this way, you believe it. When you believe it, you live it.

You enjoy life to the fullest. You make friends with people who enjoy the same things that you do. You have so much fun. Life gets better each and every day.

EMBARRASSED BY PARENTS

As we grow up, our feelings have a way of changing. When you were much younger, you may have played with the other children without even thinking about if your mom or dad were nearby. If they were, you may have felt secure and happy just knowing that they were there.

Now, you are a teenager. There is a certain amount of freedom that you crave. You want to do things on your own. You want to be with your friends without your parents tagging along. Times have certainly changed.

And, everything continues to change as you grow into an adult. Think about, imagine how you were five years ago. It was different than the way you are today. Having your parents around probably didn't even enter your mind. You played, had fun whether or not they were present. Now, go back ten years. It was much different then. You relied on at least one of your parents being with you. As a matter of fact, you probably felt uncomfortable if there weren't around.

We grow in stages. First, we depend on our parents being present; second, we don't focus on them being around; third, we don't want them around; fourth, we don't focus on them being around; fifth, we enjoy spending time with them. It comes full circle. You are now in the middle stage where you want your independence.

Think about how things will be for you in five more years. It probably won't matter much either way if your parents are around. Once you become an adult, however, you may find that you enjoy spending time with your parents. I know this is hard to believe, but then you will have more in common. You will all be adults. You focus on adult issues. You may be interested in the same things. But, now, you don't seem to have very much, if anything, in common. There's no reason to hang with them when you can be with your friends.

Now let's take a look at this situation from your parents' point of view. Imagine, just think about having a baby. You love your baby. You want to do everything that you can to protect and nurture your child. As the little one starts to crawl and then walk, you watch over them so that no harm comes their way. As they grow a little older, you are still concerned, but you can see that they are playing well with the other children so everything is fine. When your child becomes a teenager, they want nothing to do with you. Can you imagine how difficult that must be for the parents? The people who love you the most in the whole world; the people who watched over you and nurtured you so that you would be safe and healthy are now no longer needed. It happens so quickly, but the loss is so great.

It can be hard for some parents to let their children grow up. It's hard to let go. It feels sad not to be needed or wanted. It is a very big adjustment.

In five more years, you won't be giving much thought to having your parents around. You will be busy starting your career or your own family. You may be traveling or doing things that you've always dreamed about. But, ten years from now, you may find that your parents are fun and interesting. They may have some valuable insights or information that you find useful. You may even discover that you like having them around.

So, for the time being, keep in mind that where you are right now is not going to last forever. There will come a time when you look forward to seeing them. In the meantime, treat them with respect and they will treat you with respect. There is a saying that whatever it is that you want, you must give that away. In other words, if you want people to respect your privacy, you must respect their privacy. If you want someone to treat you as an adult, you must act like an adult. So the more respect you give to your parents at this time, the more they give you.

Act responsibly – like an adult. If there are curfews, honor those times. If there are rules to follow, obey them. I know this doesn't sound cool, but as you become an adult, you will find many rules and responsibilities that come with it.

Your parents love you unconditionally. They are always on your side. It may not feel like it at times when you want to do something and they're holding you back but, trust me, ten years from now you'll look back and realize that when parents discipline you and watch what you're doing, that's their way of showing that they love you.

DEVELOPING SOCIAL SKILLS

When you feel comfortable with yourself, you feel comfortable with others. It's always best to be yourself. Let people get to know the wonderful person you are.

The best way to develop your social skills is to be aware of your manners. No matter how things change in our world, "Please" and "Thank you" are words that people always like to hear. That shows that you respect others and appreciate their efforts. Everyone wants to be appreciated. It's the little gestures and thoughtful mannerisms that people notice the most.

Be thoughtful of others' needs. When you focus on someone else's feelings, you put them first. People like to be important. When you give this attention to others, they feel good about you.

Social skills are really just good manners; putting others before yourself and appreciating what others have done for you.

You have wonderful social skills. You feel comfortable in every situation. You are very versatile because it doesn't matter how young or old the people in the gathering are, you have something to share with everyone. You communicate easily.

You are very thoughtful of others. You have wonderful manners. You may find that you enjoy yourself more by being this way. Being positive agrees with you.

You learn very quickly so if there is something that you need to do in order to fit it more easily, you are able to do it. You are very aware of others' feelings. You seem to know just what to say at the appropriate time.

You are well mannered. You are proud of yourself and the way that you act. Your family is proud of you, too. You do what's right. You feel good about yourself.

Your social skills get better all of the time. You feel more comfortable. You know how to act and what to say. You are confident and secure.

SCHOOL WORK

Typically, parents tend to tell children what they do not want them to do. They say, *"I never want to see an 'F' on your report card"*. They create a very strong image of those "F's". Why not say, *"I really want to see 'A's' and 'B's' on your next report card"*. We're constantly implanting the suggestion of what we don't want to have happen, and then we're shocked when it does!

I have numerous children that come to me with bad grades. They've done their homework, the parents' have seen it, but they won't turn it in to the teacher. Why? Because the parent has told them they should be straight *"A"* students, nothing less is acceptable. The child feels that a particular assignment is not good enough to get an *"A"*, so they leave it in their locker. This is not a conscious decision. Internally, they have already failed by not living up to the parents' command. The child needs to feel that the goal is achievable. We give the child that's failing a goal that is achievable, sometimes as low as *"C's"* with room to bypass that goal.

CONCENTRATION

You are now using the power of your mind to help you to concentrate. Sometimes we have trouble concentrating because we are trying to do too many things at one time. There are some people who like to listen to TV or music when they are studying or doing their homework. Some people can do this, but for others it is too distracting.

Take one thing at a time. If you need to, make a list of all of the things that you want to do. Decide which one you will do first. Give all of your attention to that one task. Everything else is written on that paper, so you can put it out of your mind for the time being.

Now focus on the one thing that you have picked. Give it your full attention. Do whatever needs to be done in order to complete it. Then, go to the list, scratch off this item and go on to the next. By doing this, you get things done much faster. You eliminate distractions.

If you are having difficulty concentrating in class, you may want to ask if you can sit up front. If not, be aware of the teacher in front of the room. Focus on the teacher's mouth as they speak. If you cannot see their mouth, realize that your ears are like radar and can hear all of the important words and sounds that you need.

You find that it is now easy for you to concentrate when you are reading. You understand and remember everything. You may surprise yourself and find that learning is becoming more interesting.

You concentrate more easily now than ever before. It doesn't matter if it is schoolwork, or concentrating on what someone else is saying. Everything that you do is getting easier for you because now you concentrate very easily.

Whenever you need to be aware of what is going on, just think about the word, **"Concentrate"**. Say it to yourself several times. Each time that you think about this word, it is easier for you to do. You concentrate very easily. You learn quickly. You understand and remember everything that you need to know. You have a great mind.

IMPROVE GRADES

You told me earlier that most of your grades tend to be about "D's". There are some "F's" in there, too. I wonder if you really try, if you are capable of doing better. Now, when we are in this room together, you have to tell me the truth. If you really tried, could you do better? **(Wait for response.)** I thought so.

From now on, you are going to find that most of your grades are going to rise up to "C's" and "B's". Now and then, if you make a mistake and get an "A", that will be okay, too. But, you are going to find that your grades are going to start to get better.

You already know what to do to have the poor grades, so let's see if we can't learn from that. In order to get "D's" and "F's" what did you do? Or maybe, what didn't you do? Let's make a list together.

Didn't do homework.
Didn't study for tests.
Didn't listen in class.
Didn't try as hard as you could.

So, it really is pretty simple. Let's change those four things you didn't do to things that you are going to do. **Number one** is going to be, doing homework. **Number two** is going to be, study for tests. **Number three** is going to be, listen to the teacher. **Number four** is going to be, try as hard as you possibly can.

I am the first person in the world to admit that it is going to take work to get those grades up to a good level. Let's see what type of good things will happen once the grades start to get better. As I say something, if you agree with me that it will happen, I want you to nod your head "Yes". If you think that it won't happen, then shake your head "No".

Okay. Here we go. By getting your grades to a good level, you will be happy? (**Wait for response.**) *By getting your grades to a good level, will your parents be happy?* (**Wait for response.**) *By getting the grades to a good level, will your teacher be happy?* (**Wait for response.**)

So far, you have been nodding your head "Yes". That means you agree. Let's try some more. By getting the grades to a good level, it will rain every day? (**Wait for response.**) *No, you're right again.*

So now we see that by working hard and getting your grades to a good level, only good things will happen. Nothing bad will happen by having good grades.

HOMEWORK

Homework can be a drag at times, especially when you have a lot of it. But, if you do it every day, it gets done. Then, you are free to do the things that you want to do.

When you schedule your day to fit everything in that needs to be done, it's easier to keep up. You may find that if you do your homework as soon as you get out of school, you get done sooner. There will be some nights that you have more homework and it may take longer to get things done. But, if you wait until the last minute, there will never be enough time to catch up.

You are now getting all of your homework done in a timely manner. You focus on what needs to be done and you schedule time in your day to do it.

Everybody is different. Some people like to start with the homework that goes quickly; you know, those assignments that don't take much time to complete. Then they have the majority of their homework done. They can put all of their attention on the longer assignments knowing that they're near the end.

Then there are people who like to do the longer assignments first. Those are the ones that are harder to do or have more time involved in completing them. Once that have that done, it's down hill with all of the easy assignments that follow.

Which way would be better for you? You may find another way to do your homework. Either way, you are now getting your homework done easily. You learn and understand everything that you are studying. You are so proud of yourself that everything is turned in on time. You are giving it your all.

When the time comes for tests or pop quizzes, you are prepared to pass with ease. From doing the homework, you know the answers easily. You feel so good that you are in control. You do your homework and pass your tests easily. This may very well be your best year in school. You get better each day that passes.

MEMORY

Today we are going to play a game. It is called "The Memory Game". My name is **Don***. I'm sure you can remember that. It's a very easy name. I spell it* **"D – O – N"***.* **Don***. There may be other people in your life you know that have the same* *name as me. I know someone who has the same name as me. Can you guess who that is?* (**Wait for response.**) *His name is **Donald Duck**! He is a lot of fun. Do you remember what my name is?* (**Wait for response.**) *That's right. My name is **Don**.*

You are a very smart person. I bet you already know the secret that I'm going to tell you about remembering things. Can you guess what it is? (**Wait for response.**) *If there is something that you really want to remember, just say it to yourself over and over again. That's right. By repeating the information, you remember it more easily.*

In school, sometimes the teachers show us how to do this when we learn math. "Two times two equals four." That's what they will say. They give us all kinds of neat things to remember. If you say that over to yourself several times, you remember it more easily.

Another way to remember is to pay attention when someone is talking to you. If your teacher is saying something, you pay really close attention so that you hear and understand everything. You may just surprise yourself how easily you are remembering now. You focus on your teacher's mouth as they speak. If you cannot see their mouth, your ears are like radar picking up everything that you need to know.

READING

When parents bring a child in who hates reading, we try to make it a fun thing. We may have the child when they're out riding in the car to see how many signs they can read. We make it a game. For each sign that they can read, they get a point. If there is more than one child in the car, you may want to take turns, otherwise, they will all be yelling at the same time. Everyone will want to get a point for the same signs!

When you see the *"Golden Arches"*, are they able to read the sign that says *"McDonald's"*? Have them spell the word first, then say what the sign says. Signs like *"speed limit"* or *"yield"* seems less like a challenge than a schoolbook. This can get a child reading on a regular basis. They feel more confident because they are proving to themselves, and you, just how much they do know. Always praise them for a job well done, or for the effort they made in attempting it.

IMPROVE READING

Today some wonderful, magical things are going to start happening. You are going to find that you are going to be reading every day. Now don't get worried. This is going to be fun.

In fact, to be honest, you already are reading every day, but sometimes we don't think of it as reading. When you are out with your mom or dad in the car, and you pass McDonald's, without even knowing it, you are reading the sign. When you drive down the road, there may be a Burger King. You are reading that sign. If you are going to the mall and you may see a sign that says "Sears".

Everywhere you go there is something you can read. Each time you read, you are going to want to read more. This is going to be a building process. You'll start by reading things on signs and labels. As you begin to read a word or two, here and there, you will realize that this is fun. You will then want to read more.

You will be looking for places that have more than just one or two words. You will realize that the place to find a lot of words is in a book. You enjoy being able to look at those letters and, magically, turn them into words. You will have a great time turning those words into sentences. You'll have fun understanding that the words in the sentences are telling you something.

You'll start looking at reading as being on a secret mission. At first, look at the letters and then make them into words. Make the words into sentences and finally, you will understand what the message is.

The more you read, the more you enjoy reading. The more you enjoy reading, the more you'll read. You are a very fast learner. You read very well. You understand what you are reading. You even remember what you read. You are so proud of yourself. You may even surprise yourself how fun it is to read. You can read a story to your parents. That's fun!

Every day you are going to want to read just a little bit more, just a little bit longer. Reading books, papers and magazines can be fun. You have the right to have fun. There are so many interesting people, places and things to read about. Each one is a new adventure.

TEST ANXIETY

Test anxiety is so common, we use the following script that utilizes the post-hypnotic suggestion, **"red"**. This is a powerful post-hypnotic suggestion that can be used with adults, as well as children. This is a technique that can be used with any type of session. Create a positive feeling that the child needs or wants and give the suggestion that whenever they see the color **"red"**, they feel that same, wonderful way.

TAKING TESTS

There are many people in the world that could study for a test, be prepared for the test and then still, not do well on the test because they get nervous and worried and frightened when it is time to take the test. But, there is a way to become free of the nervousness or anxiety about tests. It is a secret that I am going to tell you about today.

I want you to spend a few moments, and I want you to think about the color "red". That bright, "red". Think about things that are "red". It might be a taillight, a stoplight, the color of a car, clothing, a lady's nail polish or it might be something large like a big sign. But, think about things that are "red". You will find that the color "red", that nice, bright, sharp color "red" is going to become clearer to you than ever before. It is going to seem brighter to you than ever before.

Each time you see the color "red", you are going to be more relaxed. You are going to be calm while taking a test, a quiz or an exam. For grown-ups out driving, the color "red" means stop. So the color "red" for you is going to mean stop being nervous.

The next time you get ready to take a test, a quiz or an exam, you'll look around for just a second and find something "red". You will look at it for just a moment and you will automatically feel more relaxed. You become comfortable. You are relaxed and at ease.

Everything that you have ever seen, read, heard or studied comes back into your mind. You do better on tests than you have ever done before. This makes you very, very happy. Whenever you see the color "red", you remember easily everything that you need to know.

WRITING

Not all children like to write, but most children do enjoy drawing. Since there are more children who enjoy drawing, we can use that information to make a comparison and help a child feel differently towards writing.

IMPROVE WRITING

You told me earlier that you enjoy drawing pictures. Drawing pictures is always fun because we can take a pencil or a crayon and we begin to make lines on a piece of paper. I want you to think about how much fun that really is. Imagine yourself with a pencil in your hand. In front of you, there is a blank piece of paper and you are getting ready to draw. What happens when you draw? You put the pencil on the paper; you begin to make the lines, the straight lines or curved lines, perhaps circles. And as you draw, you form a picture. It is fun to do.

You are now beginning to think of writing as being kind of like drawing. Because again, we take a pencil in our hand, put a piece of paper in front of us and we make lines-straight lines, curved lines and circles. When you draw a picture, you want it to be the best it can possibly be.

You are starting to think about writing in the same way you do drawing. Number one, it is going to be fun because you get to do the same thing you do with drawing. Number two, you are going to keep getting better at it each day because it is more fun each time you write.

SELF-IMAGE

It is very important for children to have a healthy self-image. When they feel confident and good about themselves, they do wonderfully in all areas of their lives. If a child has a poor self-image, they tend to be withdrawn, negative and not live up to their potential. This can affect all areas of their lives.

Self-image and body image are two different things. But, as children are growing up, especially when they reach their teens, they feel that they are one and the same. Children's bodies are going through constant changes. Their nervous systems and brain development are still under construction. Some children progress quicker or easier than others. We cannot compare our children to anyone else, not even their siblings.

As long as we are loving and supportive, we can help our children through these trying times. Sometimes, it helps for them to know that other children are going through the same things, too. It is not unusual for a fifteen-year-old teenager to come to us for bedwetting. That may seem surprising to some, but when you think about how many changes their bodies are going through, you realize just how common it is.

BEDWETTING

One of the first types of sessions. I want to discuss is **bedwetting**. This is one session where the desire for change is equally strong for the child, as for the adult. The child will be extremely motivated, so there will be no need to use an *"Add-on"*, such as getting better at video games or soccer.

STOP BEDWETTING

You are a very smart person. You knew that some day, some way, somehow, you were going to be free of this habit of wetting the bed. You knew all along you were not going to become a thirty-year-old adult still wetting the bed.

So really, it has not been a case of whether or not you were going to stop, but rather when and how you are going to stop wetting the bed. Well, we are answering the question here and now, today. Today is your day. You knew that once you became older you would stop wetting the bed. Everyone told you this.

Did you know that you are older today than you were yesterday? In fact, you are one year older today than you were last year. You are becoming older with every minute. So, you honestly, already have become older. Since you knew you would stop wetting the bed once you became older, it must be time to stop now. You're gong to enjoy waking up each morning with a dry bed. You are going to be very happy with yourself.

*Spend a moment now and think of the wonderful things that are going to happen now that you will never wet the bed again. It's going to be wonderful to spend the night over at your friend's house. You'll be able to relax, play games and have fun like everyone else. You are so proud of yourself. You knew you could do it and **now you are**! If you have to go, you wake up and go to the bathroom. When you are finished, you return to bed and go right back to sleep. You feel great waking up with dry sheets! You are great!*

SETTING GOALS

A study was conducted with high school students; part of the group wrote down their goals and things that they wanted to do; the others did nothing. Years later the graduates were contacted to see how their lives were going. The ones who had written down their goals not only reached them, but were more successful than their classmates who did nothing.

When setting a goal, make sure that it is something that you really want. The more desire you have, the more energy you put into getting it. Is it a job that you want, or maybe a new car? Whatever you think about you put energy into. Think about what you want on a daily basis. Think about all of the details that go into your goal. Imagine achieving it. Think about enjoying what it is that you want.

Make your goal realistic. Break it down into step-by-step things that you can do to reach your goal. When you break it down, you can do one thing at a time. It becomes easy to reach your goal. Make a commitment to do at least one thing each day toward reaching your goal. You have it before you know it.

Make a deadline. When you have a time limit that something must be completed, it makes it easier to gauge your progress. It helps you to keep on track. Take one thing at a time. Do what needs to be done. When you discipline yourself in this way, you become more efficient. You may even find that you are ahead of your deadline because you are getting things done quicker than you thought.

Write down your goal. By putting it on paper, you are making it real. You can see what it is that you are working toward. You can see all of the things that you have completed by checking off what's been done. Each day you are getting closer to achieving your goal. You are doing this so easily.

You are focused on reaching your goals. They are practical and worthwhile. You are so proud of yourself because you know that by following this pattern, you can have whatever you want. If you change your mind, that's fine. Create a new goal to replace the old one. Keep working toward something that is important to you. This is how you create success.

HANDLING GOSSIP

Many times we may hear others talking about someone else. They are eager to share information that can be hurtful or embarrassing to that person. They laugh and joke about the individual and seem to be very entertained by the mistakes or tragedies of others.

If you join them in this activity, it doesn't mean that you are safe from them doing it to you. There's an old saying, "If they'll do it with you, they'll do it to you." Be careful not to do something that can hurt someone else. The next person who gets hurt may be you.

Before getting involved in gossip, ask yourself, "Would I like it if they were doing this to me?" If the answer is, "No", then don't do it. Have more respect for yourself and others. Learn to stand up and be the best person you can be. If you don't participate, others may learn from your example. They may follow your lead and respect you for standing up and doing the right thing.

If someone starts to talk badly about another person, you can either walk away, or defend that person. After all, they are not there to speak up for themselves. Isn't that what you would want someone else to do if you were the subject of conversation? Treat people the way that you want to be treated.

People who gossip are usually insecure. They want to make someone else look bad so that they feel better about themselves.

Imagine, just think about some classmates talking about another student. What they are saying is mean; for no reason. That student has never said or done anything to deserve this treatment.

Now imagine that you say something to one of the gossips, like, "You are so popular. Everyone likes you. I wonder how it felt when you were new at school. You are so easy to talk with. I'm sure you made friends very easily. I'll bet that they would feel better if we were nice to them. Maybe we should go out of our way to show them just how friendly we can be." Say this in a very confident way as you smile at them.

What can they say in response? They don't want to say, "No, I want to be mean." Everyone would think that maybe they shouldn't be so popular. Unless they say something positive, others may wonder why they're even hanging around with this person.

Now what do you do if you are the person they are talking about? It's not so fun to be at this end, is it? No. Why are they picking on you? Probably because you are a very nice person. They think that you won't stand up for yourself and they'll get away with it.

Remember, when someone gossips it's because they are insecure and want to look or feel better about themselves. Sometimes, they're just bored and want to get some excitement going. Well, whatever the reason is, it still hurts.

Ask yourself, "What is it that they're saying about me? Is it true?" Maybe it is, maybe it isn't. If it is true, is it something that you would like to change, or does it even matter what they think? Let's say that they are making fun of an outfit that you're wearing that you don't really even like yourself. You may go up to one of the people in the group when they're alone. Pick the nicest person or the one that you think you could talk with the easiest. You could say, in a friendly, confident way something like, "Hey, I hear that you don't like my outfit. Neither do I. Do you have any constructive suggestions on how I can make it look better? I'd appreciate your input." Give them a nice smile and listen to what they have to say.

Sometimes they may be just as rude as they were before. Don't take it personally. They do this with everyone. But, if they feel that it doesn't bother you, they'll pick someone else the next time. If they think it doesn't upset you and you stand up for yourself, they will leave you alone.

If they say something that isn't true about you, let them know. Here again, be confident and friendly. Talk to them with a smile on your face.

You could say, "I hear that you think I'm the one who told the principal what you did at lunch. Just wanted to set the record straight; it wasn't me."

Sometimes we get picked on just because we are different. That's what we call being "unique". You don't want to be like everyone else. Be proud that you aren't like them. You are the best that you can be. You feel good about who you are. Each day you are feeling better about yourself. You have decided that anyone who is mean and rude is not worth your time.

You have decided today, right now, that you are confident and self-assured. You are happy with the person you are. You are honest, intelligent, positive, trustworthy, kind, fun to be with and so many other wonderful things. Each day you focus on something about yourself that is positive; something about yourself that you like.

You are learning to stand up for yourself in a friendly, positive way. You take care of yourself. You may surprise yourself and find that others are treating you better when you treat yourself better. They are getting to know the real you. They are getting to like you because you are letting them see all of the positive qualities that you possess.

If they don't like you, then you don't need them. You want to be with people who are worth knowing. You make friends with people who appreciate you. If they are mean to you, it makes you even more determined to be the best person that you can be with everyone. You can look at yourself in the mirror with pride that you never did, and will never do, anything to make another person feel bad about themselves.

Each day with each breath that you take, you are feeling more confident and better about yourself. Gossip is not worth your time. You are better than that. You have more important things to focus on. You are setting positive goals for yourself. You associate with people who are worth knowing. You are worth knowing. You are a wonderful person. You feel good about who you are. You treat others well and you are respected and treated well in return. You are a great example to your classmates. You always do the right thing. You are proud of yourself for being the best that you can be.

BEING WELL GROOMED

There was a man shopping in an electronics shop. His clothes were torn and shabby. He was unshaven. He looked sloppy. He hadn't even combed his hair. When he asked a salesperson for assistance, the man behind the counter didn't take him seriously because of the way that the shopper looked. He determined that this man wouldn't be able to afford anything in the store, so why waste any time on him? The salesman was uninterested and very short with his answers. He dismissed the shopper and walked off to help a couple standing in front of the home stereos.

Unfortunately, this salesperson was wrong. The shopper was actually a very wealthy man. He could afford to buy the entire store if he wanted to. Looks and appearance do make an impression on others. The salesman made an error in treating this shopper the way that he did. People do, however, form opinions on the way that we look.

We should be respectful of everyone no matter if they are poor or wealthy. We should treat everyone the way that we would want to be treated. But, if you want to be taken seriously, you need to put effort into your appearance.

When you look for a job, it is said that you should dress for the position that you desire to have in the future, not necessarily the job that is open at the moment. In other words, let's say that you are going on an interview to work in the mailroom for a major company but, in the future, you see yourself as being a top executive. Dress as an executive in that company would dress when you go for the interview for the position in the mailroom. The employer will see that you have potential; you will not be in the mailroom for the rest of your career.

Be proud of yourself. Show others the many wonderful qualities that you have. Look your best and you feel your best.

You dress appropriately for every situation. You have wonderful tastes in clothing. You look so sharp. Others may ask for your opinion on their appearance because you look so good and have such wonderful taste in clothing. You always put your best foot forward. You look like a winner. You are a winner!

POSTURE

We're going to do some magic today that is a lot of fun. In a way, it's kind of a secret, too, because no one else will know that you're doing this. Are you ready? **(Wait for response.)** *Okay.*

I want you to imagine that there is a magic string attached to the top of your head. No one can see this string, not even you, but you know that it's there. Imagine that you can pick up this string on the top of your head. When you pull the string up, you hold your head up high. You sit and stand with good posture. It's like this string helps you to stand and sit straight and tall. Your shoulders are back. You look confident.

You feel more comfortable with good posture. You look better. You have more energy when you need it and you're able to relax easily when you want to.

Your parents are so proud of you because you look so much better with good posture. You are proud of yourself because you feel better with good posture.

You may surprise yourself to find that pretty soon, the string works all by itself. You no longer need to pull the string on the top of your head to improve your posture. You automatically have good posture.

It's like the string on the top of your head is attached to a star in the sky, keeping your posture perfect at all times. Your head is held high; shoulders are back. You look and feel comfortable and natural with great posture.

SELF-ESTEEM

As we go through our lives, we meet many people. Some people are very positive and happy. There are some people who are very negative and depressing. We can't control what others do, but we can control how we perceive them.

Sometimes someone may say something to you that makes you feel bad about yourself. It doesn't mean that it is true because they said it. Just because they say something mean to you doesn't mean that their word is the last word.

Your mind is now working with you to establish healthy self-esteem. If someone makes a negative statement about you, simply think the word **"reject"**. *You no longer accept statements that are negative about you. You choose to be the very best that you can be. So, if you hear something negative about yourself, you turn it in to something positive.*

Let's say that you are in an argument with someone, or someone is mad at you and calls you "stupid". Your mind will quickly, automatically think the word **"reject"**. *You do not accept this statement. However, your mind analyzes the situation very quickly. You may think to yourself, "Why would this person call me "stupid"? I know that I have a powerful mind. I know that I am intelligent so, therefore, I am not stupid. This statement is false. What did I do that would cause this person to say such a thing?"*

When you think of what you have done, you may discover that you could have done something in a better way. So, therefore, this is a "learning experience". Next time, if you find yourself in a similar situation, you know how to handle it in a better way. You have learned from this experience.

You are a wonderful person. You always do the best that you can do. You are thoughtful and considerate of others. You do what is best for all concerned. You are capable of many great things.

Each day you feel more confident and better about yourself. You make wise decisions. You know what to say and when to say it. You know what to do and when to do it. You feel good about yourself. You are in control of your thoughts and actions. You like yourself more and more each day. You have healthy self-esteem.

UGLY DUCKLING SYNDROME

You may be surprised to hear that many of the movie stars at one time considered themselves to be an ugly duckling. It's hard to imagine when we look at them now looking so good. We can't imagine that they ever felt bad about themselves.

Beauty is in the eye of the beholder. If you think that you don't look good, you project that feeling to others. When you feel good about yourself, people can pick that up, too.

Take a good look at yourself. What is it that makes you think that you aren't attractive? Everyone goes through a period of time when they would like to change just about everything about them. Then there comes a time when you start to feel good about yourself. You focus on the things that you like. Each day you feel more comfortable until you feel confident about yourself.

Go ahead. Pick one thing that you like about yourself. It can be your beautiful eyes or great smile. It can be your shining hair or your long legs. It doesn't matter what you pick. Everyone has at least one feature that they like. What's yours? **(Wait for response.)**

Now focus on the best feature that you have. Think about it. Imagine your best feature. What have people told you in the past about this feature? I bet they had some nice things to say to you. **(Wait for response.)**

Now pick another feature. Give it your full attention. What do you think about this one? You may be surprised to see that this feature is pretty good, too. Start to look at yourself as a beautiful work of art. You are unique and special. There is no one else like you.

You are now appreciating yourself in a new way. You may take each feature separately and find the beauty that's there. When you put it all together, you are simply beautiful. You focus on the positive. You allow your inner beauty to be shown in your outer beauty. Each day you are feeling better about yourself. You are confident. You are beautiful. You are emerging as a person who is beautiful on the inside and out.

WEIGHT (Gain or Lose)

It doesn't matter if the child needs to gain or lose weight, it is a serious issue for both situations. Many times the child who needs or wants to *gain* weight may be overlooked. Since the age of *"Twiggy"* when *"this is in"*, most think that there's no problem.

In recent years, the issues of Anorexia Nervosa and Bulimia Nervosa are in the forefront in our culture. We are becoming more aware of all types of eating disorders.

I find it sad when helping children with weight loss. This seems to be more prevalent. We can look at a child and see the excess weight. We <u>know</u> there's a problem. I'm talking about children four, five and six-years-old. Up to this point in a child's life, an adult has more control than the child over the type and quantity of food that is available to the child. As the child gets older, they are exposed to more situations outside the home where they can make their own choices.

Adults and children alike tend to eat for reasons other than hunger. Emotional eating is so common. Most of us have, at one time or another, eaten out of boredom, depression, anxiety, stress, companionship, love, comfort, reward, time of day or other people. Who hasn't heard a child who's bored complain of being hungry? As we mentioned earlier, we may have the potential to be overweight, but it is our lifestyle and daily choices that create the outcome.

We eat for self-defense. I've heard people announce they were going to get something to eat, even though they weren't hungry because they might not get time to eat later when they may get hungry. Crazy. These same people would never dream of taking an aspirin when they didn't have a headache, just in case they *might* get one later.

As adults, so much of our socializing is set around food. Couples invite others to their homes and then feel as if they must put out some wine and cheese or snacks and beverages of some kind. From Thanksgiving and Christmas dinners to Fourth of July barbeques, most holiday celebrations focus on the meal. For many people, socializing without food as part of the activity would seem weird.

The energy level of children today is being compromised by an abundance of activities that are sedentary in nature. Children are often choosing video games, computers, TV with channels that number in the hundreds as activities, rather than going outside and running and playing. Everyone's activity level is decreasing. Think about it. It wasn't that long ago, that you had to actually get up and walk over to the television set to change the channel. Now we have the remote control. I prefer to call it the *"scepter of power"*.

Used to be, most homes had one telephone and you had to go to where it was installed to use it. Then you had to actually use your wrist to dial the numbers. Now, there's cordless and cell phones. Push-button dialing. Even better, some phones don't have to be dialed at all because they're voice-activated.

In our cars, we have the garage door opener, the automatic door lock, the power steering and the power windows. In the old days, when we got home, we had to get out of our car, bend over and lift up on the garage door to open it, get back in the car, pull into the garage, turn off the car, get out and go pull down the garage door. I'm breaking out in a sweat just thinking about it.

A while back they did a study involving a secretary that used a manual typewriter. They calculated the energy used to manually put the paper into the machine, return the carriage after each line of type and so on, throughout the day. They determined that replacing the manual with an electric typewriter could cause a weight gain of three pounds in one year without changing any other thing in the secretary's life.

To get started, here's a script to assist someone in **gaining weight**. It is important in the preliminary part of the session to get as much information as you can, as to the types of foods that they eat, and why they don't eat other foods. Is it the texture, look or smell of foods that deters them from eating?

GAIN WEIGHT

You told me earlier that you would like to gain weight. This is something that you can do. You are very smart. You know that you need certain types of food that your body needs to be healthy and strong. By giving your body the nourishment that it needs, your body gets stronger, healthier.

You eat the right kind, the right amount of food for you to reach a healthy weight for you. Exercise is something that you enjoy. You fit it into your life because you know that you look and feel better when you exercise.

You are now establishing healthy eating habits so that you are gaining the right amount of weight for your body. You gain just the right amount of weight and you gain the weight in the parts of your body that need it. You are healthy and in shape. You are built just the way you have always wanted to be.

You have an image in your mind of how you want to look and feel. You know that your body needs food, water and air to exist. You are now eating the right kind, the right amount of food to help you to reach and maintain your goal weight. You are getting everything that you need to be healthy and happy.

Hypnosis is the most effective way of changing a habit pattern. Many people do not realize that with the use of hypnosis you can do much more than simply change or remove negative habits. At this very moment, each and every suggestion that I am sharing with you is beginning to register in your own subconscious mind. These suggestions continue having a more positive effect on you, even after this session is completed. You may find that each day you are feeling healthier and stronger. You feel happy and fulfilled.

You focus on what you want and you get it! Allow your mind to focus on the positive results that you want. As you do, the energy that you put into your thoughts, turns your thoughts into reality. You look and feel great!

You may surprise yourself as to how great you are now beginning to feel. Healthy foods that may not have appealed to you in the past are now foods that you enjoy. The many textures and flavors are now tasty to you. You eat the right kind, the right amount of food for you to be healthy, strong and happy. You may find that you are open to trying new foods that are good for you. You feel more confident and better about yourself. Your future is looking brighter and happier each and every day.

Over the next week, you will begin to notice the improvement. Your weight level begins to increase and, as it does, your self-confidence also begins to increase. You will not become overweight, but you reach your goal weight and then are able to maintain your weight at a healthy, ideal level for you. You are feeling better about yourself than you have in years. But, this is only the beginning. As your weight begins to increase, family and friends begin to comment on how well you are looking. They see the difference in your appearance, but only you feel the dif-

ference from within. You feel loved. You ar loved. You are confident and self-assured. You can, you will, reach your goal weight and be so happy with the new you.

There is no person thought, memory, image, idea, feeling or sensation from the past, in the present or ever to arrive in the future to keep you from reaching your goal weight and feeling great. Your hunger for living a happy life is getting stronger with each passing day. You feel more positive. You are optimistic about your future. You look forward to each and every day. You have a feeling of health and wellbeing like you've never had before. This is the beginning of a whole new life for you. You are now the person you have always wanted to be. You are fantastic! You are great! You are loved!

This first **weight loss** script deals with selection. We want to help the child make healthy food choices. It's important that the child learns to choose to eat the healthier foods on his or her own and that it becomes a habit.

WEIGHT LOSS # 1

If you continue relaxing even more, we're going to play a little game. In this game, we are going to see how smart you really are. I'm going to say different types of foods and if they are foods that you should eat to reach a good weight, you will say the word "Yes". If I say foods that you should not want to eat because they are fattening, you will say the word "No".

Let's see how smart you are:

Ice cream	**(Wait for response.)**
Cookies	**(Wait for response.)**
Apples	**(Wait for response.)**
Donuts	**(Wait for response.)**
Grapes	**(Wait for response.)**
Potato chips	**(Wait for response.)**
Water	**(Wait for response.)**
Vegetables	**(Wait for response.)**

You did very well. From this moment on, before you eat any food, you will play the game by yourself. If you are thinking about a food that is fattening, you will say "No" and you will not eat it. If it is a food that can help you lose weight, you will say "Yes" and you will enjoy eating it. Many times when we play a game, the winner gets the prize. This game is going to be the same way. You are going to be the winner. You are going to get the prize.

Let's think about what the prize is going to be for you. Your prize is going to be the best prize in the whole world. Your prize is that you are going to be at a good weight. Think about that with me now. Let's pretend that you have already won.

Think of yourself being at a good weight and you feel happy. You look good and feel real pleased with yourself. Your parents are happy. All of your friends keep telling you how great you look now that you have lost this weight. This is probably the best prize in the world. You deserve this prize.

It's a proven fact that the mind responds to the time spent eating food, as it does with quantity. If you thought about sitting at a table for 45 minutes every day eating donuts, chances are you would not think you could do that. That's a long time to spend eating donuts. And, we didn't even discuss how many donuts with would entail. Actually, if we took the amount of food we normally eat, cut it in half and take five minutes longer to eat this amount of food, we would, most probably, be satisfied. This script is going to slow down the time spent eating.

WEIGHT LOSS #2

Today we are going to learn about a fun way to lose weight forever and ever. I want you to think about a race. In this race, the slowest person is going to be the winner. We're going to have these kinds of races each time you sit down to eat.

When you sit at the table, you are going to take the smallest, tiniest bite of food. Then, you are going to chew that bite of food over and over and over again before you swallow. You will then take another little bite of food and you will chew it up over and over. You will be the slowest eater in the world. You will be winning this race because, in this race, the one that finishes last is the winner.

Now some real magical things will happen by taking very small bites of food and by chewing these bites over and over. Since you're going to become full with less food, you will begin to lose weight. As soon as you lose a couple of pounds, you are going to notice the difference.

You are going to notice that you look and feel better. You continue on with this slow race until the weight of your body is exactly where you want it to be. You are doing this for yourself. You are not doing it for me, for your Mom or Dad. You are not doing it for your friends or teachers. You are doing this for you. You are doing this for yourself.

You are an important person. You deserve to weigh your goal weight. You are going to be the best slow-eater in the whole world. I know there are times that instead of being slow, you may want to be fast. If there are times that you want to be fast instead of being slow, you are going to go out and play. You will do things fast when you play, but when it's time to eat, you take those slow, tiny, little bites. You chew each bite over and over again.

You know that you are winning at losing weight. Each week you lose weight until you are at a perfect level for you. Now, let's make sure that we understand the race correctly. When it comes to eating, are you going to eat slow or fast? **(Wait for response.)** *"Slow". Good. If you want to do something fast, what will it be?* **(Wait for response.)** *"Play". Good.*

I think we'd all agree that sugar can be very addictive. Most of us have had times when we would decide to only have a small amount of something sweet, only to end up eating more. This comes up often in regards to weight loss sessions with adults as well.

Weight loss is the one type of behavior that if we mess up, we tend to go overboard and mess up even more. It's kind of a *"Oh, well. I might as well eat some more"* mentality that makes losing weight difficult. In other areas of our lives, we would never dream of such behavior.

Imagine carrying a large tray of expensive drinking glasses. Now, think what your reaction would be if one of those nice, expensive glasses fell off the tray and broke as it hit the floor. You certainly wouldn't think, *"Oh, well. Might as well throw down the whole tray and break them all."* Never. We are not as kind to ourselves as we would be to some drinking glasses. Doesn't make sense, does it?

WEIGHT LOSS #3

We have decided that the way to lose this weight is to stop eating all of those sugary types of food. You need to help me, because you know what the sugary sweet foods are. You know the ones that you need to get rid of. Earlier you told me what they were. Let me see if I can remember. Cakes, cookies, ice cream, sodas, pies and candies. I think that is most of them. We know that these kinds of foods are just full of sugar.

In the past, you thought a lot about these kinds of foods. Today, if you are thinking about these kinds of foods, you are going to be thinking about how sugary, sweet and kind of sticky they are.

You wouldn't want to eat a bowl of cereal with a hundred pounds of sugar on top. We don't want to eat cakes, cookies, candies, ice cream, soda, and pies because they are filled with sugar.

Everyone knows how to work a television set. We might be watching something and, if we don't like it, what do we do? We change the channel. You are going to do the same thing about sugars. You are going to change the channels in your own mind. You are going to change your mind.

If the silly, old thought of having all of those sugars would come into your mind, **click***, you'll be able to change that so you start thinking about how good you feel now that you are losing weight. If that thought of a piece of cake should slip into your mind,* **click***, it is like changing the channel and you change your mind. You start thinking about a glass of water. Every time the old thought of something sugary comes into your mind,* **click***, it is like changing the channel. You change the way you think and you start thinking about good, healthy foods; the right kind, the right amount of food that helps you to reach and maintain your goal weight.*

SLEEP HABITS

Night Terrors (or Sleep Terrors), sleepwalking and bedwetting are very common in children because they are basically caused from immaturity of the nervous system. All of these disorders take place during the deep stages of sleep. For most, these issues are temporary. As children mature, their nervous systems develop and they grow out of these conditions.

Whether the child is having trouble falling asleep, getting up in the middle of the night, not wanting to stay in his or her own bed, waking up too early or any other sleep-related problem, this is a useful method of alleviating the situation:

FALLING ASLEEP

This has been a real special kind of sleep for you and it's been a lot of fun for you. I had a good time, too. But in this special sleep, you can hear everything that I say, isn't that right? Nod your head "Yes". (**Wait for response.**) *Good. Now, if I stopped talking to you, you would go to sleep, just like you do at night. You would fall asleep real quick. So from now on when it's time for you to go to bed, you're going to lie in bed and close your eyes.*

You are going to go into this special sleep pretty soon, because you won't be able to hear my voice. You will fall asleep just like you do at night, but you will fall asleep real quick. You won't have to get out of bed; you won't have to go to your Mom and Dad's room, because now you have your own special, secret sleep. You close your eyes and go into this special, secret sleep like you did today. Pretty soon, because I won't be talking to you, because I won't be in your room, you will fall asleep very easily. You like this very much

You get comfortable in bed and close your eyes. **_(You Yawn!)_** *You are so sleepy. It feels so good to go to sleep.*

STAY ASLEEP AT NIGHT

As you fall asleep at night, you feel so comfortable. It feels good to rest your body after a busy day. Your mind and body need time to rest. They need to get more energy so you are ready for a happy day when you wake-up in the morning.

Sleep, sleep, deep sleep. All night long, you sleep. It's easy for you to stay asleep all night long. You are so sleepy.

When you wake-up in the morning, you are ready to start your happy day. You are ready to go to school, play with your friends. All kinds of fun things to do. That's what we do during the day. At night, we sleep. We rest. During the day, we're active and play.

NIGHT TERRORS (SLEEP TERRORS)

Night Terrors, or Sleep Terrors, are harder on the parent than the child. When the child starts screaming or crying in a panicked manner and moving about wildly, a parent's first concern is that there's something wrong with the child. There isn't. Your child is probably having a Night Terror.

Ironically, the child may not remember the episode when they wake-up in the morning. If they remember anything, it may be a vague feeling of being chased or feeling trapped. That seems so hard for us to believe when we've witnessed this frightening, dreamlike experience.

It occurs during the deep stages of sleep, usually within fifteen minutes to one hour of your child's falling asleep. It can last anywhere from five to twenty minutes. The longer the child is in a non-dreaming state before the Night Terror strikes, the more scared the child will be when it occurs. Your child will still be asleep, even if their eyes are open! Your child may call for you and even though you are right there in front on them, may appear to be looking straight through you. They may not recognize that you are there. They look confused or upset.

Some parents describe this crazed expression as looking as if they are *"possessed"*. (Don't worry; they're not!)

They are not, however, dreaming. This stage four of the sleep cycle is a non-dreaming state. Although in some situations you may think that your child is having a nightmare, there are some differences between the two. Night Terrors occur during the non-dream stage of sleep, where Nightmares occur during the REM or dream state. Night Terrors will occur earlier in the evening, while Nightmares would occur much later. Night Terrors are not usually recalled the next morning, where Nightmares may be vivid and real.

Night Terrors often run in families. It is more common in boys. As a rule, Night Terrors occur more often in children between the ages of three and five, but studies have shown that they can occur from 6 months to 100 years old! Basically, Night Terrors are caused by the immaturity of the nervous system. Once their nervous systems develop, they usually outgrow this condition. Night Terrors are much less common after the age of seven.

If an adult would have Night Terrors, it could be linked with Post Traumatic Stress Disorder (PTSD) or other forms of stress. Certain medications, being overly tired or eating a heavy meal prior to going to bed can trigger the Night Terrors.

To avoid Night Terrors, keep your child's sleep schedule as regular as possible. Being overly tired or having their sleep schedule shift irregularly can trigger this condition.

Night Terrors are **not harmful**. Be careful, however, that they do not bump into something or have an object around that can be harmful to them. Be sure to move anything that could be harmful to them out of their way. Clear the path so that they don't run into anything. They will not know what they are doing during this time, so keep their environment safe.

Research varies on the proper way to handle Night Terrors. Some say that you should **gently wake the child**. While others say <ins>**do not</ins> try to wake the child**, as this may just prolong the episode. As a rule, the child will go back to sleep with little or no difficulty once the Night Terror is over. There are times when the child may wake briefly before returning to sleep.

It is best to talk to them in a relaxed voice to comfort the child. It is important for you to allow yourself to relax so that your child can hear your slow, soothing speech as you reassure them. This may seem strange, but turning on the lights sometimes can help to calm them down.

Don't try to hold or restrain them, since this experience may already make them feel as if they are trapped. They might just push back or struggle more to try to get away. If you find, however, that your child wants to be held, by all means, do so.

There are no sessions for Night Terrors, as a rule. They are usually short-lived, and since children out grow them, there is no need. If, however, your child has more difficulty with this issue, you may want to set an appointment for a session for your child with a hypnotist.

NIGHTMARES

It is a proven fact that the state closest to hypnosis is the state we're in just as we are about to fall into sleep, or just as we are waking up in the morning. This is the alpha state.

Nightmares take place during REM sleep, the dream state, which is later in the evening or before waking in the morning.

As you tuck your child in at night, help them to get all cozy and comfortable. Give them a hug and a kiss and tell them *"Sweet dreams"*. Depending on their age, either read them a nice, peaceful, bedtime story, or have them think about something they enjoy doing. Set the tone for the type of things they think about as they fall asleep.

Positive suggestions before going to sleep can be very effective in determining the type of dreams we have while asleep. The goal with this type of session is to give the child positive expectations of having good dreams.

STOP NIGHTMARES

At night when we go to sleep, we have dreams. We can have good dreams or we can have what some people call nightmares or bad dreams. Many people don't realize that they have a choice of which one they are going to have. Although you are in a special kind of sleep now and you can hear me, you can also have a dream.

Let's decide if you would like a good dream or a bad dream. Which one would you like? Say either "Good" or "Bad". (**Wait for response.**) *Good. I thought that is the one you would say. I am going to count from one to twenty. As I count, you are going to have a dream. Since you have chosen, it is going to be a good dream. When I get done counting, I want you to tell me about this wonderful, good dream.*

One, that's it. You are starting to have a dream.
Two, you are going to be able to tell me about it.
Three, of course, it will be a good dream.
Four, you're going to remember the dream.
Five, the dream is becoming more enjoyable.
Six, you are enjoying this kind of dream.
Seven, it's becoming really clear.
Eight, it is kind of a fun dream.
Nine, as it becomes happier; it sort of makes you smile.
Ten, you are halfway through this dream.
Eleven, you are going to like telling me about this dream.
Twelve, you know that you are making the dream.
Thirteen, it's nice to be able to choose to have a good dream.
Fourteen, it is a good dream because you chose a good dream.
Fifteen, the dream is starting to end.
Sixteen, since it was a good dream it is ending happily.
Seventeen, there is goes.
Eighteen, fading away.
Nineteen, the dream is almost gone.
Twenty.

Now spend a moment and tell me about that good dream. (**Wait for response.**) *Good. From now on, since you know that you can have good dreams or bad dreams, each night as you get ready to go to sleep and you are lying there with your eyes closed, I want you to say three times, "good dream, good dream, good dream" and guess what? As you fall asleep you will have only good dreams.*

IN THEIR OWN BED

Children need to be independent. Sleeping on their own helps them to develop their own sense of confidence. A lot of times it seems that the parents are the ones who feel better when the child is sleeping with them! There is no greater joy than being a parent. We don't want our children to grow up too fast, so we hang on to every moment we can.

In order for your child to stay in their own bed, it would be easier when you spend time with your children during the day. By having your attention during the day, they won't give you any trouble at night. They miss being with you. It's their way of getting what they need.

Transition the child out of the parents' bed and into their own bed at an early age. If you need to take small steps, put their mattress on the floor in your room next to your bed. The child still has the comfort of knowing that you are there. As they feel more comfortable, move them into their own room.

It is important that the parents agree that the child should be in their own bed. Just like all areas of discipline, when the parents are united in their approach, the better for the child. The easier it will be for all concerned.

Talk with your child about moving into their own bed. Start a nighttime ritual to get them to feel comfortable. This makes them feel special and loved. Reading a peaceful, bedtime story is always a great way to get your child to go to sleep. So is singing them a lullaby.

Whatever the parents decided, it is important to agree with your choice and be firm. Your child will benefit in the long run.

SLEEP IN YOUR OWN BED

*As you go to sleep in your own bed, you feel so good because this means that you are a big (**girl/boy**). During the day is the time to spend with Mommy and Daddy. At night, it's time for you to get nice and comfy sleeping in your own bed.*

*You have plenty of room when you sleep in your own bed. You have your own special pillow. Your own special blanket. You feel special sleeping in your own bed. You are a big (**girl/boy**).*

SPEAKING HABITS

I hear a lot of people today say that they can't understand children when they talk. Many complain because, especially teens, seem to almost swallow their words, or mumble, whenever they try to communicate.

Speaking clearly at a proper speed and volume is important for children to learn. It will help them immensely as they grow up and cultivate their communication skills.

When it comes to volume, we get the child to talk during the session and they are able to establish for themselves a level that is more acceptable. The child is in control and able to monitor his or her volume when speaking.

Many times the reason that children have poor speaking habits is because they feel shy or insecure. They are not confident that what they have to say is important or correct. We need to instill confidence in them so that they realize that we are interested in what they do have to say.

When parents have the habit of talking with their children about the everyday, little things in life, children will then come to their parents when there are big issues at stake. They need to know that they can trust you and not be afraid of what you might say or do if you don't agree. They are afraid of getting into trouble or being corrected.

MUMBLING

As you open your mouth to speak, you want to make sure that people understand what you have to say. You are an important person and people are interested in your thoughts and ideas.

You feel confident about what you want to communicate. You speak clearly. You are easy to understand. You have a wonderful way with words that keep people interested. You speak at a comfortable speed and volume so that people want to listen to you. You speak clearly so you are understood.

SPEED

So much to say, such little time! Kids always seem to be in a hurry. I guess that's because we seem to be more rushed now than ever before. Children want to get in what they want to say before the conversation goes onto another topic.

Anyone who knows me knows that I tend to speak a tad fast, to say the least. Matter of fact, when I'm around others who tend to speak rather slowly, I have a tendency to want to speed them up. Sometimes this manifests itself in a circular arm movement that, I guess, is a subconscious XE "subconscious" desire to crank them up to a faster pace. When we're dealing with a child that speaks way too rapidly, it helps to emphasize to them that they are important and what they have to say is important enough that we want to hear them.

SPEAK SLOWLY

When we are talking with someone, we need to be able to do two different things. We need to talk, but we also need to listen. From the time we spent together, I can see that you are very good at listening.

Most people want to be good at listening, just like you. Wouldn't it be nice if you could help other people become better at listening? You are such a nice person that you really do want to help people listen better. The one sure way that you can help other people listen is to begin talking slower.

Sometimes you talk so fast that the people who want to hear what you have to say cannot listen as quick as you can talk. You now begin to talk slower, so that other people can listen better.

VOLUME
AM I GETTING YOUR ATTENTION?!!

Yelling is one way to do it, but not the most effective. It seems that if there are other children, they seem to talk over each other and louder so that they are the one getting heard. It can be an eternal headache!

We've all heard parents tell their children, *"Use your inside voice."* This is the best way to change any bad habit; become aware of what you are doing so that you can change it. Sometimes, children need to be reminded about their volume. Once they are in the habit of catching themselves, they will be able to make the needed change.

OVERCOMING LOUDNESS

I know sometimes when I get excited, or maybe when I think somebody is not listening to me, my voice tends to go up and up until it gets really loud. Sometimes it just gets louder and louder because I think maybe if it gets louder, then they'll be able to hear what I'm saying.

Has that ever happened to you? (**Wait for response.**) *Yes, I thought so. Well, let me tell you what I found that will work really good for you. It works for every-body. I'm going to come over and touch your right ear, and then I'm going to touch your left ear. As I touch your ears, you are going to have kind of super hearing. That's right, almost like Superman.*

If your voice starts getting too loud, you will know it because you have super hearing. You will lower your voice back down to a good level. In fact, from this moment on, it is going to be impossible for your voice to get too loud because with your super hearing, you will know when it is getting too loud and you will be able to lower it back down to a good level. This is going to work forever.

SUBCONSCIOUS HABITS

Things that we do automatically without thinking about them are subconscious habits or behaviors. In order to change a habit, we need to become conscious of what we are doing. By becoming aware of these subconscious movements, we can change the habit by catching ourselves. Hair twirling, nail biting and thumb sucking are similar because they all involve the movement of the hands.

HAIR TWIRLING

This is a nervous habit that people do when they feel unsure about themselves, or when they are trying to make up their mind about a situation. It's harmless by nature, but can be annoying to those around them.

STOP TWIRLING HAIR

Your mind and body are now working together. You may find that if your hands were to reach up towards your head to play with your hair, you will automatically become aware of your hands and stop that movement. You move your hands to another position and realize that playing with your hair or twirling it serves no purpose.

You may surprise yourself and find that you can think more clearly when your hands are down by your sides. You make better choices, better decisions when you are not playing with your hair. When your fingers are free from your hair, your mind is free to make good choices.

Every day you feel more confident and better about yourself. No longer do you twirl or play with your hair. It serves no purpose. You make better decisions when your hands are free from your hair.

NAIL BITING

Nail biting is a behavior that is almost always subconscious. Whether dealing with a child or an adult, an important element in overcoming this habit is to make the person conscious of the action before it gets to the mouth.

You are going to be very happy to realize that you have already stopped biting your nails. That's right, you realize how good you feel right now even though you are not chewing or biting or picking at your nails. This nice, good feeling that you are experiencing right now is a feeling that you made happen.

No on else may ever make you relax, just as no one else can ever make you bite your nails. You are in control. You are the boss. You have control over the movements of your hands and your arms. If you wanted to, if you decided to, you could move your hands and place them on your legs. If you wanted to, if you decided to, you could move your hands and place them on your tummy. If you wanted to, you could move your hands and place them right on the top of your head. Yes, you have control over the movements of your hands.

If your hands or arms would ever begin to sneak up towards your mouth for the purpose of biting or chewing on your nails, you will become aware of it and you will then move your hands to another position. They can never move up towards your mouth without you realizing it. Once you notice that they are sneaking up towards your mouth for the purpose of biting or chewing on your nails, you move your hands away and feel good.

As you continue to relax, let one of your hands try to sneak up towards your mouth and notice how you catch it. When you catch that hand moving up towards your mouth, move it away. Bring it back down to the arm of the chair. Let's see if it is going to be your right hand or your left hand that is going to try to sneak up without you knowing it. There they go. As soon as you know that it is moving up towards your mouth, you catch it and move it back down to the chair.

That was good. So, if one of those hands and arms try to sneak up towards your mouth for the purpose of biting or chewing your nails, you know it and you move it to some other position.

I love to tell the child, *"Now, before you leave the office, one of your hands is going to try to sneak up to your mouth, but you will catch it and move it, right?"* They love this. Pretty soon, they will have one of their hands crawling up their shirt or flying through the air, they'll catch it with their other hand and exclaim, *"I caught it!"* I'll ask them if they think the other hand will try as well. Sure enough, the other hand will start to sneak up and they'll catch it with the same enthusiasm.

STUTTERING

If you are going to do any work with someone who stutters, I recommend you record his or her speech before you begin. People who stutter tend to only notice the words that give them trouble and when they have an improvement, tend to discount that improvement. If you have a recording that shows the before and after, you can demonstrate to them their own progress.

Stuttering can result from an imprint. Remember, an imprint is a thought that has been registered at the subconscious level of the mind, causing a change in behavior.

There is a case history of a child that had a severe stuttering problem. When the child was regressed, it was discovered that the stuttering resulted from an event in his past. The child lived on a farm and had decided to fill a little swimming pool so the ducks could go swimming. His father came home and began to hit and yell at the child for drowning the chickens. What happened was, the child mistook the chickens for ducks. (Apparently, chickens don't swim as well as ducks!) But the father thought the child was simply being cruel.

Every time the child tried to speak, the father would cut him off, yelling at the child. Both the child and the father were quite upset at the time. The child was only able to get part of his words out, producing only stammering sounds as he tried to explain his good intentions to his father. He stuttered constantly after that experience.

STOP STUTTERING

Some people don't realize it, but stuttering is a habit that is learned. That's right. There has never been a baby born with a stuttering habit. It is something that is learned. Like anything else that you learn, you can re-learn, too.

It really doesn't matter what caused you to begin stuttering. It really doesn't matter what caused you to continue stuttering. You will find that you are going to be more relaxed when you speak. Your words are going to be clear. You will be confident with your ability to talk to other people.

I want you to spend a moment now and I would like you to mentally, just in your mind, think back to a time that you did not stutter, a time when you spoke clearly. As you begin to think of that time, I want you to nod your head "Yes" for me. **(Wait for response.)** *Real good.*

Now, I want you to pretend like you can look forward in time. I want you to think of a time in the very near future when, once again, you are speaking clearly. You are not stuttering any longer. As you think of yourself in the future speaking clearly and speaking easily, I want you to nod your head "yes" for me. **(Wait for response.)** *Good.*

We know that in the past you didn't stutter and we know that in the future you will not stutter. Let's now turn the present into the future. You can now begin to talk clearly, precisely, easily and freely. You'll never again have to stutter and once you are sure, once you are certain, once you know that you won't have to stutter anymore, I want you to nod your head "yes" and let a big smile come across your face. **(Wait for response.)** *Good. You can speak clearly now.*

THUMB SUCKING

I would like for you to try something for me. Clasp your hands together. Now, look at your thumbs and see which thumb is on top of the other. This positioning of your thumbs is a subconscious XE "subconscious" habit. At some point in time when you were younger, you clasped your hands together in this fashion and now you always do it the same way. Try again, but this time, clasp your hands so the opposite thumb is on top. How does that feel? Probably, pretty weird. For the most part, thumb sucking is a subconscious habit. A child may want to stop sucking his or her thumb, but when they're sleepy, or even in their sleep, in goes the thumb.

STOP SUCKING THUMB

You have decided that the time has come to stop sucking your thumb. You are doing this because you know it is the right thing for you to do. In the past when you were smaller, sucking your thumb seemed like the right thing to do, but now that you are older, the idea of sucking your thumb has become kind of silly. It would seem silly to sit around and suck on our toes. It would seem silly to try to suck our elbow. Of course, it would be awfully hard to try to suck on your ears. It really seems kind of silly to be sucking on your thumb.

*From this moment on, if you have the thought or idea of sucking on your thumb, you are going to take in a really deep breath and just hold it for about two or three seconds. **One, two, three**, let it out and you will find that the thought, the idea, of sucking your thumb just disappears. What you are now doing is sucking in air. Air is good. We need air. We don't need to suck our thumbs.*

Without fail, if you have a thought or idea of sucking your thumb, you take in a deep breath, hold it for one, two, three seconds and let it out. Without fail, if the old thought of sucking your thumb would pop into your mind, you know what to do.

SUBSTANCE ABUSE

This is probably one of the most tragic situations a parent can witness. When your child is involved with substance abuse, part of you may feel helpless. You know that they're going to do what they want. We worry about what we can do to stop them.

This issue is serious because it harms our children and, possibly, others. As your children are growing up, be sure to make time for them. Talk about everything under the sun. If they grow up feeling comfortable talking with you, there is a better chance that they will share life-changing issues with you. When they grow up with a good sense of self and a feeling that they are loved and belong, they may not choose to go with the crowd in this destructive lifestyle.

Love your children, be a good listener and be supportive. Know when it's time to seek professional help and get them into rehab as soon as possible. Their life is in your hands.

DRUG & ALCOHOL ABUSE FOR TEENS

You may think that drinking or doing drugs is the answer but, really, it is a question, "What are you running away from?"

When people look to drugs and alcohol to help them to feel better, they are not able or willing to look at what they don't like in their lives. There is something that they are trying to escape. What is that for you?

Your friends may be drinking and doing drugs, so you're just doing it because they are, right? Well, that may be how it started, but you continue for other reasons. You are in control of your own actions. If you stopped drinking and doing drugs, do you really think that it would matter to your friends? Of course not. They don't care what you do. If they don't want to hang around with you anymore because you stop, then they weren't really your friends in the first place.

You need to do what's best for you. You want to live a healthy life. You want to be successful and happy in all areas of your life. Drugs and alcohol are not the way to get to what you want. They change the way that you act. They change your personality. You may find that the people who you care about in your life change the way that they look at you. Your life is so much better when you are clean and sober.

Make a promise to yourself that you do what's best for your own health and wellbeing. There is nothing in drugs or alcohol that your body needs. You are determined to eliminate drugs and alcohol because you respect yourself. You care about what happens in your life. You want to be the best that you can be. You are your best when you are free of drugs and alcohol.

There is no person, thought, memory, image or idea from the past, present or ever to arrive in the future that can keep you from being free of drugs and alcohol. You are in control of your own life. You are healthy, happy and successful in every area of your life.

You are free of drugs and alcohol. You are in control of your life. You are healthy and happy. You are the best that you can be. You feel better about yourself when you are clean and sober. You are so proud of yourself.

DON'T START SMOKING

While we've never had a parent book a session specifically for this next script, we have used it as an "Add-on" and the kids really love it. It points out that sometimes children can be smarter than adults, especially adults who smoke. This is an especially fun thought for a child, to be smarter than an adult.

DON'T START

I have heard that some people think that all grown-ups are smarter than children. You and I know that this is not true. If all adults were smarter than children, then adults would have never started smoking. I see adults every day who say that they wish they had never started smoking. They tell me that smart people do not smoke.

I know that you do not smoke. This means that you must be smarter than some of the adults that do smoke. You kind of like being smarter than some adults, don't you? It will be interesting to see if you can continue being smarter than the adults that smoke.

I guess there are two different kinds of people in the world. There are the really smart people who do not smoke and then there are the people who do smoke.

Are you one of the smart people? **(Wait for response.)** *Yes. Good.*

Will you be one of the smart people next month? **(Wait for response.)** *Yes. Good.*

Will you be one of the smart people next year? **(Wait for response.)** *Yes. Good.*

Will you be one of the smart people forever and ever? **(Wait for response.)** *Yes. Good. That makes me feel happy that you are smart now and that you will always be the smart one.*

STOP SMOKING FOR TEENS

You may be surprised to hear that most people who started smoking did so when they were in school with their friends. Most of these people tell me that the friends who got them to start smoking no longer smoke themselves. They quit the habit years ago, but they are still smoking.

When I ask them how they feel, they tell me that they wish that they had never started to smoke. They tell me that if they could do it all over again, they would have told their friends that they had no desire to smoke. They would have spoke up for themselves and not smoked just because everyone else was doing it.

You are a unique individual because you are standing up for yourself today by eliminating the smoking habit. You may find that others quit when they discover that you did. You are a wonderful inspiration to your friends.

There is nothing in cigarettes that your body needs. As people get older, it can affect their health and ability to breathe. But, you already know all about that; that's why you're here. You have decided for yourself that you do not want to put yourself in a position that adversely affects your health. You are planning to live a long, healthy, happy life; able to do the things that you want to do and have fun doing them.

You are now releasing the smoking habit. You don't want anything in control of you. You are eliminating the smoking habit because you have decided that you are in control. You feel better being a non-smoker.

It is easy for you to quit smoking. You are determined to be healthy and happy. By releasing the cigarettes, you improve your health. You are in control. You are a non-smoker.

You are free from the smoking habit. You feel better now that you are in control. You look and feel better as a non-smoker. You are choosing to be healthy and happy by being a non-smoker.

You are a non-smoker and you feel great being a non-smoker. You are in control.

About the Author

Don Mottin is the director of one of the most successful hypnosis centers in the U.S. Through constant evaluations and hours of professional practice, Don has created proven strategies that have resulted in a successful practice that has gained international recognition.

In 1972, while serving in Japan with the United States Marine Corps, Don had the opportunity to view a few demonstrations of hypnosis, and was amazed at how different hypnosis was from his previous notions. He discovered that he was not asleep, did not float around the room and he was not out of control. He was, however, able to create total anesthesia in his own arm, recall events from the age of five as if they had happened yesterday and he was free of all stress and worry. He was hooked, and spent the next year studying hypnosis.

Around 1976, Don joined the police force and began refining his hypnotic techniques in the field of criminal investigations. With hypnosis, the witness may be regressed back to the time of the crime and recall the event without experiencing any of the emotions. Don was soon appointed to the Major Case Squad. He has since used hypnosis to help the police with cases involving murder, rape, kidnapping, robberies, burglaries and other major crimes.

By 1980, Don found himself working eight-hour days with the police department and another eight hours with his therapeutic hypnosis. He then chose to leave the police department to concentrate on hypnosis and to teach others how to use this wonderful tool. His practice grew quickly; he was seeing as many as eleven clients a day with over a month-long waiting period for clients. Don spent the next five years training new hypnotists and delivering his hypnosis services to the public.

As a result, by 1985 hypnotists from every state in the country, as well as hypnotists from Canada, Mexico, England, New Zealand, Korea, France, Australia, Japan, Italy, Germany, Ireland and Saudi Arabia had trained with Don Mottin. He is one of the most sought-after instructors in the hypnosis profession today. More than 1,000 hypnotists take advanced training with Don every year. After hypnotizing over 50,000 people, Don has learned what does and does not work.

Over the last 25 years, Don Mottin has gained an international reputation as one of the foremost experts in the field of hypnosis. Every major hypnosis organization has honored Don with awards for his unique teaching abilities. His awards include "Educator of the Year", "Instructor of the Year", the prestigious "Ormond McGill Award" and, in 2003, the National Guild of Hypnotists' revered "President's Award".

Although he no longer conducts private sessions, Don has trained the hypnotists that do the sessions in his office. Don now focuses on teaching and sharing his wisdom and experience with other hypnotists, as well as the general public.

Don serves on the Advisory Board of the National Guild of Hypnotists, founded in 1951 and based in Merrimack, New Hampshire. He has earned the designation of Fellow from this esteemed organization, serves on the NGH Board Certification Committee, is an adjunct faculty member and is a columnist for the Guild's generated publications. Don's advanced training classes at the annual NGH convention gain some of the highest attendance every year. He teaches individuals to become hypnotists twice a year in St. Louis, Missouri. Don also conducts a year-long advanced training course, Clinical Hypnotism, to already Certified Hypnotists.

Don and his lovely wife, Brenda, live happily in New Florence, Missouri. They are both fun-loving individuals who enjoy the simple things in life. As Don has said, *"There are no adults living in this house!"*

Don's love of children and his contagious optimism create the perfect blend to work with children. When Don was conducting private sessions, working with children was his favorite type of session.

CPSIA information can be obtained at www.ICGtesting.com
Printed in the USA
LVOW08s1212191013

357682LV00002B/587/A